Architectural Voices

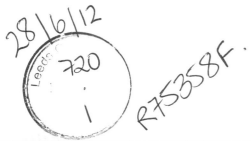

Published in Great Britain in 2007 by Wiley-Academy,
a division of John Wiley & Sons Ltd

Copyright © 2007

John Wiley & Sons Ltd, The Atrium, Southern Gate, Chichester, West Sussex
PO19 8SQ, England
Telephone +44 (0)1243 779777

Email (for orders and customer service enquiries): cs-books@wiley.co.uk
Visit our Home Page on www.wiley.com

Anniversary Logo Design: Richard Pacifico

Other Wiley Editorial Offices

John Wiley & Sons Inc., 111 River Street, Hoboken, NJ 07030, USA

Jossey-Bass, 989 Market Street, San Francisco, CA 94103-1741, USA

Wiley-VCH Verlag GmbH, Boschstr. 12, D-69469 Weinheim, Germany

John Wiley & Sons Australia Ltd, 42 McDougall Street, Milton, Queensland
    4064, Australia

John Wiley & Sons (Asia) Pte Ltd, 2 Clementi Loop #02-01, Jin Xing
    Distripark, Singapore 129809

John Wiley & Sons Canada Ltd, 5353 Dundas Street West, Suite 400,
    Etobicoke, Ontario M9B 6H8, Canada

Wiley also publishes its books in a variety of electronic formats. Some
content that appears in print may not be available in electronic books.

Executive Commissioning Editor: Helen Castle
Content Editor: Louise Porter
Publishing Assistant: Calver Lezama

ISBN 978 0 470 01673 2

Cover design by Liz Sephton

Page design and layouts by Ian Lambot Studio, UK
Printed and bound by Grafos SA, Spain

Architectural Voices

Listening to Old Buildings

David Littlefield

Saskia Lewis

WILEY
Publishers Since 1807

BICENTENNIAL
1807
WILEY
2007
BICENTENNIAL

Contents

6   Foreword
       Alain de Botton

8   Introduction
       David Littlefield

16   The Round Foundry
       Leeds, Yorkshire — *David Littlefield*

24   Riflemaker
       Soho, London — *Saskia Lewis*

34   Autistic Modernism
       Peter Stewart

38   The Moor Street Hotel
       Soho, London — *Saskia Lewis*

48   The Pro-Cathedral
       Clifton, Bristol — *David Littlefield*

54   Memory, Consciousness and Trace:
       Interview with Peter Murray — *David Littlefield*

58   Bomb Shelter
       Busselton, Western Australia — *Saskia Lewis*

64   The Young Vic Theatre
       Southwark, London — *David Littlefield*

72   Morphology and Matter: Working with Existing Structures
       Simon Henley

82   St Catherine's Chapel and Almshouses
       Exeter, Devon — *David Littlefield*

86   St John-at-Hackney and St Barnabas
     Hackney, London — *David Littlefield*

98   The Power of Absence:
     Interview with Gerry Judah — *David Littlefield*

104 Clock House
     Coleshill, Oxfordshire — *Saskia Lewis*

120 Battersea Power Station
     Battersea, London — *David Littlefield*

124 Interview with Eric Parry
     Saskia Lewis

136 *Milky Voids:* The reinterpretation of a Cornish mining building
     David Littlefield

142 Royal Mail Sorting Office
     Victoria, London — *David Littlefield*

148 Of All We Survey: Drawing out stories of place
     Carolyn Butterworth

152 Park Farm / River Cottage HQ
     near Axminster, Devon — *Saskia Lewis*

164 The Royal Military Asylum
     Chelsea, London — *David Littlefield*

172 The USA and Mexico: Through the eyes of Funda Willetts
     David Littlefield

180 Gibo and The Boathouse
     Westminster and Ladbroke Grove, London
     David Littlefield

184 Ditherington Flax Mill
     Shrewsbury, Shropshire — *David Littlefield*

194 Random Thoughts on Background Noise
     Lawrence Pollard

198 Taming the Monster:
     Interview with Julian Harrap — *David Littlefield*

204 The Soundscape of 2 Marsham Street
     Westminster, London – *Mathew Emmett*

208 Hoxton Cinema
     Hoxton, London — *Saskia Lewis*

222 The Power of the Real:
     Interview with Peter Higgins — *David Littlefield*

228 Epilogue
     Saskia Lewis

232 Further Reading

235 Index

239 Acknowledgements

240 Credits

Foreword

Alain de Botton

John Ruskin once remarked that every good building must do two things: firstly, it must shelter us. And secondly, it must talk to us, talk of all the things that we think of as most important and that we need to be reminded of on a regular basis.

Ruskin's idea lies at the heart of *Architectural Voices* and helps to lend this book its originality and value. In a period that still has difficulty discussing buildings as anything other than giant pieces of technology, this book focuses our minds on the idea that buildings *speak* – and on topics that can readily be discerned. They speak of democracy or aristocracy, openness or arrogance, welcome or threat, a sympathy for the future or a hankering for the past.

In essence, what works of architecture talk to us about is the kind of life that most appropriately unfolds within and around them. They tell us of certain moods that they seek to encourage and sustain in their inhabitants. While keeping us warm and helping us in mechanical ways, they simultaneously hold out an invitation for us to be specific sorts of people. They speak of particular visions of happiness.

To describe a building as beautiful therefore suggests more than a mere aesthetic fondness; it implies an attraction to the particular way of life this structure is promoting through its roof, door handles, window frames, staircase and furnishings. A feeling of beauty is a sign that we have come upon a material articulation of certain of our ideas of a good life.

Similarly, buildings will strike us as offensive not because they violate a private and mysterious visual preference but because they conflict with our understanding of the rightful sense of existence – which helps to explain the seriousness and viciousness with which disputes about fitting architecture tend to unfold.

The benefit of this book in shifting the focus of discussion away from the strictly visual and technical towards the values promoted by buildings is that we become able to handle talk about the appearance of works of architecture rather as we do wider debates about people, ideas and political agendas.

Arguments about what is beautiful emerge as no easier to resolve, but then again no harder, than disputes about what is wise or right. We can learn to defend or attack a concept of beauty in the same way we might defend or attack a legal position or an ethical stance. We can understand, and publicly explain, why we believe a building to be desirable or offensive on the basis of the things it talks to us about. The notion of buildings that speak helps us to place at the very centre of our architectural conundrums the question of the values we want to live by – rather than merely of how we want things to look.

Opposite: Reflections suspended in a film of dust evoke a sense of timelessness.

Left: Buildings are expressions of self, society, status. At Coleshill, an English country house, amongst an assembly of workshop tools, a note on the wall reveals that Queen Mary paid a visit in 1938.

Introduction

David Littlefield

So silence can, according to the circumstances, speak!

Robert Bolt, *A Man for All Seasons*, 1966

A mill, two centuries old and reputedly the world's first iron-framed building, quietly settles into the earth, leaking, rotting, cracking. The building, in the former industrial heartlands of the English Midlands, is suffering from old age and a number of wounds inflicted carelessly during its working life. Now empty, it is in need of rescue, of being nursed back to health. This mill has been measured, photographed, probed and subjected to a thorough medical examination. It has also been touched ever so lightly, gazed at, listened to. It is the subject of a meditation. The architects are taking their time. Deconstructing the building, scrubbing it up and reassembling it (like the pieces of a dead engine; like the old London Bridge, now sunning itself in Arizona) seems unconvincing. So, too, does the application of bionics, a steel and glass counterpoint to the original brick and iron. In listening to the mill's gentle whispers, its screams of agony and frustration, the architects are posing a rarely asked question: 'What does the building want?'

This book is an exploration. It deliberately contains more questions than answers, and it is built upon the shifting sands of memory, association and metaphor. It is, perhaps, an unconventional witness in the matter of architecture; a collection of testimonials which suggest a route rather than a destination. This book turns on the uncertainties within architecture, a subject which is more commonly seen as a business of absolutes – of weights and dimensions, a practice of intent and relative precision. It looks behind, beneath and within the fabric of buildings in the search for what makes these things, these constructions, come alive.

All the observations and contentions which follow are predicated on the single belief that buildings are more than an assembly of construction materials – more, indeed, than just composition, volume and form. That is the paint-by-numbers view of architecture. All buildings are products of the human imagination and the role of the imagination does not cease once the design has been committed to paper. All buildings are, more or less, psychological entities – projections, even. They are expressions of ideas, skeletons on which we hang notions of self, society, status, heritage, value … Buildings are not merely *there*, as coordinates of space and time; buildings live most powerfully in the mind and we constantly process them, assimilate and digest them, reimagine them.

'In vain, great-hearted Kublai, shall I attempt to describe Zaira, city of high bastions,' writes Italo Calvino in *Invisible Cities*. 'I could tell you how many steps make up the streets rising like stairways, and the degree of the arcades' curves, and what kind of zinc scales cover the roofs; but I already know this would be the same as telling you nothing. The city does not consist of this, but of relationships between the measurements of its space and the events of its past; the height of a lamppost and the distance from the ground of a hanged usurper's swaying feet … As this wave from memories flows in, the city soaks it up like a sponge and expands.' (Italo Calvino, *Invisible Cities*, Vintage, London, 1997, p 10.)

We constantly invest buildings with meaning (or at least adjectives), often to the point where these meanings appear to gain a certain independence. Churches are holy; brothels are seedy; Stonehenge is enigmatic, a provoker of questions. It is largely in this

Right: The voice of a building
emerges through an amalgam
of what is there (the orderly rows
of seats) and what isn't there (a
congregation). St Barnabas, a
church in Hackney, east London,
has become a museum of itself.
It is abandoned but its voice lives
powerfully in the mind of the
occasional explorer.

capacity that a building begins to accumulate something of a 'voice'. These voices penetrate deeper than straightforward symbolism – it is more than a matter of identifying railway stations with the happy prospects of travel, of office towers with commercial success, of ruins with mortality. It is, rather, a matter of reimagining the building as a personality and asking, 'If it could speak, what would it say? What would it sound like? Would it be worth listening to?'.

Questions such as these are particularly relevant for architects embarking on projects of renovation, interpretation or expansion. Very often architects see their role in anthropomorphic terms: as 'performing surgery', 'breathing new life' into and restoring the 'soul' and 'heart' of elderly buildings. These are vigorous, dynamic and determined acts which require the building to adopt a submissive role, to remain prone (perhaps anaesthetised) while work is visited upon it. Anthropomorphising the building in terms of 'voice', however, reverses this power structure, if only temporarily. The act of 'listening' makes the building an agent in its own reinvention, and the architect has to work hard to hear what is said. 'It's about letting a building talk to you and not walking inside with a lot of preconceptions,' remarks architect Paul Davis (p 164). It

is an exercise in full immersion, in much the same way as language is learnt – it can be an uncontrolled affair, one of hearing a multitude of voices and making judgements about which make sense, which have a comprehensible syntax, and which are just noise. Some buildings, in spite of our listening particularly hard, even appear to be mute. But discovering the curiosity of an absent voice is still worth the effort. Listening remains, however, an unorthodox thing to do: 'Despite the expressive potential of objects and buildings, discussion of what they talk about remains rare. We appear more comfortable contemplating historical sources and stylistic tropes than we do delving into anthropomorphic, metaphoric or evocative meanings. It remains odd to initiate a conversation about what a building is saying', writes philosopher Alain de Botton in his book *The Architecture of Happiness* (Hamish Hamilton, London, p 97).

More commonly, the conversation will focus on what the occupant is saying through their ownership of the building. But what is intriguing is the possibility that occupant and building begin to merge, in a manner that is pushed to the limit in Roman Polanski's 1976 psychological drama *The Tenant*. All inhabited spaces become loaded with biological debris – the dust of flaking skin, the hair, the exhaled air, the humidity, heat and bodily fluids that get left behind by generations of occupants can only combine to form a peculiarly human trace. And this is a trace, one which fades gently over time, that is surely detectable by others from the species. It is an arresting thought that part of the experience of being within an elderly space is sensing these human residues – the warmth, grease and breath of past inhabitants will have contrived, however subtly, to alter the fabric of the place.

As buildings continue to be occupied, like a well-worn coat they become more human (in the Parisian apartment of *The Tenant*, there is a tooth in the wall, while the strangeness of the building and the central character become evenly matched). Non-human traces also cram themselves into buildings (smells of cooking, machine oil, pigeon droppings, mould, damp, cleaning fluid, the mustiness of ageing books) which wrap around the visitor and, quite apart from the power of the raw dimensions and geometries of the architecture, conjure the fullest range of emotional and poetic responses. The kitchens of the former Royal Mail sorting office in London's Victoria smelled evocatively of chip fat long after the building was vacated (see p142). Perhaps the voice of a building is always unique to the visitor, a synthesis of what is verifiably there and how these presences are processed in the mind.

In his novel *Slaughterhouse 5* (1969), Kurt Vonnegut describes the arrival of American POWs in Dresden, prior to its bombing: 'The boxcar doors were opened, and the doorways framed the loveliest city that most of the Americans had ever seen. The skyline was intricate and voluptuous and enchanted and absurd. It looked like a Sunday school picture of Heaven to Billy Pilgrim. Somebody behind him in the boxcar said, "Oz".' The voice of a building (and a city) floats between documented evidence, personal and cultural memory, association and an emotional response to hard architectural facts – the language of style, scale, materiality, texture and light. It is such a complex blend it becomes baffling and it is simpler to consider buildings in more focused terms: fitness for purpose, or for their purely architectural merits or historical significance. But there are buildings, or building types, which resist these categories and make it their business to be experienced on all levels simultaneously – churches, for example. A well-made church deploys the tools of architecture (such as the control of light and acoustics, the drama of perspective, volume and rhythm) in such a way as to have a substantial effect on the attitude and behaviour of the visitor. It slows the pace, lowers the voice and lifts the eyes. It induces reverence. When loaded with religious iconography – with all its social, cultural and personal implications – churches transcend the matter of their construction, which is what they are supposed to do.

Professor Robert Tavernor, director of the cities programme at the London School of Economics, recalls a church from his youth: 'The buildings I probably enjoy the most, those that give me a "shiver", are probably those from my childhood – Gothic churches in particular. One of the wonderful things about being in [my local] church was that you were often left on your own there. I remember the sense of being in that place, the dark, the smell of it, the particular kind of light, the sound. Also, the church music gave it a particular kind of magic. It wasn't at all frightening and there was a real sense that people had been worshipping in the place for a thousand years. There was a sense of the sacred.'

Above: Buildings and their spaces are more than spatial coordinates. This room, in the Round Foundry in Leeds, is a place of texture, light, colour and odour.

For Tavernor, hearing the voice of a building is a very personal affair, requiring a sort of selflessness and a sensitivity to a building's physicality. Partly, it is a process composed of a fundamental human need to find one's roots in the past, and elderly buildings can be deployed almost in the manner of religious relics – tangible expressions of that which is valuable and significant, bequeathed from long-departed generations. It is a process not only of identifying yourself with the past but of positioning yourself within the timeline of the building, of imagining yourself from the perspective of future generations, as part of the past to come. In this sense, you not only hear the voice of the building, but become part of it. Tavernor also imagines one's experience of a building not necessarily as a coherent memory of a single place, but as a collection of individual memories and responses to materials, forms, textures, sounds – the coldness of stone, for example, or the quality of light.

Each time a memory is triggered, it is renewed and revised by the new experience, and our sensitivity to buildings becomes an amalgam of recall and reinterpretation. Buildings are networked through the ever-changing associations of the mind; places can be linked by memory trails, and buildings as diverse as churches, banking halls, coastal gun emplacements and even the US immigration centre of Ellis Island might be bound together through the association of, say, an echo. 'You are alert to a whole set of visual signals, clues and smells, each of which can trigger memories of, for example, "happy" or "unhappy". I don't think there are happy and unhappy buildings, or evil buildings. A building's voice can be very potent, but it is ultimately the inner voice you are hearing – your own voice,' said Tavernor.

If this is true of an individual response to a building, the same can also be true of a societal response to a place. Many buildings are overlaid with association so effectively that they are entirely transformed; they cease to be buildings at all, but become rather three-dimensional representations of an event or an idea. Again, churches are the most complete examples of this phenomenon, but they were actually conceived in this way. Key locations relating to the Second World War are further examples of this tendency (Nuremberg, Auschwitz), while Neoclassical German architecture is often the subject of some distaste because, according to de Botton, 'it had the misfortune to be favoured by the Nazis' (2006, p 96). The occasion of a murder, or murders, also has the power to completely reinvent a place, and society hears a voice so shrill that only demolition will cause it to stop. In the UK, the homes of two notorious child murderers, Ian Huntley and Fred West, were not only demolished but the rubble was taken away in secrecy and pulverised to help erase the memory of the events which took place there. It is an extreme response, and one which ignores the possibilities of other voices within these buildings. Yet buildings rarely have a single, clear, unambiguous voice; and any voice that is detectable is often amplified by demolition. The World Trade Center, New York's twin towers, through their absence have a far greater presence than they ever did while standing.

These socially agreed associations and demolitions do, however, imply that the idea of an architectural voice is not such a strange thing; de Botton is almost certainly right that trying to identify what a building is saying might be 'odd', but it is not ridiculous. What would be ridiculous is to destroy a house out of a misplaced sense of revenge, or in the

ARCHITECTURAL VOICES

hope that erasing the building might help to erase the events which took place there. What these demolitions imply is a sympathy for a more complex view of the relationships between people and buildings. There is, weaving its way through the warp and weft of this book, a difficult and unanswerable question: is the building's voice merely a metaphorical device, or an identifiable phenomenon capable of isolation? That is, do buildings continue to speak even when there is no one there to listen? Conceivably, like Calvino's city of Zaira, buildings soak up memory, events and human presence and undergo a subtle and barely detectable transub-stantiation. Peter Ackroyd, author and historian, has some sympathy for the idea ('It is a possible theory and, like all such theories, it can do no harm'), while architect and journalist Peter Murray has a deep conviction that the notion contains a significant element of truth (see p 54). Mathew Emmett (p 204) also wonders if the

physical sounds imposed on a place over time can remain as the faintest echo, part of an unseen sound-scape. Whether these ideas are robust enough to stand up to scientific scrutiny is debatable; they are, therefore, a matter of faith.

The idea embodies something of the haunting or the curse, the tactic often deployed by horror writers to create a close relationship between the nature of a place and the behaviour of its inhabitants – the one forcing its character on the other. Often, these stories are deliberately vague on the matter of culpability; has the life of a building been transformed through acts of cruelty and unholiness, or is there something 'other' within the fabric of the place which drives people to despair and madness? It is a chicken-and-egg question, emphasising the notion that the lives of people and their buildings are impossibly intertwined. In HG Wells's short story *The Red Room*, the narrator experiences a fear so real that it appears to have its own independent presence, and the horror lurking in the room *is* fear. Stanley Kubrick's *The Shining* (based on the novel by Stephen King) is a more complex example of this blurring, where fearsome apparitions, the sublime immensity of the landscape and isolation within empty space conspire to create a horror which is both real and imagined.

What make these narratives so potent is not the facts of the stories (this happened, then that happened), but the magnitude of the meanings which underlie those facts. In architectural terms, buildings can be suggestive of narrative potency simply by being there – the Egyptian pyramids, the medieval cathedrals, the towers of Manhattan, represent a 'triumph of the will' and the voices of their creators speak through them. This is not merely a recognition of style or symbol (that is another layer of language entirely) but an appreciation of the endeavour that went into these buildings' construction. These are stories which do not have to be related but which visitors to these places instinctively *hear*. There are, though, stories that are not so explicit, which need to be told; stories which can be vaguely imagined or guessed at but which amplify a building's voice only when they are made clear. The peculiarities of the buildings in London's Soho (see p 36) cannot be fully appreciated until their use as a brothel is graphically laid out; neither can the drama of the now defunct Chatterley Whitfield coalmine be understood until oral history comes into play.

Chatterley Whitfield, near Stoke-on-Trent, was once one of the UK's most productive pits and the first in the country to produce more than 1 million tons of coal per year. Its buildings are redolent of danger, physical labour and a sense of community, but it is only through personal accounts[1] that the buildings are revealed as places of sorrow, song and practical jokes:

I lost my brother in the pit and [this is how they had contempt for people]. I'd come through the baths, just had a towel wrapped around me, and a boss bumped alongside of me. 'Tha'd better get to the pit head. Tha's brother's been killed,' and he carried on walking. That's how they broke it to you. And they didn't stop drawing coal. I don't know what happens in normal places when people get killed. (Harry Allen)

In the pit head baths, when the miners were changing shifts, with a lot of them attending churches and chapels and being in the choir, they used to sing. It was beautiful. Hymns. (Sid Boulton)

You had to be very selective on who you'd get to wash your back. Say 'wash mine' and you'd wash his. Some of them would get a scrubbing brush – really dig it in, see if you were a man … One guy used to bring a Brillo pad to see if he could make you scream. Some would wash your back and leave a piece in the middle, a big black mark. (Paul Sherratt)

The danger here is that the idea of a building's voice slips into the realm of sentimentality, a trap which lurks

---

1   Collected by historian David Souden in 2000 as part of the regeneration and conservation plan for Chatterley Whitfield, commissioned by English Heritage and Stoke City Council.

within any consideration of the historical merits of a building. But the value of history and memory, in an architectural respect, lies not in the fact that something notable once occurred, but in the fact that notable events might continue to occur. This is what might be called the 'authentic' building. The authentic building does not live in the precision of the drawing or the computer model; nor does it live, devoid of inhabitants, in the newly completed structure. The authentic building is the one which continues to accommodate life. It grows out of its history and becomes more alive because of it, but the authentic building is not in thrall to that history – that is where meaningful engagement stops and any voice is extinguished. One has to be careful with history and the voices one encounters, otherwise what begins as a set of poetic clues ends as an intellectual straitjacket, what architect Robert Adam

Below: 'Churches are holy; brothels are seedy.' A red light bulb hangs from the ceiling of a former brothel in London's Soho – to be redeveloped as a hotel.

describes as 'the study of wildlife through taxidermy'. To uncover the joy and sorrow of Chatterley Whitfield is enough and one need not memorialise it.

This book examines a wide range of elderly buildings, many of which were on the cusp of redevelopment when visited. All have a voice, of sorts; some speak loudly and powerfully, others softly or barely at all. In all cases, the architects have left room for listening in their contemplation of these buildings, although there is rarely any agreement about what they are trying to hear or by what mechanism buildings can speak. Most will agree, though, that the voice of a building emerges slowly through a fusion (an alchemy) of imagination, metaphor, association, memory, sensory experience, emotional response and hard architectural and historical facts. The mix varies from architect to architect, from building to building, and the ratio of ingredients can vary considerably. What is important, though, is that architects leave room for listening in their contemplation of elderly spaces, to immerse them-selves in these places and make themselves a little submissive.

'[Buildings] are not simply assemblies of dull stones but are powerfully affected by human inhabitation and human practice,' wrote author Peter Ackroyd in correspondence with the authors of this book. 'Certain buildings have a moral value, for example, as a token of human will and human idealism. Other buildings are moulded by a sense of the sacred. Others are dedicated to the pursuit of profit. Each of them then acquires an identity which, through the years, becomes as integral a part of the structure as the bricks and stones.'

If architecture were as simple as bricks and stones, it would be a dismal subject indeed.

The Round Foundry

Leeds, Yorkshire

David Littlefield

Built in the1790s by the industrialist Matthew Murray
Redeveloped by architects BDP, 2004–7

Above: The cast-iron newel of a
Round Foundry staircase, freed
of paint and polished by years of
handling.

Opposite: An assembly floor in the
Round Foundry: oil-stained floors,
peeling plaster and the stench of
ammonia from pigeon droppings.

Celebrating and romanticising the patina of decay could
easily become a dangerous cliché in a book like this: the
complexity and peculiar beauty in the patterns of mould
and rot; the displacement engendered by seeing
commonplace objects (like the sign: 'conference room')
lose all sense of meaning in the wreckage of a long-
empty building; the utter stillness. Ruined and
abandoned buildings are often marked by things like
this and it is tempting to fantasise that the slow process
of dereliction be allowed to progress unhindered. It is
largely an idle and pointless fantasy, of course – if decay
goes unchecked, the building will eventually fall apart
and become a ruin.

The point at which buildings become ruins is a
philosophical question. When precisely does a building
cross the divide which separates a need for repair from
the requirement to do nothing? Ruins obviously have
their own charm and resonance, and have for the last
three centuries been read as symbols of vanitas and
entropy. Dilapidated buildings can operate in much the
same way, but by not being ruined enough they still
contain the possibility of habitation. There is also the
thought that ruins are never (apart from the wild
indulgences of poetic aristocrats) deliberately created –
ruins tend to be the result of war, catastrophe, social
upheaval or epic and uncontrollable neglect. Buildings
are built for, and by, people; serving the needs of people
is what buildings do, and wilfully turning a building into
a ruin is a reversal of its most fundamental purpose.

The post-industrial economy has left us with a
surplus of empty buildings, many of which display the
characteristics described above. The north of England
is particularly marked by empty warehouses, mills and
engine sheds, and Leeds boasts perhaps the finest
collection of the lot. One of the UK's first purpose-built

engineering developments, begun in the 1790s, is the
Round Foundry complex close to the centre of Leeds.
Acquired by developer CTP St James, these buildings
are slowly recovering from decades of abuse and
abandonment. Inevitably, the developer is working hard
to maximise its return on investment, but BDP architect
Ken Moth, a man who is unashamedly sensitive to
the requirements of historic buildings, is largely
untroubled: 'They know the historic character and
value of these buildings, but they have to deliver a
commercial return. Otherwise, they're not businessmen, they're philanthropists,' he says. 'Conservation is
generally misunderstood. A lot of people think it's about
preventing change – it's not. It's about managing
change when change is neccessary.'

At the time of writing, the Round Foundry site
had already been partially developed. Phase 1 was
complete and this early industrial warren of factory
buildings, service roads and courtyards had become a
mixed-use development of offices, cafes and
apartments. Four architectural practices had set up
offices there. Phase 2, however, had barely begun.

Phase 2 contains, essentially, a domestic-
looking Georgian building flanked by a pair of much
larger, more overtly industrial sheds. This early industrial
house – neglected, abused and coated at ground level
with a disastrous cement render – is a forlorn object.
Such is the building's state, with its 'bleak walls' and
'vacant eye-like windows', that it wouldn't be a bad
image to have in mind when reading Edgar Allan Poe's
1839 tale *The Fall of the House of Usher*.

'Its principal feature seemed to be that of an
excessive antiquity. The discoloration of ages had been
great … Yet all this was apart from any extraordinary
dilapidation. No portion of the masonry had fallen; and

The Round Foundry, near Leeds city centre, was built in the 1790s by the industrialist Matthew Murray for the manufacture of static and locomotive steam engines. The complex of buildings was expanded and adapted throughout the following century. When first laid out, the site attracted the attentions of Birmingham firm Boulton & Watt. Concerned that Murray might be infringing the company's copyrighted designs, a Boulton & Watt industrial spy lodged in the Cross Keys pub to keep an eye on this new rival. The pub is still there. In 1875 the circular 'Round Foundry' burned down and a brass ring now marks the footprint of the building, which slides beneath a later Victorian structure.

The site fell into decline after the Second World War, and by the 1980s the buildings were typically used for metal bashing, car repair and spray painting. In the 1990s a small local firm of architects, Regan Miller Associates, drew up a redevelopment plan and attracted the attention of developers. Too large for the firm to take on, BDP was brought to the job by developer CTP St James in 1999.

The work on the site was quickly divided into two phases. Phase 1 provided a mixed-use scheme of offices, apartments, cafes and bars, and was rapidly occupied by design and media firms. The principal Phase 1 building provides a media centre for new businesses aided by the regional development agency Yorkshire Forward. Phase 2, which will tackle the oldest buildings on the site, will add more office space and provide a more prominent public face for the development.

there appeared to be a wild inconsistency between its still perfect adaptation of parts, and the crumbling condition of the individual stones. In this there was much that reminded me of the specious totality of old woodwork which has rotted for years in some neglected vault, with no disturbance from the breath of the external air. Beyond this indication of extensive decay, however, the fabric gave little token of instability.'[1]

Two centuries ago these buildings were at the forefront, to use an anachronism, of the 'white heat of technology'. But they were both traditional and experimental. The visible timber roof trusses are fine examples of Georgian carpentry and are clear descendants, with their wooden pegs and the arrangement of principal members, of a much earlier woodworking tradition. Elsewhere, though, there are the remains, if you know what you're looking at, of one of the earliest overhead cranes.

Founded by Matthew Murray in the 1790s for the manufacture of static and locomotive steam engines, this site was conceived as a way of rationalising the production process. Murray quickly

Above: 'This door to be kept locked and bolted.' The Round Foundry, empty for many years, still contains locked doors and notices like this retain a sense of authority even now.

Left: Within the Round Foundry's old administration centre, the door to the conference room, marked 'private', gives on to nothing but dilapidation and emptiness.

ARCHITECTURAL VOICES

began challenging the supremacy of engine makers Boulton & Watt of Birmingham and, in 1812, produced the locomotive used on the world's first commercially successful railway. Murray's innovation extended to his buildings: the need for fire-proofing encouraged the use of iron as a structural material, while slim metal rods tied his buildings together in a way rarely seen before; meanwhile, his nearby home was heated by the steam produced by his manufactories.

But there is much that is still unknown about these buildings. It appears that Murray kept little paperwork, although some architectural decisions can be extrapolated from his products and the more extensive archives of his rival Boulton & Watt. However, Moth and a team of industrial archaeologists are sometimes left scratching their heads. There is a stone staircase that rises directly into the roof, indicating that there was once an extra storey or a tower of unknown use. Moth indicates a large piece of ironwork bolted to the outside of the largest building: 'What on Earth was that for?' And inside he points to an unexpected piece of brickwork: 'What's that corbelling doing? Haven't got a clue.' Even the Round Foundry itself, a circular building elsewhere on the site which burned

1   *Tales of Mystery and Imagination, from the Stories of Edgar Allan Poe*, Usborne Publishing, London, 2002, p 68.

down in 1875, is a mystery – no one knows for sure why it was round.

Today, the undeveloped buildings on this site are so sad and decrepit they are mute. Like a person who has suffered a trauma that causes loss of memory and the power of speech, these buildings are inscrutable. The largest is now the domain of pigeons and it reeks of ammonia from the carpet of droppings. There are very few traces of human habitation. On a dirty window sill there is a page torn from a pornographic calendar, dated 1999, from the company 'Bolt and Nut Supplies Ltd'; the occasional sign advises caution on steep stairways; and a plastic bottle of drink which has long since lost its fizz lies covered in dust. Some signs of life are older – vast chunks of softwood are stacked on the ground floor, each of which contains a set of scratches which (again, if you know what you're looking at) contain centuries-old shipping information from Baltic timber merchants. But it is not like the *Marie Celeste* – these buildings were largely stripped out first and then abandoned. They lost their human warmth long ago. You have to work very hard to reimagine these spaces filled with the heat and noise of industrial production.

Whenever Moth visits an elderly building, he likes to touch it. As a conservation specialist, there are sound professional reasons for this, but Moth also believes that touching a building brings you into closer

contact with the people who once inhabited it.
Buildings, he says, are the 'skeletons of history', a
framework around which we can develop an understanding of the past. Moth believes that what makes
the past so interesting is the people who lived there;
and what provides the best possible understanding of,
and connection with, the people of the past is physically
experiencing what the dead have left behind.

'As a species we're very visually focused. I do
feel the act of touching a building brings you into a
deeper understanding of it. You get a sense of all the
people who have ever lived there,' says Moth. 'Every
one of these bricks was made by somebody – there
was soft clay and someone pressed it into a mould,
someone put them in a kiln, someone loaded them onto
a wagon.' Moth is not superstitious about these things,
and neither is he attaching a mystical quality to the act
of touching; but he does believe that this sensitivity to

the human attributes of a building provides one
motivation for 'bringing the building back to life'. So he
leaves the dents, imperfections and scratches as he
finds them ('We're not trying to make it pretty. It is what
it is') because a building is about as good an expression
of how people have lived as it is possible to get.

For this reason it is almost a waste of time
moving a building brick by brick and re-erecting it
elsewhere. The London Bridge of Arizona's Lake
Tacoma is not the London Bridge of the Thames.
Exercises like this certainly preserve the form of a
building, and its spatial qualities are, more or less,
retained. But a building – and this is essentially the
whole point of this book – is more than the sum of its
spaces; the smells and accretion of dust and other
residues of a de- and re-constructed building will
disappear; the sun will penetrate the building differently
and any relationship with context will be lost;

archaeologically it will lose most of its value and even the ground on which the building sits will be different. 'A building is an entity. If you pull it up and move it somewhere else, it's no longer the same thing. A building is also a place – it's fixed there, it's part of the surface of the Earth,' says Moth.

But there is a point at which the life of a building starts to fade. Architect Paul Davis talks of buildings losing energy (see p164), but simple abandonment might suffice. This can manifest itself in a catalogue of absence: of heat, for example, of smell (both human and of food), of function and even, through the disappearance of furnishings, of human scale. Stripped of these elements, buildings can be rendered almost meaningless. There are some buildings where the power of geometry, or some vital relationship with the landscape, or a deeply embedded myth will sustain a voice through a prolonged period of abandonment. Not here. The undeveloped buildings at the Round Foundry site are voiceless, even lifeless – a fact that was powerfully reinforced when contractors had to stop work because a murder victim had been found in a skip. At the Round Foundry, Moth's job is less to do with listening to a building's voices and more to do with imagining the voices he can recreate through a process of architectural rescue.

Right: The forlorn administrative heart of what was once Matthew Murray's steam engine factory – a domestic-looking building exhibiting 'the discoloration of ages'.

'The buildings of the Round Foundry were once filled with furious activity, the smell of burning coal, hot machine oil, noise and sweat. The things that were made there were of high value, technologically advanced and beautiful,' says Moth. 'After a century and a half of use foundry operations ceased and other lower-key uses were introduced – car body shops, tyre depots and signmakers. Coal and oil smells were replaced by spray paint and the clatter of hammers by transistor radios. Eventually even these low-key uses faded away and the buildings became cold, silent and lifeless. At this stage the buildings are at their most vulnerable – likely to be destroyed by fire through chance or arson, or demolished as so much old rubbish. The challenge … is rescuing the buildings and their memories, repairing neglect and adapting the buildings to new uses in a way which expresses both the old and the new.'

Moth does not have a predetermined work method. For him each project represents a unique set of circumstances. Sometimes the object is to preserve as found, with the lightest of visible touches, so that after extensive repair it's hard to see what has been done. This was the case at Plas Mawr, Conwy, which Moth describes as Britain's finest surviving Elizabethan town house. He was so overawed by the building, the absence of alteration, the sense of history and weight of human presence that he frankly admitted to the client that he hardly dared begin. Almost a year was spent learning about the building, probing carefully, before an approach to repair was worked out. Repair involved carefully exposing parts of the building that had been concealed for centuries. From beneath the floorboards 400 years of debris had to be removed to allow the ceilings to be secured, but in one room the debris was left tantalisingly in place for future generations of archaeologists. The Round Foundry is not a 'preserve as found' project. It is, instead, a project of 'layering' new on to old.

'I am aware of being first in, and it's wonderful. It is a bit like being Howard Carter, peering into Tutankhamun's tomb fo the first time, and you have a sense that you are about to change things forever,' says Moth. 'In changing a building or place you must retain its special qualities and significance. Historic places are part of the material culture of the past, what our fore-bears made, the places they knew. If you go to the National Maritime Museum in Greenwich, you can see the musket ball that killed Nelson – it's still got some of his gold braid on it. You see that and you establish a connection with the real man and the real event. That's what the historical environment does – it gives us that connection.'

Below: A battered laminated poster, detailing the laws of Health and Safety, blends into the fabric of Leeds' Round Foundry.

Right: In recent years the Round Foundry has been used by sign-makers. This skin of paint flaking away from the brickwork contains a thin layer of spray-can blue, applied over the older, hand-painted white.

Riflemaker

Soho, London

Saskia Lewis

It was dark. They stood opposite 79 Beak Street in London's Soho.

'Where?' she asked and looked at him.

'That's your gallery,' he said. She looked across the road and then back at him.

'That dirty old building? What is this, Riffil-makka?' in her curious accent.

'Rifle Maker,' he said.

'The long guns?' she asked, and as he nodded she picked up an imaginary rifle and took aim across the street, made the noise of firing a shot, and concluded, 'Not a bad name for a gallery ...'

Tot Taylor and Virginia Damtsa had only just met. Damtsa had plans to open a gallery away from the frenzy of Hoxton in the East End of London where the contemporary art scene had moved at the turn of the Millennium. Taylor had been aware of this discreet gunmaker tucked away in the heart of Soho, London's West End, and that they had recently closed. He had

Above: A John Wilkes & Son rifle – ornate and beautifully crafted.

Right: The basement was packed with useful materials, spare parts and machinery for turning, working and calibrating bespoke guns.

had his eye on the vacant property, but just out of curiosity. He had had no plans for it at all. Three months later they were in business together.

'Riflemaker' does not make rifles, not any more. For 150 years it was home to John Wilkes & Son, gun- and rifle-makers to the hunting and fishing gentry. As the 20th century rolled on number 79 stayed static. By the Millennium it seemed to be an anomaly, an incongruous entity huddled in among the newsagents, the hairdressers and shops selling trainers – a throwback in time. The fast pace that people adopt while walking London's streets meant that only a few noticed the dusty workshop.

Making guns is a craft, a detailed business of meticulous precision and fine-tuning. You imagine that that sort of work goes hand in hand with a meditative rhythm and a sober silence. It is not a garage. No Radio 1 here; Radio 4 perhaps, at a push, occasionally, at low volume. Guns are instruments, mechanisms, tools. There is a slow spiral etched on the inside surface of the barrel of a rifle, a barely noticeable scratch, a meticulously drawn line that starts the bullet spinning on firing. A spinning bullet follows a straighter line, a more accurate trajectory. Load, aim, fire. This was repeated

again and again in the basement of the workshop, the walls were grazed with the evidence and thousands of spent cartridges were strewn over the floor.

More unexpected was the overwhelming smell. It took the burning of dozens of candles to begin to eradicate a confusing olfactory patina that had built up over years. The smells of gunpowder, metal, oil and grease from John Wilkes & Son, underlain, maybe, with a hint of lavender. Before being a workshop, number 79 had been a lavender depot, a point of distribution, supplying the lavender girls who walked the streets selling posies to ward off harmful ills and the stench of urban life. So maybe there was still a little lavender smell hovering, bled into the floorboards amongst the meticulous grime of the crafting of guns.

A gallery has now taken over the space and the previous occupant's identity, a good disguise in the contemporary world of art, and a memorable name in this context. *Rifling* is the drawing of the slow spiral line in the barrel of the rifle, it is the process of forming the groove in the steel. It is a technology that is contemporary with the opening of this building as a gun shop in 1850. Before the mid-19th century all guns were smooth-bore. At its naissance this gunsmith, this

Riflemaker, was absolutely at the cutting-edge and it is the drawing of a line that makes this distinction.

The premises opened as a gallery in May 2004. Taylor and Damtsa, the directors, wanted to avoid the formal trappings of an immaculate white cube and make use of an existing interior with minimal intervention. It is an intimate space even though partitions have been stripped out. The door is locked, so you ring the bell and the temporary custodian lets you in and returns to their desk at the back, facing away from you. It is one of those galleries where you can spin on your heel in the middle of the room to take it all in and then browse around the perimeter to get the detail. The domestic scale is certainly unintimidating and that was one of its aims. The content is often unexpected and unrepeatable.

The way that you approach the building as a visitor is unchanged. Roger Mitchell of Holland & Holland (gunsmiths) had known the Wilkes brothers and their dusty Dickensian workshop. They were an artisan outfit, making only around 20 bespoke guns a year themselves, but were trusted craftsmen who could repair or recalibrate, adjust, clean, test and finely tune a gun at late notice, as an emergency. In such a case someone would run east from Holland & Holland in Bruton Street, London's Mayfair, cross Regent Street and slip into Soho to go to number 79. Mitchell describes how you would ring the bell to be let in, how the ground floor was divided into two, front and back. The front room was a reception with a work-bench behind a desk; the back, full of tools and clamps, files, lamps and oils, hammers, springs and stocks – the walnut butt of a gun. Mitchell says the walnut has to come from Iran, Turkey or the south of France, somewhere with stony soil and a warm climate that would produce a richly decorous patterning

Right: The restored ground-floor entrance hall is now used by the gallery as exhibition space. During the *Riflemaker Becomes Indica* exhibition, a television showed film footage shot by Peter Whitehead of *Wholly Communion*, a 1965 event featuring seminal poets from that era. Allen Ginsberg's voice reverberated in the sombre light of the corridor.

Left: The new gallery occupies the basement, ground and first floors, while the stairs are shared with the occupants of the residential properties on the top floors.

in the wood. English walnut is too bland. During the 20th century, the front window was empty as the police discourage the display of guns to the street and the doors and windows were barred as an extra precaution against breaking and entering.

The ground floor and basement are both now used as gallery spaces. They have very different characteristics. The gallery at ground level is fully glazed to the street, with a shop-front that is prettily divided into four decoratively arched panes, and glass that has been stripped clean. You can see right through the space from front to back from the pavement. There are two doors side by side – one goes straight into the gallery and the other, less used and private, leads into the corridor towards the stair and basement. The main door and fan light above are still barred from the premises' gun-maker days.

The building's street presence is still unassuming but at night, when the gallery is shut, it can be transformed with lighting. The stair to the basement is tiny, reminding you that you are much bigger than your 18th-century compatriot, and leads directly into a more dimly lit subterranean space into which only a little light penetrates through glass blocks in the pavement. This space is entirely removed from the street: quiet, enclosed, contained. This duality is perfect for Riflemaker which is developing a playful reputation for shows that cross-reference work by unknown artists with that of historic legends, and presents them side by side with fun and intelligence. They are unafraid, making it up as they go and creating a new attitude to showing work, a stimulating atmosphere, inviting curiosity.

Not at all convinced that buildings have a voice, in fact sure that they don't, Taylor certainly researches and enjoys the narrative attached to the property and

Above: The Firearms Act 1937 signed by John Wilkes on 3 June 1941. This sits in the inside cover to the *Riflemaker Everyday Book & Diary 2006/2007.*

Opposite: The gallery spills into the more subsidiary spaces – on the stair to the first storey a narrow painting sits propped up on the floor to the right of the door.

Above: There is a sombre darkness to the subsidiary entrance to the gallery, which is used only by gallery staff and the residents of properties on upper floors.

Above: The stair to the basement is very steep and dark. On a winter's day, the glow of artificial light creeps up the stair to meet the failing daylight that spills over the threshold of the back door, which is slightly ajar.

Opposite: Ground-floor gallery during the *Riflemaker Becomes Indica* show. A piece by the Boyle family hangs on the wall to the left of the image.

locale and has used it to advantage. He thinks of the gallery as a shed, transported into the centre of London, a workshop, a place to test things out and experiment. He does know what he likes about space, a human volume maybe, how the proportions of a Georgian room, for instance, are so comfortable. The importance of the height of a ceiling and how spaces can accommodate stuff without feeling overly choked, claustrophobic. How, for example, the Soane Museum can be so madly packed, literally littered with paraphernalia and not have you running for the door to get out, but make you happy to peruse the collection and examine the quirks.

This is what a building can do for you if you handle it right and appreciate it. Riflemaker does and has been. It has been stripped back and cleaned – just enough – and the timber panelling has been painted a soft white. It has retained a sense of timelessness. It is a couple of rooms neither dominated by the past, nor overly bright or sterile; it is not cursed with fussy shadow-gaps or shamed by a dent or a crumpled edge. There are more important things to do and see. Taylor is interested in a space that can accept a wide variety of experiences without compromise.

The *Riflemaker Everyday Book & Diary 2006/2007* dovetails the history of the building and the local area and firms up the growing reputation of the venue as a gallery. On the outer cover is an image of the Wilkes brothers in the back room of the ground floor, 'stocking & checkering tools, examining gun action and action filing'. Inside is a colour image, slightly askew and bled to the edge, of the dealer's certificate signed by John Wilkes and dated 3 June 1941. The book is peppered with images – of the gallery, of guns, of art, photos, flyers, essays by Matthew Collings and Adrian

Right: The basement glow is framed by darkly painted timber panelling and a steep domestic stair. Visitors tread carefully and in silence as they descend slowly to the lower floor.

Far right: Battered timber frames are left rough while doors are repainted – the repaired or redecorated sits next to the distressed, the old against the new. There is no fear of worn space; the gallery does not succumb to the tyranny of desire for the immaculate surface, the pristine showcase.

Below: The Riflemaker gallery holds regular talks on a wide variety of subjects. The modest interior space becomes packed with people and those who arrive too late to find a seat must stand outside and watch through the window.

Above: A spinning sculpture by Conrad Shawcross dominates the first-floor gallery; the audience, of necessity, skirts around the edge of the room.

Left: As night falls, candles are lit on the stairs to provide just enough light to see by. Artificial light is kept low and at dusk, as daylight fades, shadows install themselves as part of the show. This movement of light throughout the day has been caressing these interiors since the building's construction in the early 18th century.

Right: Riflemaker renamed itself Indica in homage to the gallery that existed between 1965 and '67. The gallery has a chameleon-like character, shifting its identity from show to show – its spirit creates an exciting synthesis of historically significant work, established names and current young practitioners.

Above: Reviews and notices are tacked onto the back of the door that separates the ground-floor gallery from the hall, emphasising a type of domestic informality that is part of the spirit of the gallery.

Dannatt and interviews with Dunbar and Miles (Indica) and Anthony Fawcett. A plethora of attitudes and angles, known and unknown, home and abroad. Past shows and future content, facts and possibilities. The building's history lives on in its present.

In October 2005 Riflemaker showed *The Unseen Art of William S. Burroughs: Paintings, Targets, Soundworks, Scrapbooks, Cut-Ups, Fold-Ins, Film and Documentary Evidence*. He had lived a few streets away in Duke Street, St James's, SW1 for a time in the mid-1960s. Famous for shooting his wife Joan Vollmer dead in a drunken game of William Tell in Mexico on 6 September 1951, he later said that shooting her had been a pivotal event in his life, and one which had instigated his writing: 'I am forced to the appalling conclusion that I would have never become a writer but for Joan's death … I live with the constant threat of possession, for control. So the death of Joan brought me in contact with the invador [sic], the Ugly Spirit, and manoeuvered me into a life-long struggle, in which I have had no choice except to write my way out.' The tale has a curious resonance in this building with the slugs in the wall of the basement and the filings still gathered behind gaps in the floorboards. But there is a lot of that. In a gallery where the past is not swept away but included, you get the opportunity for a richer datum line, a point of cross-referencing that seems unpretentious yet stimulating.

In November 2006, Riflemaker showcased the work of Indica, in its time a pivotal gallery born on 25 November 1965 and dead by 3 November 1967. What is charming is how Riflemaker dresses up, tries on other identities, accesses different eras, and invites contemporary artists to join in. This gallery doesn't just show the existing work of artists but introduces people to one another and commissions work that is the result of surprising and unexpected partnerships that they, the directors, have created. The gallery is not the end game. It is significantly more than that – which is why it is becoming so popular. The space holds around 70 people at a push, and yet more than 1,000 turned up for the opening night of *Riflemaker Becomes Indica*. The human contents spilled into Beak Street, reversing the invisibility of the once dusty old workshop. People stopped to look and join in – next time they go past, they will, just maybe, ring the bell.

Autistic Modernism

Peter Stewart

Peter Stewart is an architect. Formerly director of design review at the UK's Commission for Architecture and the Built Environment, he now runs his own consultancy advising on architecture, planning and urban design. Here, Stewart considers the role of architectural language (particularly Modernism) in the stylistic sense. Modernism is a 'problematic' style, Stewart argues, 'autistic' even. Perhaps, he suggests, architects should learn to become more comfortable seeking inspiration from the past.

One of the more obvious kinds of voice to be found in a building comes from the architectural language deployed by the architect. That language may be modern or old-fashioned, engaging or distant, loud or soft. When a second architect extends or adapts a building, they have to decide how to respond to the voice that they find: whether to use the same language, or a modified version of it, or to use a different one.

In the past, this was a private matter for the architect, or the architect and their client. Today, particularly in the case of an existing building of significance or architectural interest, the choice of architectural language can assume a far wider aspect, forming part of a discussion involving not just the client but also the public, public agencies, pressure groups and amenity societies. Today's architects are used to the idea that they will have to negotiate their designs with professional representatives of various bureaucratic bodies who may hold firm views about the right and the wrong way to approach existing buildings.

At the beginning of the 21st century, the language of architecture is eclectic – even confused. The banalities of Post-Modernism have been discarded, but no strong and coherent alternative has emerged. If there is a prevailing language, though, it is that of Modernism in the broadest sense – even if that underlying voice is increasingly presented in new forms.

On the face of it, Modernism is an architectural style which, when applied in a relatively pure form to extensions or conversions, cannot easily establish a relationship with what is already there. One would think, therefore, that such an approach might not be easily accepted by those who have more interest in the old than the new. Oddly, though, a strange sort of consensus will often be found in which Modernist interventions, if implemented with exquisite taste, will be felt to be more appropriate as a response to existing situations of various kinds than something stronger and more personal with an individual voice.

Yet in its engagement with the past, the language of Modernism remains problematic. Modernism in its purest form has such a strong intellectual and ethical base, and generates such distinctive visual imagery, that at times it can seem almost autistic in its

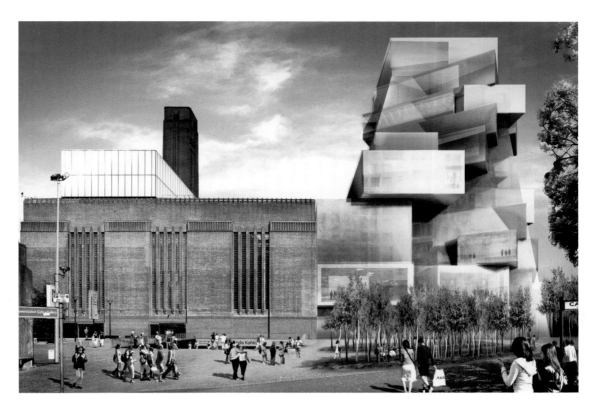

Opposite: Manchester City Art Gallery, Manchester. Michael Hopkins's 2001 extension to the gallery which was built by Charles Barry in the 19th century.

relations with buildings and neighbourhoods that predate it. That intellectual and ethical base was, in the movement's origins, often expressed in terms of superseding the architecture of the past rather than engaging with it, and such sentiments are still echoed today in the more provocative statements of the '*épater les bourgeois*' tendency still to be found within the architectural avant-garde.

I have always been fascinated by those English architects who have been prepared to plough their own furrow and experiment with architectural languages which clearly derive from those of the country's past yet do not simply revive past styles. A tradition of strong and distinctive personal voices of this kind can be traced through the past 40 or 50 years of English architecture. Architects such as George Pace, William Whitfield and Michael Hopkins have, successively, been drawn to qualities of mass and solidity in architecture that are difficult to realise within the canonic languages of Modernism, and as a result have been able to design in the context of historic buildings in a way that establishes a clear visual relationship between old and new. In each case, however, the results have been inventive, original and related equally strongly to the architect's own personal voice.

George Pace's Palace Green Library at Durham, hailed by some as a masterpiece on its completion in 1966, today passes largely unnoticed as part of the range of stone buildings that link cathedral and castle in a group which, Pevsner wrote, 'can only be compared to Avignon and Prague'. A heroic and masterly example of 'both/and' architecture, its Modernist planning strategy, with a clearly articulated circulation tower looming over the river valley, is nevertheless not so far in spirit from the medieval architecture which surrounds it. The eclectic language, which pays close attention to the spirit of Durham's older buildings, allows this connection to be made readily in the mind of the viewer.

William Whitfield's St Albans Cathedral Chapter House (1982) is a comparable example of a 'strong' response to a powerful existing building. Its impressive solidity is clearly inspired by the medieval architecture of the cathedral, which is of the solid rather than soaring variety. Yet while there is little in Whitfield's building that is drawn from the language of Modernism, there is not much that is taken literally from the architecture of the

Below: Inside Michael Hopkins's extension for the Manchester City Art Gallery. The rhythm, composition and materiality of the exterior, which are drawn from Charles Barry's original build-ings, do not prevent the interiors from being unashamedly contemporary.

Below: Inside Michael Hopkins's extension for the Manchester City Art Gallery. The rhythm, composition and materiality of the exterior, which are drawn from Charles Barry's original build-ings, do not prevent the interiors from being unashamedly contemporary.

past. His architecture is relaxed about making use of the structural properties of reinforced concrete, which is beautifully crafted in a manner that might have been appreciated by medieval masons.

Michael Hopkins is an architect who, from about the time of his projects for Lord's Cricket Ground and Portcullis House, attracted the opprobrium of some critics who felt that the new-found interest in tectonic qualities – and thus in history – was a betrayal of what they thought was represented by his earlier high-tech projects. To me, the later projects are far more interesting in their more complex responses.

Hopkins's Manchester City Art Gallery project (2001) provided a major extension to Charles Barry's original 19th-century Art Gallery and Athenaeum build-ings, completing the urban block. The project makes an interesting contrast with Richard Meier's Frankfurt Museum of Applied Arts, which also extended an existing architecture of calm cubic volumes (in this case, a 19th-century villa) with further cubic volumes. The two buildings are similar – in each case a rational and seemingly obvious, yet skilful planning strategy was suggested by what was there already.

Their approach to architectural language, however, is rather different. Meier's architecture does little to modulate or inflect the Modernist language he had already developed in other projects elsewhere. Hopkins, by contrast, adapts a language of expressed structure with infill panels used in earlier projects to sit comfortably with Barry's solid stonework. In each case smooth planes of stone are contrasted with carefully articulated detail. The interiors of the building, as is characteristic of Hopkins's best projects, demonstrate at least as much tectonic quality as is found on the exterior – something rarely achieved today when buildings are increasingly stuffed with the paraphernalia of mechanical servicing. His interiors offer a clear and straightforward reading of contained volumes – adding to, and comparable with, Barry's – linked by open glazed connections which unite the various parts, in contrast with the much more ambiguous relationships of Meier's project.

Many architects respond to the challenge of a strong existing voice with the safe and tasteful neutrality of Modernism. The examples here suggest that it is possible for serious architects to develop stronger and more characterful responses to the voices they find in existing buildings so that they are at the same time original and, in a relatively clear manner, derived from what has gone before. Such approaches make many architects and critics nervous because of the perceived dangers of errors of taste, or of a descent into pastiche or kitsch. If there is to be a 'strong' response with a distinctive voice of its own, rather than a 'polite' one, these critics tend to prefer something along the lines of Herzog & de Meuron's Tate Modern extension project (2006), which proposes striking architectural imagery that is largely unrelated to either the original building or the architects' own earlier conversion of it.

Post-Modernism (exhibited in Venturi Scott Brown's Sainsbury Wing extension to London's National Gallery and Terry Farrell's building for UK security service MI5) was an architectural movement the stated intentions of which had something in common with the approaches referred to above. Yet the output of PoMo in England is now seen as adding up to little more than thin and trivial gimmickry, and its defining projects, with one or two honourable exceptions, already look as dated as the period red braces of the City stockbrokers of Mrs Thatcher's Britain.

In what way do these projects which I admire differ from the now largely despised flurry of Post-Modernism? The answers lie in a number of areas: the seriousness of the intentions of the architects and their clients, and of the programme; the site-specific nature of the response; and in the quality and the solidity of the results. The examples above demonstrate that there are architects who can listen to the voices that they find in existing buildings and engage with them, not in order to imitate them but as a part of the 'usable past' – in a way that has always been part of the architect's working method.

Government planning policies in England set store by 'local distinctiveness' – the idea that architecture should be place-specific, in contrast to the 'anywhere and nowhere' housing built all over England by volume builders. As with so much central planning, thoughtful architects find themselves caught up in the consequences of a policy intended to deal with thoughtlessness. Yet while such policies respond to a popular desire for continuity and familiarity, examples such as those given above show that a search for rootedness is not incompatible with invention, creativity and architectural integrity.

Just as Modernism has been critically reassessed and now flourishes again as the architectural language of the Establishment in spite of its egregious failures, there is scope to reconsider the opportunities for an architecture that avoids both the autistic qualities of the purer forms of Modernism and the superficiality of Historicism – that is, an architecture which achieves a distinctive voice connecting it with the past not through abstruseness and metaphor, but by plain and direct, but inventive, reference to visual precedent.

The Moor Street Hotel

Soho, London

Saskia Lewis

Soho is an island. Major routes flow around it like a moat – Oxford Street to the north, Shaftesbury Avenue to the south, Regent Street to the west and Charing Cross Road to the east. It is an intimate knot of streets supporting small independent trades and hiding a wealth of secrets. It has a reputation – albeit considerably distilled these days – for the renegade, for an underground culture that has lubricated the imaginations of artists and writers for centuries and provided an environment to collapse the constraints of class and decorum. In a celebration of hedonism and freedom people have collided here from all walks of life. The *Rough Guide to England* (4th edition, Rough Guides Ltd, 2000) describes it as retaining 'an unorthodox and slightly raffish air born of an immigrant history as rich as that of the East End' and 'a nightlife that has attracted writers and ravers to the place since the eighteenth century'. In *The Forsyte Saga*, Galsworthy describes Soho as '… untidy, full of Greeks, Ishmaelites, cats, Italians, restaurants, tomatoes, organs, coloured stuffs, queer names, people looking out of upper windows, it dwells remote from the British Body Politic'. Soho has never felt very English. Initially it was inhabited by Huguenot refugees – French Protestant communities who fled France following the revocation of the Edict of Nantes by Louis XIV in 1685. The Great Fire of 1666 and the plague the previous year had had devastating consequences for London, and the subsequent restoration of the city set the scene and pace for the rapid development that would result in the creation of the West End and much of what we know as Soho today. Many of the residents were artisans, creating busy retail streets with cafes and restaurants and a social buzz, a place that promised continuous entertainment of many kinds, day and night.

At the south-eastern edge of Soho there is a triangular block of buildings that by the late 1980s had gained a fearsome reputation for all kinds of renegade activity. Moor Street defines the southern edge of this plot, Charing Cross Road the east, and Old Compton Street the north. Fifteen buildings made up the facades of three streets and hid a shared central void that provided light to the back of all the properties. It behaved similarly to a Bastide town, a local fortified environment, a stronghold, and it was this physical characteristic that helped the site to become a venue for all sorts of legal and illegal goings-on that were not readable from the street. The upper floors dealt in the sex trade, more or less legitimately. There were unofficial drinking clubs that provided floorshows and gambling. But the catalyst that forced the redevelopment of the site was the minicab office on the first floor

Below: Facade of 13 and 14 Moor Street. Nor 13 is a listed building that once housed a Chinese restaurant at street level with accommodation for staff above. No 14 contained a hairdresser's at street level and a mini-cab office at the first floor – a front for drug dealing and prostitution carried on upstairs.

of 14 Moor Street which was a cover for the dealing of drugs. By the early 1990s this address had become as infamous for selling crack as Billingsgate is famous for fish, Smithfield for meat or New Covent Garden for flowers. The smoke screen of a cab business was perfect for illicit activity – people milling around everywhere, constant comings and goings and the dealers merging in among their punters, both those looking for chemical substances and those ordering a lift home. The police referred to the site as the Moor Street Triangle.

Determined to take back control of the block, Westminster Council threatened a compulsory purchase of all the buildings, to eradicate unauthorised businesses and create residential property on site. However, the developers had been gradually buying up leases and partial freeholds among these properties and by the Millennium had the opportunity to redevelop the site themselves. Planning discussions have taken roughly a decade, seen several architects come and go, and are only now being implemented. Form Design Architecture secured planning for the site and Earle Architects are currently overseeing the building work. This project will see the creation of the Moor Street Hotel, a new bijou central London destination, a restaurant, retail units and some residential accommodation, renegotiating the boundaries of 5, 7, 9 and 11 Old Compton Street, 13 to 17 Moor Street and 95, 97 and 99 Charing Cross Road. The site is pinned in its corners by buildings that will remain unchanged, but act as witness to the redevelopment – namely the Cambridge pub, Ed's Diner and Lovejoy's bookshop.

This layout of streets first appears defined in William Morgan's map of 1682 when Charing Cross Road was called Hog's Lane. The earliest evidence for rates being paid in Moor Street and Old Compton Street dates from 1683, but there are no clear records of who built the streets originally. The present buildings on site all date from the 18th and 19th centuries. William Dunn, carpenter, and William Lloyd, bricklayer, both local men, took 65-year leases from the Portland family and rebuilt most of the houses on the north side of Moor Street around 1736, although William Bignell is thought to have erected No 13 in 1738 which is now a Grade II listed building. While constructing during these periods, it was common to rebuild on the footprint of a previous property and stitch into the neighbouring party walls, and this is exactly what has happened here. These buildings all rest on the sites of their ancestors, rather like wearing an old pair of shoes. No 7 Old Compton Street, for instance, is leaning on No 5, its neighbour. They are like a gang of old familiar friends.

There is no doubt that there is a cacophony of voices in this environment but not all of them are full of laughter. Some speak of loneliness, desperation,

Below: View from the first floor of 95 Charing Cross Road. Although on a level with the top deck of a London bus, views are either prohibited by a build-up of dirt on the glass or are crudely painted out.

Above: No 14 Moor Street, a late-night unofficial drinking club with pole dancing. The windows have been partly painted out to prevent people looking in.

Above: A shaft of sunlight slowly shifts across the shabby Artex ceiling marking the slow passage of time.

Opposite: Second floor, 9 Old Compton Street. Unofficial alterations to these buildings have created a surreal space where the doors and windows span the 6 feet from floor to ceiling. To stand in these rooms is to seem oversized, larger than life.

scraping by in the world. Everyone who visits the site is touched by the romance of the decay and titillated by the illicit nature of what used to take place here. They seem saddened by the plan to clean up this fragment of renegade Soho, but acknowledge that its attraction is based on neglect and voyeurism – these buildings have witnessed as much pain as joy. Malcolm Clayton of Form Design Architecture said that it reminded him of a very accomplished set for the National Theatre, a seedy Dickensian scene insulated from modernity. Herein lies the problem – how do you use these voices, how can you create a dialogue with them?

Nos 95–99 Charing Cross Road have an arcade on the ground floor that will stay. From first floor up these properties were a warren of rooms and corridors that had housed unauthorised late-night drinking clubs cheek by jowl with rooms used by prostitutes. At the time of writing, the majority of detritus in these buildings had gone, but there were still notes Sellotaped to the backs of doors reminding girls to protect themselves – the practical side of the credit card-size fantasy advertised in public phone boxes. More poignantly still, on the second floor of No 95, there was a red heart tacked above the security spy-hole on the back of an apartment door – for a moment the sun streamed in through the window and illuminated the back of the heart so it seemed to float. The attempt to introduce the idea of romantic love into an interior that had been cheaply subdivided to facilitate the servicing of as many clients as possible seemed incongruous, a waste even. The windows were veiled in dirt screening the interior view from the top deck of the buses passing by in the road outside. A non-stop din, a soundtrack of sirens and wails, piercingly penetrated the first floor from the arcade below. There had been no thought to dividing

Above: Plans of the Moor Street Triangle – at the top the existing site with all the areas marked in green due for demolition, and the proposed scheme above.

Below: The floor level had been dropped in part of 14 Moor Street to accommodate pole dancing – the windows no longer bear any relation to finished floor level.

space with regard to sound or heat, no insulation, just thin walls acting as screens.

The restaurant, hairdresser's, comic shop and sex shop that had occupied street-level premises on Old Compton Street were all closed down in 2004. The oldest of these, number 5, had had the restaurant operating from its ground floor. The early 19th-century facade hid an unusual late 17th-century chimneystack among the tables and chairs dividing the front from the rear of the site. The restaurant had made DIY extensions into the shared central void, adding a series of preparation, cooking and storage areas. It was rumoured that at one point staff had dragged a whole dead cow out into the courtyard space where they kept it under a tarpaulin, hacking off chunks of flesh to cook as orders came in. The same *ad hoc* kitchen gave up a dead, dried-out python during renovation – a 6 foot long prop to an exotic dancing show that had escaped and lived the rest of its days in a heaven of food and vermin. The first floor of the building had been home to one of the last tailors resident in Soho, a man who is said to have made suits for the Krays and a host of film stars. Most bizarre, though, was the top floor. The policemen who eventually stormed the property described an Oriental club which they had suspected of acting as a front for the dealing of narcotics – it was equipped with a steel cage in the interior of the room and a solid steel door at the top of the stair with a sliding panel. A strong room. In stripping this away, some early Georgian panelling was uncovered and when that was removed for storage during building work French graffiti was found in the plasterwork dating from around 1750.

Above the comic shop at No 9 was a large salmon-pink room with a bidet and an unpainted patch of wall where a blackboard had been. A dulled shaft of

Right: As plasterboard is stripped away during demolition, temporary views reveal themselves: a window painted out in red is visible through the exposed studwork.

Above: A door on the first landing with a sign that reads 'First Model' – here there was room for a bed, a basin and a frilly lampshade. A 'Second Model' was signposted on the stair with an arrow pointing to the floor above – generic inter-changeable girls.

sunlight slipped across the dirty Artex ceiling acting much as a clock, ticking away the seconds, minutes, and hours as it must have done every day. The second floor was barely 6 feet high, its doors and sash windows sitting absolutely flush with floor and ceiling like an *Alice in Wonderland* parody, a curious dream, an unsettling joke. The spaces were unnervingly horizontal which, given the circumstances, was all that was needed. The ceiling at first floor in No 9 had been raised to allow for a more spectacular pole dance and a sizeable audience, leaving the floor above reduced in the style of the film *Being John Malkovich* where clients would be served more intimately.

The interior layout was partly the result of 9 Old Compton Street and 14 Moor Street having been unofficially joined together, on the sly, by professional builders in the 1970s and 1980s. A confusing series of twisting stairs and corridors joined the two properties with the pole dancing somewhere in the middle – you could be left feeling entirely disorientated regarding your relationship with the street if you were not familiar with the venue. If you were more savvy you could enter one door and literally disappear, leaving via another address entirely, hidden from view. This is more the sort of physical arrangement seen in movies such as those by Alfred Hitchcock, or reminiscent of Ken Adam's sets for *The Ipcress File* and the James Bond films.

So, a trip from 9 Old Compton Street could take you to 14 Moor Street without the need to leave the block, and it was because of this address and its handling of narcotics that the whole site had become known for serious crime and had been shut down. There was a hairdresser on the ground floor and a minicab company operating from the floor above. The rest of the building was a craze of disorienting rooms with labels reading 'First Model' on the landing and 'Oriental Model Here Today' up the stairs. The rooms had a lampshade, a basin and a bed. Since the building work in the late 20th century, windows no longer bore much relation to floor level in the facade to this street – some were 2 metres above floor level and others disappeared behind floorplates; these were either boarded over or painted out in black, green or red. There were no original floors in this building. The puce pink walls gave a dark and cloying atmosphere in the continuous absence of natural light.

A more tame recent history and a more domestic identity characterised 13 Moor Street. A food bar had occupied the premises at street level with accommodation for several families above the cafe. It had a tight winding stair dating from the early 18th century and what is thought to be the only example of a Yorkshire sash window to have been found in London. This is a sash that slides horizontally from side to side

Right: First floor, 9 Old Compton Street. Located above the space where a bed once stood is an unpainted square patch where a blackboard used to be.

rather than vertically but it looks out into a narrow light well just behind the chaotic extension of a diner that has quietly grown larger over a period of years – not a view to relish. Families had been living in studio flats opening directly off the stair. The rooms were decorated with chimes and bells hanging from the mantelpiece and paper decorations. On the first floor was a huge *Kill Bill* poster of Uma Thurman in skin-tight black rubber holding a sword in pseudo-martial stance.

Perhaps the most dramatic change to site has been the demolition of 15, 16 and 17 Moor Street. Number 15 had become the Community Safety Office and during its latter months took on the guise of resident mole as part of the operation to close down illegal activities within the Moor Street Triangle. This type of continuous police presence was a tactic first modelled in Holland and it marked the end of the block's existence as an independent state. A website on 'classic cafes' mourns the loss of Nos 16 and 17, independently run cafe/restaurants of which people had been genuinely fond: Centrale with its intimate atmosphere and battered brown vinyl seats and memories of Malcolm McLaren as customer with his 1980s band Bow Wow Wow; and No 17 next door, Cappuccetto, a patisserie whose owner claimed to have been first to import pesto to London in 1962.

Day by day these buildings were demolished – they were deconstructed by a small team who acted as if paying for the indulgence and misdemeanours of others. At one point a man stood on a fragment of wall half a metre wide and three storeys high that he was reducing brick by brick, methodically pick-axing the mortar joints at his feet. Every brick that could be removed intact was, and they were sold for £1 each, a process that measured the pace of demolition and

Below: In the late 1970s and early 1980s, 14 Moor Street was subject to building work joining it to 9 Old Compton Street. Spaces are cut up and rehashed creating a warren of fantasies. In daylight the interior looks like a crazy film set.

Below: Entrance hall to the brothel and entertainment club that was 14 Moor Street.

Left: First floor, 9 Old Compton Street, early afternoon. In a pink-painted room 10 metres by 5 there stands a lone bidet, now looking rather shame-faced, apologetic, naked without all the other props.

Right: A chaos of debris in the shared lightwell at the heart of the Moor Street Triangle.

Above: The party walls between buildings on Old Compton Street were punctured momentarily, opening up to one another adjacent buildings and creating new routes at first-floor level for the safe movement of materials. Once the job was completed the party walls were reinstated.

tamed the site. The stronghold has been breached by the removal of these buildings – the new building, the entrance to the proposed hotel, reads essentially as one mass even though on the facade reference has been made to the original party walls. The shared void at the back of the properties has been opened up more directly to Moor Street and the whole dynamic of the interaction of space and sequence of spaces has been changed for good.

The lowering of the basement floor slab to achieve adequate head clearance from floor to ceiling, especially in the vaults that slip deep under the street at 11 Old Compton Street, necessitated considerable underpinning and excavation. When clearing the central void and lowering the basement level, the contractors found that the buildings were not set in the clay that is common in this area of London but on a gravel terrace. According to the description provided by the Museum of London: 'The Lynch Hill gravels were formed by the Thames during the glacial period. These were overlain by a deposit of brickearth, a mixture of sand, silt and clay, laid down as alluvial and Aeolian deposits during the last glaciation around 26,000 to 13,000 BC.' The site has consequently provided its own very high-quality gravel to use as aggregate in the mixing of concrete on site; it is being extended from its own footprint. Extra gravel has been sold for profit, over a hundred 20-tonne trucks have been filled, their contents exported to other sites for use in construction.

The rears of the buildings revealed a shared void full of discarded jumble, *ad hoc* detritus that had never been cleared: air vents, aerials, satellite dishes, ladders, broken brushes, abandoned cans, discarded clothing, rags, buckets, condoms, plastic chairs, mattresses, armchairs, pots of paint, lengths of cable. The whole site is tied together with myth. Rumour has it that a cache of weapons is hidden on site and huge sums of money stashed away. At least one murder in Moor Street has resulted in conviction and a series of fires has been both deliberate and accidental. This is the stuff of movies. And yet, inevitably, development strips the narratives away and the voices become very distant, if audible at all.

The buildings are now tied together using the central lightwell as shared circulation space instead of central dumping ground, accessing hotel rooms and accommodation from what would have been the back elevations of the buildings. Earle aims to retain the irregularity of the roof profiles and stitch the buildings together with a series of walkways keeping the void as an external space. He cites the description of Zenobia from *Invisible Cities* by Italo Calvino (Vintage, 2007) to illustrate his aim: 'platforms and balconies of various heights, crossing one another, linked by ladders and hanging sidewalks'. The stainless steel stair and walkways, using a material called Amron originally designed for oil rigs, will bolt on to the existing structure to span the void, ramping from one building to another as few share the same floor level. The cables for servicing the building are held underneath the walkways in trays rather than hidden behind coving, making reference to the fact that each girl had had an individual wire winding directly from her room to the street. Lighting designer Kate Wilkins has been commissioned to animate the facades of the buildings with shadows of figures moving around. They will be visible at night, prompting people to imagine past lives, as the hotel allows its flow of transient characters to move on through. There is, of course, the possibility that all the old trades will just move back, if into more sanitised environments.

Below: Two sections through
the proposed scheme by Earle
Architects.

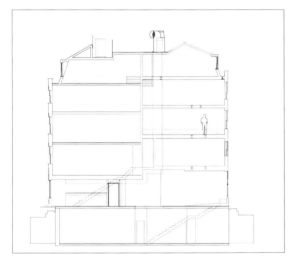

Above: Demolition is slow and
done by hand. One of the team
stands precariously on a fragment
of wall which he is demolishing
brick by brick.

Right: The dead and dried-out
6 foot python found in the kitchen
of what had been a restaurant at
5 Old Compton Street.

The Pro-Cathedral

Clifton, Bristol

David Littlefield

Designed by HE Goodridge and Charles Hansom and built in stages, 1834–70
Remodelled as housing by architects Atkins Walters Webster, 2006

The Pro-Cathedral in Bristol's Clifton is an unhappy building. Deconsecrated in the 1970s and re-equipped as a Steiner Waldorf School, the building has been empty since the mid-1990s, since when it has been stripped down, vandalised, daubed in devillish graffiti and subjected to increasingly damaging incursions from the weather. The building is a mess: its altar has gone, the adjoining Bishop's Palace (now roofless) is scheduled for demolition and parts of the vaults consist of churned earth, the result of the savage and unsympathetic removal of bodies during the deconsecration.

There is something fatalistic about this building. It didn't have a good start. It's even oriented wrongly. Usually churches face east, either to the cardinal point or directly towards Jerusalem. The Pro-Cathedral faces south-west. This anomaly is undoubtedly due to the constraints of the site and there is nothing doctrinally wrong with this 'reverse orientation' – it is merely unusual, even curious. Begun in the 1830s as a grand monumental gesture by Bristol's Catholic congregation, the church ran out of money, partly due to the unpredictable geology of its elevated and sloping site. So the heavy basilica-like walls were topped by a cheap, lightweight roof to quickly and easily make it weather-tight. It wasn't until the 1870s that the building, renamed the Pro-Cathedral (meaning temporary), began providing comprehensive community services with the addition of a school and other accommodation. But less than a century later, the authorities were planning a replacement structure, a building which was to become one of the biggest projects undertaken by the Percy Thomas Partnership.

From the outside, the present condition of the building is unclear. The Pro-Cathedral is on such a scale that from a distance it's hard to imagine it is derelict; up close, locked gates, the proximity of adjacent buildings and a private car park make it impossible to circum-navigate. Meanwhile, uncontrolled tree growth and the presence of a vast and uncompromisingly brutal municipal car park shroud the building and help shield us from its embarrassment. By 2005 the Pro-Cathedral was best known locally for being Number One on Bristol's Buildings at Risk register, and for its appearance on Living TV's programme *Britain's Most Haunted*. At the time of writing, the reclamation website www.salvo.co.uk was advertising a pair of 'finely carved' Bathstone angels, sourced from the building and retailing at £1200 (plus VAT), that 'would serve to enhance any fireplace or decorative situation'.

Because of its condition, the strength and rigour of the religious architecture lacks the impact to hush

Below: An altarpiece. Curiously, graffiti artists, in brutal homage, often repeat the colours and proportions of their setting.

visitors or slow their pace. The height, the rhythm, the elevated light sources, the strong perspectival views, the temperature and acoustic of stone – what ought to be a powerful combination of architectural forces simply fails. Instead, like an awkward silence, there is a palpable sense of a lack of awe – where you expect to feel reverence, you experience shock. Philip Johnson once wrote in the *New York Times* that architecture was 'the art of how to waste space'; here, though, the building has become a waste of the art of how to waste space. Like the mad King Lear, 'crowned with weeds and flowers', the Pro-Cathedral has become 'A sight most pitiful in the meanest wretch'.

This is a place of multiple voices singing in unison, but not in harmony. Darren Sheward (joint director with Jonathan Brecknell of local developer Urban Creation) argues that the Pro-Cathedral has passed through four distinct 'chapters' in its short life: its early, troubled birth; its later expansion; its decon-secration and take-over by the Steiner movement; and, finally, its abandonment. But that is not to say each chapter presents a single voice; each phase inter-weaves with the others and therefore generates odd combinations and discords. Memorial plaques, such as

the slab entreating 'Of your Charity, Pray for the Repose of the Soul of Mary Simmons who died June 28th 1850 Aged 74 Years RIP' take their place alongside marker-pen scrawl like the daub 'ghost chillin'. A Steiner-era printing press, complete with piles of its last print run (advertising a summer fair and school open day), adjoins that vault containing the disturbed earth of disinterment. In places, such as the main volume of the Pro-Cathedral, the building appears long-abandoned, while smaller and more discreet spaces are obviously still occupied intermittently; in spite of the efforts of security, graffiti still appears, like stigmata. This is a multivalent place, at once rich in meaning and possi-bility while proving difficult to pin down. Sheward and Brecknell, in converting the Pro-Cathedral and its narthex buildings into offices and 38 residential units, are having to tread very carefully.

Sheward admits he has never really entertained the idea of buildings accumulating a voice: 'Do I believe buildings have voices? I don't honestly know. In some respects I'd like to think they do and I certainly believe the Pro-Cathedral sends a message to us.' The content of that message is hard to establish, apart from an anguished cry for help. Sheward prefers the metaphor

Above: Like the Round Foundry in Leeds, Bristol's Pro-Cathedral is home to a thriving community of pigeons. Every surface within the nave of this building is encrusted with droppings.

of breathing new life into old buildings, and both he and Brecknell happily reimagine the real voices of the schoolchildren who once inhabited this place as an antidote to the obvious difficulties of tackling the building. Without this reimagining, on which the hopes of a youthful and animated residential scheme are pinned, the Pro-Cathedral is almost too sad to contemplate.

Sheward and Brecknell purchased the site for £2.1 million in April 2005. They inherited a scheme drawn up by Edward Nash Architects which forms the basis of the present development. Essentially, the scheme centres on the idea of a building-within-a-building: after the fabric of the Pro-Cathedral has been secured and the roof made weather-tight, the building will act as an envelope for a contemporary, two-storey insertion in the nave whose geometry is predicated on the grid of the present roof-supporting columns. Although the rose window above what was the altar will be preserved, the cathedral shell will not be hermetically sealed – the intention is to remove the glazing at clerestorey level to create a semi-open volume while at ground level new (glazed) holes will be punched through

the massive walls. The architectural intention draws on the idea of the covered city, most recently explored by Lifschutz Davidson's 'Legacy' proposal for the Millennium Dome (a scheme which placed modular, experimental buildings beneath the weatherproof canopy of that Teflon tent). Metaphorically, though, the strength of the Nash scheme rests on a literal interpretation of the role of the church – that of protector.

When complete, around 2008, the development will be a curious place. This is not like the conversion of a bank into a pizza restaurant – the intervention is much stronger and, through the commercial imperative, the original intention of the building is quite the reverse of that to which it is being put. In one sense, the biggest attraction of this place is its volume. But Sheward and Brecknell are applying a sensitivity to the space in much the same way as architect Matthew Lloyd did at the much smaller St Paul's in Bow, East London (see p 86). At St Paul's, Lloyd filled a good deal of the volume of the church with a contemporary, timber-clad 'ark' which draws out the religious intent of the building at key moments. In a peculiar way, the new insertion knows where it is and tactfully reinforces, or amplifies,

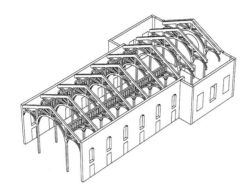

Right: Sequence of axonometric drawings illustrating the 'building-within-a-building' concept – here the walls and roof structure of the Pro-Cathedral as found.

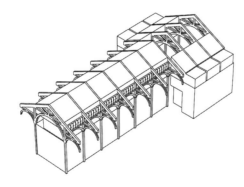

Right: The new volumes to be inserted into the nave and transepts.

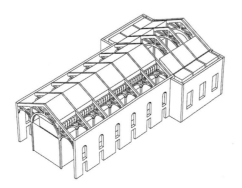

Right: An amalgamation of the two views above, showing the new spaces within the existing structure.

Although the construction of Catholic churches became lawful in 1790, it wasn't until the Catholic Emancipation Act of 1829 that conspicuous places of Catholic worship became possible. Construction of Bristol's Pro-Cathedral, designed by HE Goodridge as a Corinthian temple, began in 1834 but work ceased the following year after the foundations failed.

Eight years later building work recommenced; an attempt to reinforce the foundations failed once more and the half-complete building was abandoned. Architect Charles Hansom redesigned the building as a less ornate and lighter structure and, once sufficient funds had been raised (partly through selling adjacent land for private housing), work restarted in 1846. The smaller building was completed in 1848 and the first Bishop of Clifton was appointed two years later.

Hansom returned to the Pro-Cathedral in the 1870s, remodelling it as a Romanesque basilica and adding a school – he even planned a 200-foot campanile, which never materialised.

The building survived Second World War bombing unscathed and plans were hatched in the 1960s to update it and finally consecrate it as a fully fledged cathedral. The cost of this exercise proved prohibitive, however, and in 1965 the Percy Thomas Partnership began design work on a replacement building which was completed in 1973.

The original Pro-Cathedral was then used as a store and later as Bristol's Steiner Waldorf School, which withdrew from the building in 1996. Developer Urban Creation bought the building in 2005 and commissioned architects Atkins Walters Webster, as well as conservation architect Richard Pedlar, to revise a scheme already drawn up by Edward Nash Architects. The scheme will locate office space in the narthex of the building, while contemporary insertions containing apartments will be set inside the Pro-Cathedral's nave and transept. Further apartments, making 38 in all, will be added to the south of the building on the site of a roofless Bishop's Palace.

its envelope to the benefit of both structures. Sheward and Brecknell hope their scheme, though much larger, will work in a similar way. Also, most religious relics will be preserved as a deliberate reminder of the history of the building, while the full height of the chancel (to become the principal entrance) will be retained. The south-westerly rose window will still drop colour into the space.

This sensibility to the site has also caused Sheward and Brecknell to make a significant departure from the Nash proposal. In the original scheme, the floor of the church was to be turned over to car parking, while apartments were to be constructed on a new floorplate above. Sheward and Brecknell have moved the cars underground, to the vaults which would otherwise have remained empty, allowing the apartments to sit at ground level. 'Using the ground

floor as a car park just didn't seem the right thing to do,' says Sheward. Partly, this is because he sees his intervention as simply another chapter in the life of the building – and by no means the last. While Urban Creation's scheme is hardly reversible, it is not as heavy handed and uncompromising as the Nash proposal.

More poetically, though, packing cars into the very space once occupied by church pews is no better a response to the place than the multi-coloured murals of graffiti artists. The painted vampire displaying the pentagram, colourfully and disturbingly applied to these lime-washed walls, is arguably a more pertinent response to the building than the parking of cars. This is the harshest discord of all – that some of the graffiti, with its overtly anti-Christian flavour, actually helps amplify the original voice of the building. The parking of cars would be merely banal.

Memory, Consciousness and Trace
interview with Peter Murray

David Littlefield

Above: Peter Murray

Peter Murray trained as an architect but is best known for communicating the architecture of others – he is a writer, editor and curator and is enormously respected for his energy in helping to raise the value of architecture within the public consciousness. He has worked on journals including *Architectural Design* and *Blueprint* and more recently founded the architecture communications agency Wordsearch. Murray obviously cares deeply about the subject but he is, perhaps, more associated with the hard facts of architecture (towers in London, the role of developers, the publishing of magazines) than with the soft invisibility of architecture's psychology, the strangeness of spaces, the uncanny sensitivities of people to particular places.

During the 1970s Murray edited *Building Design* magazine, and he recalls its culture editor reviewing a BBC drama based on the premise that buildings could, conceivably, soak up momentous events that happened within them. Provided the events were significant enough, and were imbued with sufficient emotional energy, they might reside within the building's fabric and, once triggered, be played back. The drama, *The Stone Tape* (1972; Peter Sasdy, director) starred Jane Asher and featured a group of scientists who had been charged with uncovering a new recording medium. Having discovered that their own ancient building was haunted, they began to explore the idea that the stone of the walls appeared to have 'record' and 'playback' facilities. Although Murray never saw the programme in question, he remembers the reviewer being sympathetic to the concept – Murray himself, though, considered it a clever piece of nonsense.

Later, however, Murray visited the Canadian National Vimy Memorial in France, the site on Vimy Ridge that commemorates a bloody First World War battle. During the war, the Allied forces dug a warren of tunnels to allow soldiers to live, seek shelter and deploy right up to (and beyond) the front line. From these tunnels, at 5.30 am on 9 April 1917, Canadian forces attacked the German lines, resulting in 3,600 deaths and a further 7,000 casualties on their own side. The battle of Vimy Ridge was considered a significant Allied victory. According to Murray, fear, anxiety, nervous energy, even tragedy, oozes from the chalk walls of those tunnels. It is as if, after all, *The Stone Tape* had a basis in historical fact.

'There was definitely something physical in that space related to what had been there before. Maybe it was the softness of the stone that made the difference, but definitely something had been absorbed into that space that still echoed 80 years later,' says Murray. 'I don't have any particular solution, but I definitely believe that somehow the experiences of buildings are deposited into their fabric in some way. There are aspects or characteristics of buildings' spaces to do with events that have happened before – spaces where you feel comfortable and [spaces where you feel] uncomfortable.'

Murray suggests a whole range of alternatives which may account for the power of the tunnels at Vimy Ridge. The porosity of the chalk would have acted as a sponge, soaking up blood and other bodily fluids, and the humidity of soldiers' breath, which may prompt an alarm signal from a hypersensitive receptor within the living. There may even be something of the immensity and danger of the undertaking, of the digging of tunnels in secrecy and under fire, which survives intact through some unaccountable aura. People do leave traces of themselves, says Murray, which may last longer in an organic setting like one made of chalk than in a

Below: Vimy Ridge battle site, France. During the First World War, Canadian soldiers inhabited a maze of subterranean rooms and tunnels carved out from the chalk of the Vimy Ridge in northern France. Here a tunnel divides into two – that on the left leads to an exit 150 metres behind the main battle line; the right-hand tunnel contained medical posts for the walking wounded.

contemporary enclosure of non-absorbent glass and steel. Indeed, chalk is a sedimentary material – a sort of memory bank of many lives – and perhaps it continues to accumulate layers ... traces. The trace, he continues, is as subtle and poetic (but somehow palpably *there*) as music which resonates in a cathedral long after the organist has stopped playing. 'I think there is a consciousness we have which doesn't have much to do with ghosts in the conventional way. In a way it's what Peter Ackroyd talks about – the sense of place. Things remain over quite a long period of time.'

Murray repeatedly employs the word 'trace', which he uses to indicate both residual matter and something of memory. Often, he uses it to indicate both. Murray was brought up in Lacock, a National Trust-owned village in Wiltshire, which is a compendium of traces. Lacock is the place where William Henry Fox Talbot developed photography, and the dreamy, rather miasmic 1835 impression of a latticed window in the local abbey (known to everyone in the village) is one of the world's oldest photographic images. The abbey itself is a repository of scars and traces, notably from the treatment meted out under Henry VIII's dissolution of the monasteries. More prosaically, Murray recalls the patina of dung that was ground into the roads before the National Trust stopped cattle being driven through the village's streets, a patina that disappeared only very gradually.

These traces require the observer to be alert to the lives they symbolise. Murray admits to finding ruins 'pretty boring', especially if they have been stripped of their humanity and are preserved as mere physical objects. Neither is he especially excited by the prospect of conservation – the recreation or preservation of spaces is not, Murray believes, as psychologically satisfying as

Above: Vimy Ridge battle site, France. Part of the Vimy tunnel complex. These steps lead down to the tunnels (or 'saps'), which were dug under German lines for the setting of mines. 'There was definitely something physical in that space related to what had been there before. Maybe it was the softness of the stone that made the difference, but definitely something had been absorbed into that space that still echoed,' says Peter Murray.

Right: Vimy Ridge battle site, France. The Commanding Officer's bedroom and office, effectively the nerve centre of the Vimy tunnel complex. Other sleeping quarters and offices were located nearby.

Above: Vimy Ridge battle site, France. A maple leaf, now protected by glass, carved into the chalk of a small Vimy tunnel storeroom during the First World War.

inhabiting them and adapting them as required. This is why Murray finds Avebury, that almost uncared-for circle of stones which straddles a functioning village, more alive and resonant than Stonehenge, Avebury's molly-coddled neighbour. In the early 1970s, Murray visited Munich, a city which still bore the marks of war: 'There was an old post office with a shattered dome, over-grown, piles of rubble. It was almost as if the war had finished only recently. If I returned and found it had been tidied up, I guess it wouldn't have the same impact.'

The point Murray makes is that the voice of a place is amplified (indeed, only heard at all) if visitors are allowed to imagine their way through to the human histories of the site. A physical and purely visual curating of a space, one which clears away all detritus in an

Right: Lacock Abbey, Wiltshire. William Henry Fox Talbot's negative of a window at Lacock Abbey, taken in 1835 and one of the world's oldest photographic images.

attempt to get to the kernel of a single truth, often has the effect of removing all truths and closing down the role of the senses other than that of sight. If the history of a place is so utterly finished, so completely out of time, devoid of a human presence or of any kind of life, it is of dubious value.

Christopher Woodward, in his book *In Ruins*, makes the same point in describing how Rome's Colosseum was stripped of its wild flowers, grasses, cypress trees and shrines in the latter half of the 19th century. '[By 1870] every tree was gone, every flower and blade of grass plucked from the ruins by cold-hearted archaeologists,' he wrote. 'The Colosseum is extinct. Today it is the most monumental bathos in Europe: a bald, dead and bare circle of stones. There are no shadows, no sands, no echoes and if a single flower blooms in a crevice it is sprayed with weedkiller.'

Evidently, it is difficult to know exactly where the voice, or life, of a building lies. It is certainly not resident purely in the architectural space itself, but in the marks, humidity, smells, miscellany of a place. The voice, if it has any physicality at all, may be just an atom thick and even a cursory clean-up may remove it. Occasionally, the voice is harder to remove, which Murray feels is the case at Vimy Ridge – that space is too condensed, claustrophobic and isolated easily to lose whatever aura is present there. But although he concedes that individuals may perceive and respond to a place quite differently, Murray is certain that the voices in the tunnels of Vimy are not prompted by the prior knowledge of what went on there – they are, he believes, bound up in the fabric of the place. 'Until somebody comes up with some sort of scientific evidence [to the contrary], I'm happy to follow my own feelings on this,' he says.

Bomb Shelter

Busselton, Western Australia

Saskia Lewis

A pale dust road stretches ahead and veers out of sight to the left. Low scrub frames the track and a ripple of hills sits on the horizon. Scale is stretched. The landscape is vast and flat, the glare of the sun to the north, relentless. A flock of birds crosses the path and out of nowhere sounds the high whine of an aircraft. The plane drops from the sky and dives towards the land, crossing the road low to the ground. It discharges a load, white dust, turns sharply and is gone …

The dirt road leads to an isolated bomb shelter, an imposing monolith. Every Easter Sunday from 1977 until 1984 the friends and family of Helen Shervington would play 'War'. They would appoint two generals. The adults would have spent days compiling the list of rules and deliberating their importance while the children would make and stockpile weapons – flour bombs, mud grenades and sticky pellets. The teams were divided with equal numbers of adults and children in each. One team would take the 'vital object' into the bush while the other would try to attack and recover it. It is hot at Easter, around 25°C. There was usually

cavalry in each army, occasionally joined by a friend in a light aircraft that swooped around pouring out flour, changing sides at will. The children adhered diligently to the rules while the adults broke them, the moral lesson for the youth being that there are no rules in war.

War was not unfamiliar territory. Indeed, the bomb shelter was born of war. In 1939 the Australian government had requisitioned land from Helen's grandfather to be developed as a Commonwealth air force base in Western Australia. The flat open country had made a perfect site for a series of airstrips and buildings to house a temporary community. The property is near Busselton, south of Perth, 2 kilometres from the ocean and 1.5 kilometres from the nearest main road. Initially this had seemed ideal. But the site proved to be too near to the ocean and it became clear that warships moored close to shore would be able to target and bomb the base. Instead of it being an operational base it soon became a training ground, preparing pilots for combat during the Second World War.

The bomb shelter was built in 1941 to serve as the administrative headquarters for the base. This was one of the few buildings on the site built to withstand the impact of weaponry, essentially to protect the paperwork and administrative infrastructure of the operation. The majority of other buildings had been timber-frame weatherboard constructions that had been quick to construct initially and subsequently to deconstruct and transport on decommissioning, leaving their concrete foundations behind as the only trace of their location. Many of them were moved to East Busselton as part of the development of the town in the 1950s. Some became family homes and a couple the quarters for the local Girl Guide and Scout troops, re-erected on stumps instead of foundations. Many are still

Right: The northern facade of the shelter shows the main entrance and the high-level windows that allowed daylight to penetrate the interior but prevented views in or out. The flat roof built in 1941 has failed and a shallow pitched asbestos roof was erected to provide temporary weatherproofing.

Right: Perspective view of the main entrance facade. The major extension is the 'control tower' that provides a living space at first-floor level and allows access to the re-instated flat roof. From here there will be an uninterrupted panorama of the surrounding landscape.

Above: In 1998 Helen Shervington built a terrace across the northern facade of the building and added a garage to the western elevation, both of which will be removed during the planned redevelopment.

standing today on their second sites and Helen can match them to the vacant plots drawn out in concrete in her paddocks. In effect, this building had been abandoned by its community, it had served a short life for the purpose for which it was built and then lay unused for over a decade. The bomb shelter stood as built, immovable, monolithic, dominant. A curious redundant relic, a freak of construction, a memory of a moment when the future seemed unreliable and threatening, even in a place as remote as this. It is the only building of its kind in the locale.

In 1956 Helen's father bought back his land from the government, reunited his 400 acres and resumed farming cattle commercially. The west end of the bomb shelter was turned into a store for fuel, tools and hay, the rest stood empty. The building is a mass of reinforced concrete, a box roughly 24 metres by 14 metres. External walls of 360-millimetre-thick concrete were cast on site, tied into a reinforced concrete roof. Windows between the beams sit just under the eaves allowing light to penetrate the interior but do not afford views out as their sills stand at 2.5 metres from the

finished floor level. The space had been subdivided into offices, stores and meeting rooms, 10 rooms either side of a central corridor. There were only two apertures to the interior, one in the middle of the north facade that was used as a main entrance and the other in the centre of the western facade. It was never clear to a first-time visitor how to get into the property and there were no views into the interior by which to hazard a guess. The reinforced glass had all been shattered as vandals had begun to use the site for shooting practice. The flat roof had started to fail bringing down the ceilings and so, as an interim measure, the structure had been clad with a secondary low-pitched asbestos one. The building had begun to deteriorate through time and lack of continuous inhabitation. No bombs had dropped. It had not been directly structurally challenged. It seemed doomed to slowly disintegrate and disappear.

The building's domestic reinvention came in 1976 when the family began to visit the site during holidays and camp in the huge interior volume. Since there were only perimeter fences to the land, the animals – a few horses and a herd of cattle – would occasionally wander in through the doors or lick the cars outside. Minimal work was done to make the building livable, just some DIY plumbing to provide a basic kitchen and bathroom. Many people visited during this period and grew deeply fond of this curious construction and the open wilderness in which it sat. It had become a retreat, a venue for people to gather in large numbers. In 1985 the living space was set alight by arsonists, the interior was blackened by smoke and although repairs were made it still seemed gloomy. The attack had caused an interruption and circumstances dictated that the building once again lay fallow for a decade. But the seeds for a change of identity had been sown.

Helen has been living here full-time since 1996. Initially she repaired the rooms that she was using. The kitchen occupies what was the Commander's Office, her bedroom an old store. She painted rooms as she needed them. The existing Jarrah hardwood floor that had been damaged in the fire has been replaced with concrete, marking the scene in a sombre tone. The

northern facade regained status as the main entrance and a terrace was built along it using old foundations of what had once been a toilet block. The west end of the building became guest quarters – it was clear that with an independent entrance it could function as a self-sufficient dwelling. Since the late 1990s, the only views out have been through the original door openings west and north through a single leaf width. This is about to change.

Preparations are being made to open the building up a little and slice through the dominant skin of its envelope, to introduce into the interior views to the south and direct sunlight from the north. Existing windows will retain their original positions in plan but will be cut out, some to floor level, on the north side to provide access, others to allow for views out while sitting. The building will be stripped back, removing the temporary pitched roof and the deck and garage that were erected in the late 1990s. Internal walls will be knocked through to provide larger spaces running the full width of the building, north to south. These will accommodate communal areas for living, cooking and eating and at the heart of the space the L-shaped concrete floor that commemorates the fire will be

NORTH ELEVATION

SOUTH ELEVATION

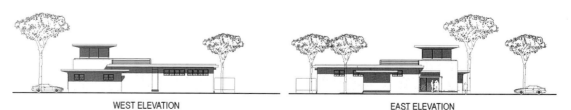

WEST ELEVATION

EAST ELEVATION

Right: Simple apertures have been cut between the rooms, with curtains used instead of doors to screen one space from another.

sanded and polished in celebration of its chequered history. Dane Richardson, who is overseeing the design, stresses that anything that is added or altered in the building at this point will be clearly readable against the fabric of the existing structure. Load-bearing walls that are removed will be replaced with steel columns and beams that will clearly identify them as part of this new phase of development. The intention is not to create an immaculate, pristine interior but a series of Modernist interventions into an existing environment, interventions that articulate a new way of living in the space. The original building will continue to tell the tale of the shifts in its use.

The major extension will be a 'control tower' on the north facade of the building. This will more clearly indicate the main entrance to the interior and provide a living space at first-floor level, access to a restored flat roof and a 360-degree uninterrupted vista of sky and surrounding landscape including the 2,000 olive trees that now occupy 30 acres of land to the east. Helen laughs that this suits her controlling personality. She enjoys the idea of being able to keep an eye on everything in sight. In being modified to become a home, the building will gain some imagery in keeping with its past, a cheeky fabrication of what there never was originally, but of what might have been. A smaller block built to the east will provide a laundry, and a garage is planned to the north-west of the building that will help to protect the front facade from the prevailing winds. Over the last few years a 2-acre carpet of lush green grass has been nurtured to encircle the bomb shelter like a moat. In summer months the surrounding paddocks bleach pale in the sun in what is partly a strategy to protect against fire but also serves to

Below: During the Second World War, the vast flat landscape was ideal for the building of a Commonwealth air force base to train pilots; this led to the building of the bomb shelter in 1941.

Below: The central corridor divides the interior space; with rooms facing either north or south. The corridor will be partly stripped away during the redevelopment, allowing the full width of the building to be united.

Bottom: Proposed plan. Internal walls will be removed to make the space more open plan and unite views to the north and south. A veranda will run the full length of the north elevation with a roof to screen the interior from solar gain during the summer months.

reinforce a new domestic atmosphere for what was once a much more industrial building.

Busselton is growing at an accelerated pace. A decade ago there were about 10,000 inhabitants, now there are 30,000. The land on which this structure sits is part of an area that has been identified and approved as suitable for new housing. An indication, perhaps, of how the surrounding area may eventually evolve, although Helen is determined to maintain acres of farmland around her property for the foreseeable future. Once transformed into a home, she has no intention of allowing the bomb shelter to change status any time soon, but it may eventually find itself embraced by the growth of the town and reattached, if at a distance, to its original neighbours that were moved half a century ago. It may, one day, become a curious town house with extensive gardens and an intricate story to tell.

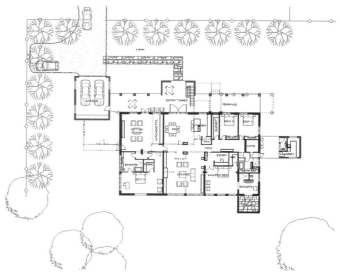

The Young Vic Theatre

Southwark, London

David Littlefield

Designed as a temporary structure by Bill Howell, incorporating a Victorian butcher's shop, 1970
Rebuilt by Haworth Tompkins Architects, 2006

Above: 'Young, gifted and back.' The theatre reopened to the public in October 2006 after being closed for redevelopment for two years.

Opposite: Conceived in the 1960s, the Young Vic was designed as a very unmonumental place – anti-iconic, classless and even a challenge to the Establishment.

The Young Vic is one of those arts institutions founded on raw commitment, low budgets and the loyalty of its clientele. Conceived in the 1960s and realised in 1970, the Young Vic (an off-shoot of the more established Old Vic theatre down the road) was imagined as a very unmonumental place, 'classless', accessible and cheap. Built on a bomb-site over the basements of a Victorian terrace and incorporating the remains of a butcher's shop, the building was a cheap structure designed for a short life. However, temporary structures have a habit of sticking around, thumbing their noses at their better-built permanent cousins, and after three decades the Young Vic had more than outlived its intended lifespan. It was a rough-and-ready place, with a roof thin enough to convey the patter of rain to the audience; in winter it could be cold, and the sirens of passing emergency vehicles were clearly audible during performances. The Young Vic was designed not as a theatre of escape, but of reality.

An element of that reality is the fact that 54 people, sheltering in their basements during a Second World War air raid, died when a bomb caused their terrace to collapse on them. This partly explains the retention of that butcher's shop as the entrance to the theatre, a design tactic that was at once an economy measure, a constructional head-start and an arresting symbol of the event which had cleared the site in the first place. When you enter this building, whether you know it or not, you enter a ruin. The Young Vic, therefore, had more than a constructional head-start – the place came loaded with memory. It was almost ripe for story-telling.

Architect Steve Tompkins describes the building as one lacking any intrinsic architectural qualities but one that, simultaneously, transmits a great deal of humanity. However, as an already powerful place, the building resists overlay – it is multilayered enough and any attempt to add new messages or play symbolic or architectural games would have felt contrived and uncomfortable. 'The building was already a palimpsest when we came to it. Intellectually, there's nothing here that demands to be treated as an important piece of architecture, and we're not a practice that feels we have to preserve as much as we can. But there is a sense of dereliction and melancholy; there is a very strong cultural memory of that bomb. I suppose we've attempted to commandeer all that melancholy and turn it into something positive and joyful. The Young Vic is a place of re-emergence, of the survival of culture. Our job was to make a building that was convincingly new that could incorporate its past lives.'

Tompkins has some sympathy for the views of Peter Murray (see p 54) who believes that powerful and dramatic human events can somehow leave a super-sensory trace of themselves within the fabric of their locations. This is more than, to quote artist Antoni Malinowski, 'the graffiti of use'; it is, instead, a subtle resonance that impresses itself upon the mind quite independently of known facts and recorded history. It is like detecting the faint aroma of food before you realise you are standing in a kitchen. It is an alertness to the traces of what has been. 'I know what Peter Murray means,' says Tompkins. 'It's something more than common knowledge. That was behind the decision not to demolish the whole site. The building's voice was very strong.'

Haworth Tompkins takes a 'slow burn' approach to its architecture; the practice engages with existing buildings as a 'full immersion' process, soaking them up and almost looking at them with peripheral vision before

Right: The graffiti of affection. Before the Young Vic was vacated in 2004, employees covered its interior in rapid scribbles – principally names: Samuel B, Naomi, Roger, Stella, Alex, Esther …

The Young Vic opened on 11 September 1970 as an often experimental theatre for younger designers, actors, writers and technicians. Built for £60,000 as a no-nonsense theatre with low-price, unreservable seats, the company was led by Frank Dunlop who wanted to create 'a new kind of theatre for a new generation – one that was unconventional, classless, open, circus-like and cheap'. The new venue was even described as a 'paperback' theatre.

Built on the site of a building destroyed during a Second World War bombing raid, where 54 people had died, the theatre was designed to last just five years. By 2000, under the direction of new artistic director David Lan, the theatre was in a poor state and a fund-raising effort was begun to rebuild the venue. The Young Vic vacated its site in 2004 for two years, co-producing shows across the UK and internationally, before returning in October 2006.

The £7 million reinvention of the building was undertaken by architects Haworth Tompkins and aimed to provide new facilities while retaining a sense of architectural ambiguity within which theatre directors could work freely. The butcher's shop (the sole architectural survivor of the Second World War bomb) has been retained as the theatre's entrance, while the auditorium has been considerably reworked. A range of new facilities has been added, including two studio spaces, offices and an enlarged foyer and cafe. The entire development was conceived as a connected group of distinct elements, articulated through the use of different materials including profiled brickwork and hand-painted cement panels (covered in steel mesh) by artist Clem Crosby.

tackling them. The firm has no particular house style and its collection of built works is not obviously the product of the same minds. The architects attempt to preserve something of the spirit of a place, not so much in terms of a *genius loci* but in the sense of extracting the maximum value from what is there. At the Young Vic, just like the practice's 1999 remodelling of the Royal Court Theatre, the building is still recognisable for what it was. It has been transformed, but not obliterated. The remade theatre still has an air of the industrial makeshift about it, an informality and a lack of polish that tries to capture the essence of the original enterprise. If ever an architect had to perform a balancing act, this is it: to draw on the chronological, physical and cultural matter of the building (Tompkins calls it 'quarrying raw material') without resorting to imitation or over-managing the ways people feel about it. The success of the Young Vic, both of the building and of the institution, is the emotional depths it can plumb inexpensively and with little effort. If the voice of the theatre was to be preserved, the trick was to understand the personality of the place and keep it talking – perhaps to change the accent, but not to petrify the voice as a recording or an echo.

'In some way you're an elocution teacher. The voice of the building is in the present – it's not just fixed in the past. But you can silence a building if you hit a wrong note,' says Tompkins. 'I think the butcher's entrance, for example, had acquired a significance; the semiotics of it were well established and we could see no reason why a piece of new architecture would do the job any better. In fact, quite the contrary. Honesty is the issue here. If you're making architecture that is somehow knowing, or condescending, the preserve of the cognoscenti and the cultural elite, you've got a big

Opposite: Long section through the Young Vic, running through the main auditorium, the foyer and a new rehearsal studio to the left. The old butcher's shop appears at the centre of the drawing.

Opposite: Plan of the redeveloped theatre. The entrance, still through the old butcher's shop, is shown at the bottom centre of the drawing.

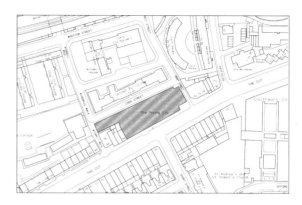

Right: The theatre (the shaded area in the centre of this image) occupies the site of what was once a row of terraced houses.

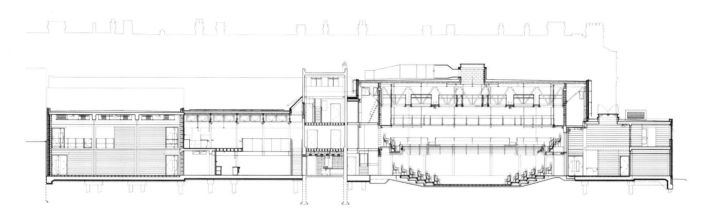

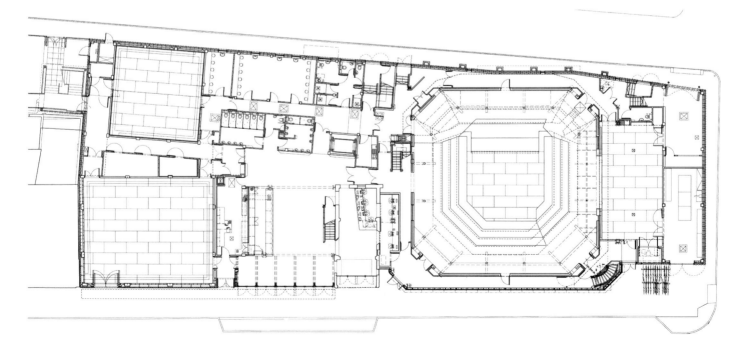

Below: Cross-section through the foyer of the redeveloped building.

Right: The main theatre space prior to closure in 2004.

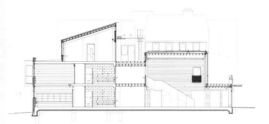

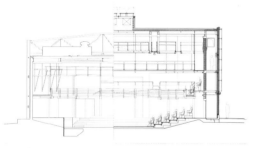

Above: Section through the main theatre space, showing the original 1970 structure on the left; and the new Haworth Tompkins building on the right.

Right: Prior to redevelopment, photographer John Collingwood recorded the building in a series of long-exposure images. His pictures are often high contrast and veer towards the ghostly, as in this image of the costume department mannequins.

Right: The theatre after reopening in October 2006. The redeveloped building incorporates elements from its past lives, including the tiles from the former butcher's shop which serves as the theatre's main entrance.

problem. The architect has got a duty to make work that is accessible.'

In this respect, for a building that has been almost completely demolished and reassembled, Tompkins has exercised a curious restraint. Pre-existing surfaces have not been cleaned and the edges between old and new are not only apparent, but a little rough. Wall treatments record the presence of lost partitions and the practical, operational fixtures of the building (steel beams, bolts, electrical conduits) are exposed – this is a theatre, after all, and any deception that is to take place is confined to the stage. Builders were even encouraged to stop working on certain jobs when they were not quite complete, handing over to the Young Vic production team which finished the job under the supervision of the architects. In this way, the theatre was not 'tidied up too soon' and small details are simpler, more direct and somehow more convincing. Patching-up jobs have been done in a way that is deliberately unsentimental. 'A lot of detail at the Young Vic is builders' detail,' says Tompkins, who admits you have to 'stay confident' when adopting a position such as this. 'If you can leave a certain amount of detail to chance, interesting things will start to happen.'

The hope is that the remade theatre is as suggestive of possibility as its predecessor, that it can be occupied (and appropriated) in the manner of the last 40 years. Before the Young Vic's employees vacated the old building in 2004, to make way for its reinvention, they wrote all over it (principally names: Samuel B, Naomi, Roger, Stella, Alex, Esther ...). Very few, if any, of these daubs were poetic; the poetry lay in the act, which was one of affection.

Photographer John Collingwood, who captured the theatre prior to the rebuilding work, looks for traces, evidence of people in the spaces he photographs. His objective is to record not the space as such, but the role of space as an extension of the mind. Banal as they are, these little acts of graffiti become an authentic part of the place. 'The building becomes something else,' says Collingwood. 'The traces of the people who pass through the building constantly change it.' That remark is interesting: it is not the people who change the building, but their traces. This is, perhaps, the point of the Young Vic. It is a conduit, perhaps even a catalyst, for memory and little more. It is an unmonumental, very uninstitutional place where people are encouraged, gently, to look beyond what is in front of their eyes.

ARCHITECTURAL VOICES

Left: The new theatre space has been designed to echo the 1970 original. The form of the space, the seating plan, wall materials and the studio quality of the place embody memories of what went before.

Below: The new Young Vic has a greater street presence than its forebear, but its entrance remains almost innocuous, apologetic even.

Morphology and Matter
Working with Existing Structures

Simon Henley

Simon Henley is a director of London-based architecture practice Buschow Henley, a firm which has developed a knack of responding sensitively and thoughtfully to given spaces. Here, Henley explores how contemporary architecture can grow out of the old, not as pastiche but in a more ambiguous, even 'perplexing', manner.

In 1928 Alois Riegl wrote the essay 'The Modern Cult of Monuments: its Character and its Origin', in which he defined the 'intentional commemorative' monument and the 'unintentional' monument. He described an intentional monument as a memorial constructed expressly to commemorate a person or event; the 'unintentional' acquires 'age-value' with time or 'historical-value' due to its association with past events.

As an architectural practice conserving existing buildings for adaptive reuse, we are in effect dealing with monuments of the unintended variety. They are old and exhibit 'age-value'. But we recognise that these buildings have a voice; furthermore, their conservation and reuse can strengthen that voice. Not only does the act of conservation imply an interest in age and historical value, but our work may also be seen to translate the unintentioned into the intentioned (the search for collective meaning) by devising an analogue (something that resembles something else) which may be latent within the form and fabric of the existing structure. The analogue is superimposed, but onto a building whose order lends itself to that situation or expression and to any collective understanding which results. Each project described in this essay may be read morphologically, that is in terms of its spatial structure, and materially, for the atmosphere it seeks to create.

Riegl notes that a building (or 'monument') that is no longer useful can be preserved for its age-value alone. However, he acknowledges that the 'situation is more complicated where use-value comes into play', because there is a conflict between age-value, which requires signs of decay, and use-value, which depends on the robustness or completeness of a building.

On our first encounter with 10–22 Shepherdess Walk and 20–22 Newman Street, the heavy masonry facades were quite evidently old-fashioned and the fabric showed obvious signs of weathering. This was true also of EW Pugin's St Monica's Board School in Hoxton, designed in the 1860s, but in this case its association with the architect's father, AWN Pugin, and the school's part in an ensemble of buildings for Augustinian friars mean that its 'historical-value' is cemented with a Grade II listing.

However, the idea of a monument becomes more problematic when referring to newer structures such as the 1960s concrete-frame, brick-panelled Buckland Court housing estate in London's Shoreditch and the 1980s steel portal-frame extension to the listed Goole market in Yorkshire. These structures have aged, but neither has done so gracefully. They are perceived as neither old enough to be attributed age-value and historical-value nor new enough for the 'masses' to enjoy.[1] Their newness is, of course, suggestive of how useful they should be or, as Riegl describes it, their 'use-value'.

---

1   Alois Riegl. 'The masses have always enjoyed new things and have always wanted to see the hand of man exert its creative power rather than the destructive effects of nature'. *Oppositions 25* (4), tr. KW Forster and D Ghirardo, 1982, pp 21–51.

Right: View of the central courtyard of 10–22 Shepherdess Walk
prior to Buschow Henley's intervention for The Factory.

All five of these buildings had use-value that lent each to adaptation, but in the case of the Victorian and Edwardian load-bearing masonry structures, age and use were in the balance. In the case of the two more recent examples, use dominates over age. Conventionally, architects conserve load-bearing masonry buildings and complement historic elements with distinctive contemporary additions. By contrast, new structures are demolished, over-clad (rewrapped like a present) or stripped to the frame and reclad. If much of the fabric is to be retained unaltered, few designers have sympathy for its innate language but prefer to employ an arbitrary, often glib and jolly approach to distract our eye from the original structure.

The Factory, 10 – 22 Shepherdess Walk, London
This 10,000 square metre warehouse is located in the canyon-like streets of Shoreditch, East London. In volume, the building describes a rhomboid at the centre of which lies a courtyard. To the west, the building rises six storeys, and five storeys to the east. In turn, the west block is divided by load-bearing party walls to create four 'tenements', each with an entrance and stair. The east building is divided into five similar 'tenements'. At the same time one, two and nine different buildings, it has now been adapted to accommodate 50 loft apartments with basement parking and workspace on the ground floor.

This project is an interesting exercise in roofscape. The local planning authority was in favour of replacing the existing skylights and we began to investigate the possibility of creating a series of detached pavilions on the roof. Our initial ideas depicted an ironic setting of monopitch bungalows, picket fences, lawns and kitchen gardens. These structures evolved into 13 gardens, each with a detached or semi-detached

Left: The Factory's roofscape after reinvention by Buschow Henley. 'The loft apartment, this most urban of living conditions, is transformed by the invention of a garden suburb on the roof.' (Simon Henley).

pavilion. The loft apartment, this most urban of living conditions, is transformed by the invention of a garden suburb on the roof. New pavilions are treated as detached houses with their own gardens to cultivate; a counterpoint to the very urban streets below. Poet John Betjeman wrote that 'Outline is the most important part of British scenery'. Yet buildings characterised by their rooftops – plateaux dotted with lift and plant room housings, drying rooms and caretakers' flats – surround 10–22 Shepherdess Walk. The pavilions give the building an 'outline' with an innovative and strange sense of scale, and an analogue of British domesticity that influences the residents' way of life.

The new construction uses structural rolled steel sections to graft place and circulation onto the found building, mediating demonstratively between the building's original and proposed use. The resulting construction utilises known efficiencies and is enhanced by the recognisable qualities of specific components: timber for warmth and tactility; glass for transparency; and zinc, a universal enclosure for both walls and roofs. Recalling ideas about newness-value and age-value, the materials have two lives: a short-term life which coincides with the time it takes to market the building and in which the new materials occupy the foreground; and a longer term life, the result of a gradual weathering process during which bright zinc and warm wood turn silver. This coincides with the building's occupation, where both materials and residents recede into the background and the community.

Talkback Television Offices, London

In her critique of this project, writer Irina Davidovici described it as one that 'attempts to identify and interpret Britishness, in which much of the Talkback

Below: A new pavilion (exhibiting 'newness value') set atop the older building ('age-value') for The Factory.

Above: Aerial view. The Factory's building is set within 'canyon-like streets'.

ethos is anchored, but in this case in architectural terms of urban models and language. Second, it questions the conventional and achieves richness from subverting it. Third, it uses the immediate neighbourhood as a reference, creating a small, self-sufficient universe.' She went on to write that 'The interiors operate at a subconscious level, re-creating faintly familiar situations. … All that is new…works like a cement that binds together the aggregate of the original structures.'

The site is a little to the north of Oxford Street in Central London. It consists of two adjoining buildings (20 and 22 Newman Street), each 9 metres wide and 34 metres deep. Each property is fronted by a 10-metre-deep, six-storey structure with an equally deep five-storey building at the rear – leaving a substantial central space between them, found on the flat roof of the two-storey link block. Our brief was to accommodate 250 staff, a TV studio, a rehearsal room, various meeting rooms and editing suites; to this we added a 'common room/village hall'. The design took its cue from the 'university model' Talkback employed in its day-to-day research and production of programmes. This translated into a multistorey cloister 18 metres wide and 14 metres deep.

Right: The premises at 20–22 Newman Street prior to their re-invention as offices for television production company Talkback by architects Buschow Henley.

ARCHITECTURAL VOICES

Right: In creating the offices
for Talkback, Buschow Henley
considered the analogue of the
English country house. 'The
reception [was conceived] as a
generous domestic hall with a fine
timber stair, timber panelling and
a heavy oak table.'

Below: Plan through the entire building complex for Talkback, with the two office buildings grouped around a central courtyard.

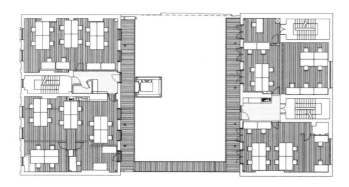

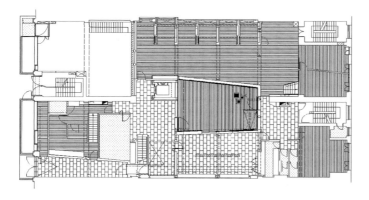

Above: Plan of the ground-level entrance to Talkback, with the central staircase and flagstones designed to suggest the English country house.

Inspired by JB Jackson's essay 'Gardens to Decipher', the central space took on the characteristics of a 16th-century garden – in essence a herb garden that placed great emphasis on symbolism, utility (medicine and cooking) and fragrance, setting little or no store on the visual aspects of the plants. 'As if to protect it from contact with the wider, undisciplined landscape [for which read Central London] the garden was usually surrounded by a wall,' wrote Jackson. Overhead, the windows in the courtyard elevations have been replaced by doors that open onto the cloister, which is broad enough to meet and work in; bridges span the space between the buildings. This layout generates a focus for circulation and the life of the organisation and every office has direct access to the outside. In the centre a new two-storey structure incorporates the reception hall, common room/village hall and offices around a sunken garden.

A second analogue, that of a period English country house, is used to conceive of the reception as a generous domestic hall with a fine timber stair, timber panelling and a heavy oak table. The stair signifies that the space is integrated into the morphology of the building and is not a conventional threshold that should not be transgressed.

The new work relies on timber cladding and decking outside and natural timber and matchboard panelling inside, painted Fletton brickwork, concrete paving ('flagstones') and floorboards, and handmade components such as plain metal railings, timber doors, windows and staircases, light fittings and traditional doorknobs. The composition of materials and components is intended to reflect the capacity of the English Arts and Crafts Movement to produce a building at the close of the 19th century, when 20–22 Newman

Street were originally constructed. The design avoids the use of easily dated building products that would otherwise fix our intervention in time.

Buckland Court Estate, Shoreditch, London

The 113 dwellings on the estate are arranged in three linked blocks around an open courtyard. Built in the 1960s, the estate demonstrates the problem of urbanisation that arises with the relative density of four- and six-storey deck-access flats set in an open and poorly defined space. In a sense there is an abundance of space, but there is neither the dimension that open land affords, nor the structure and security that a garden provides. Our brief is to secure the entrance points and to landscape the space.

Inside the newly secured courtyard we envisage a utilitarian garden of herbs and other fragrant plants at the heart of which a glade is planted with meadow grass. It is designed to remove those who live here to some rural idyll; for children, trees, a hillock and a dell might serve to conjure thoughts of the Hundred Acre Wood where Pooh and Piglet sought out a Woozle, or a Wonderland into which Alice descended.

But what language is appropriate to gate a concrete-framed, brick-panelled deck-access block? For generations William Morris wallpapers have lined city and suburban rooms, in recognition of a longing for the countryside. Heavy and fret-cut from Corten steel, our gates will be patterned with leaves, vegetables and fruit, projecting the idea of a rich garden landscape. Rich brown and weathered, the gates will at once have newness-value and age-value. On the corners of the site, next to the pavement, semi-mature pine trees will be planted, their scale designed to confront the dominant nature of the existing architecture. Intervening only by means of alterations to the landscape (including

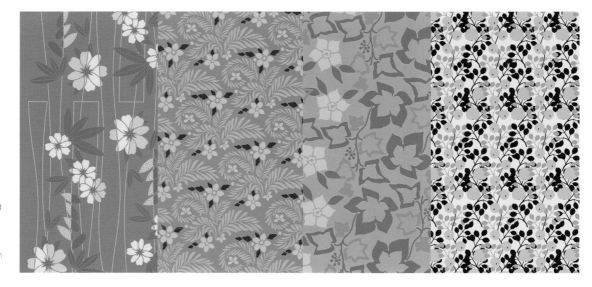

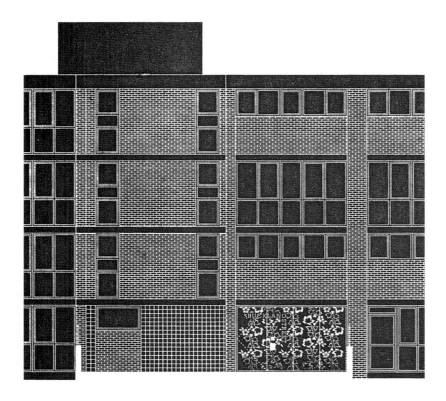

roof. It is an awful building, the material character of which diminishes its curious geometry. Our adaptation retains the ground bearing concrete slab and the steel portals. Strangely, the completed building will once again be clad in a similar corrugated sheet metal, this time in black. But beneath the carapace, the new enclosure has been reduced to a timber-framed and -clad enfilade – theatre, foyer, cafe and workshop, with offices and council chamber above – creating an external performance space and a covered area for market stalls.

The building stands next to a side street that in recent years has gained great importance as a pedestrian route between the historic high street (Boothferry Road) and the newly completed Wesley Square shopping centre (1997). Although the form of the building remains essentially the same, the decision to raise the portals where the geometry of site and building change forms a 'crossing'. The addition of a 'brim' (as in a hat) and verandah along the side street will afford visitors and passers-by shelter from both sun and rain, and also provide a place for traders to pitch a stall. The underside of the brim is lined in polished gold stainless steel and reflects the rich colour of the timber cladding beneath it. But it is the pitch of the brim, along with the addition of the crossing and the shift in the original geometry which, when seen in perspective, will result in an optical illusion that translates this prosaic corrugated metal building (whose geometry is derived directly from the site) into a very particular material and sculptural form.

the gates), but without altering the brick and concrete architecture of the estate, we intend to effect a significant change in perception.

Arts and Civic Centre, Goole, Yorkshire

The existing market structure was built in the 1980s. A steel portal frame supports corrugated sheet metal, powder-coated brown, that is used above a brick base to clad both the walls and an asymmetrically pitched

Conclusion

When conserving and reusing existing buildings we do more than repair the fabric, and replace and modernise

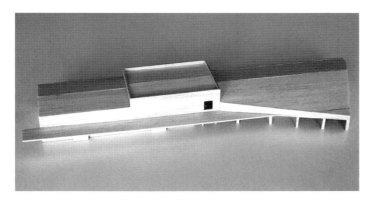

services. We seek to understand what, in Riegl's terms, is of value; we seek to know what the building wants to be. This ranges from 'what might have been' to 'what still can be'. It is an opportunity to remake the building and propose a collective understanding absent in the original by employing memory where the protagonists are type and construction materials. The original form and materials inform the nature of adaptation and extension, and the construction technique we use.

Such an approach even permits an unconventional outcome in which the point of intervention is not obvious and which, in time, will be difficult to date. The objective is not to preserve the original, and not to contrast new with old. Instead, we believe our intervention should be more ambiguous, more perplexing, a solution in which contrast may play only a small part. Our objective is to create a continuity of experience for those dwelling in the remade building, where coherent experience in terms of the analogue takes precedence over the authenticity of the 'unintentional' original. This treats the original fabric as both particular inspiration (morphology and matter) and mundane resource that can be put to new use and given previously unintended meaning.

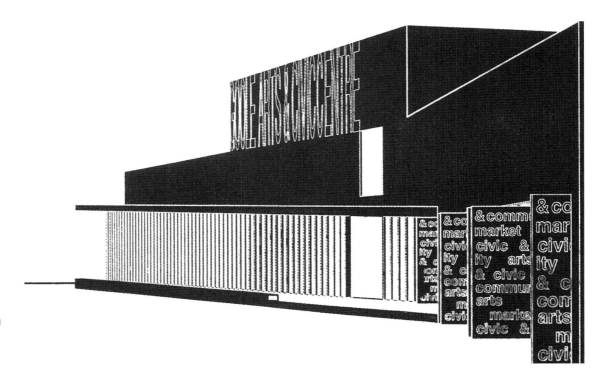

Right: Etching of the redesigned Goole Arts and Civic Centre, the geometry of which plays games with perspective.

ARCHITECTURAL VOICES

St Catherine's Chapel and Almshouses

Exeter, Devon

David Littlefield

Founded 1457 and destroyed during an air raid in 1942

Subject of an art installation by Patricia MacKinnon-Day, with lighting by architects BDP, 2005

Above: The chapel of the former almshouses, lit within by a grid of fibre optics – a lighting strategy designed to be suggestive of votive candles.

Opposite: The almshouses were founded in 1457 and destroyed in 1942. Artist Patricia MacKinnon-Day has reinvented the site, with architects BDP, by monumental-ising the position of the former doorways in glass.

In 1457 Canon John Stevens founded the St Catherine's Almshouses to provide homes for 13 men. Some 350 years later, in July 1799, William Scanes was employed to delouse the place for 'two pounds, two shillings and two pence'; in May 1804 a new well was ordered to replace the original because the latter was 'so near to the common sewer as to be frequently choked by the oozings from it'; and in May 1942 the complex of buildings, by now managed by the Salvation Army, was bombed by the Luftwaffe.

This odd collection of detail – the beginning and end of a building, flanking minor and almost irrelevant events – provides the raw material for artist Patricia MacKinnon-Day. The artist, who later enlisted the help of lighting designers from BDP, was originally commissioned by developer Land Securities to create an enclosure for the ruined site, a fence to prevent the space from continuing to be inhabited by the homeless. MacKinnon-Day, however, felt a subtle richness in the surfaces and textures of the site and the project grew into a far more interventionist proposition. Glass cases, marking the exact dimensions and positions of former doors, contain archaeological detritus and signpost spaces that are no longer present. The circulation of the building is reversed – visitors are forced to walk where once there were walls, locating themselves in relation to doorways which remain impassable.

On her first visit to the site, MacKinnon-Day was struck by the small spaces marked out by the traces of the former building. Inhabitants had squeezed themselves into rooms often measuring no more than 8 feet by 5 feet and the artist considered that highlighting the positions of the doors would draw attention to this fact more sensitively and emotively than would drawing out the closeness of the walls. The doors, or their representations, become monumental – like headstones, they become symbolic of the lives of the people they once framed.

For MacKinnon-Day the voice of a building is not always immediately apparent. Often a voice emerges over time through careful sifting of historical information and scrutinising of physical clues for their suggestive power. At the almshouses the tiny spaces defined by the remaining stonework forced the question 'who lived here?', which was in part an emotional response triggered by the claustrophobic atmosphere of Glasgow tenements, with which MacKinnon-Day is familiar. Fortunately, precise records were kept by the almshouse authorities and archived in the cathedral, and MacKinnon-Day was able to track who had lived where, and when. It is these records that reveal the requirement for a new well, that William Scanes needed to be paid, that resident Ann Gidley received a new bedstead in 1828 and that the 'chimnies' were swept by Phillip Baker in August 1810, for which he was paid 10 shillings. Curiously, MacKinnon-Day also visited contemporary local shelters for the homeless and old people's homes, comparing the schedules, rules and sanctions adopted by the almshouses with those of their modern equivalents; the language had changed but the intent was much the same, she found.

'These [records] revealed the humanity of the place, the human context. It is all very ordinary, but for me the ordinary becomes significant,' says MacKinnon-Day, who approaches her work from an analysis of faint traces. If a place has a voice, she doesn't want to amplify it too loudly – as with the site itself, she prefers to leave other listeners to do a little detective work. 'I think I wanted to give people clues, a sense that they are looking at part of a whole mystery.'

Saturday the 12 may 1804

They ordered a new Well to be dug
at Saint Catharine's almshouses
the present Well being so near
the common Sewer as to be frequently
choked by the Oozings from
it.

Left: Texts from archival records are inscribed into the stonework of the site, such as this entry from 12 May 1804.

Below: The artistic programme at Princesshay focused less on the building than on the ways in which it had been inhabited.

The 'doors' double as display cabinets and contain small objects retrieved from the history of the site: glazed and colourful Roman pottery, medieval earthenware and molten glass from beer bottles that were scattered from a nearby pub, which also caught the blast of the 1942 bomb. MacKinnon-Day even included a ring-pull from a 1970s drink can, to the consternation of the local press, to reference future archaeologists who may attribute a similar measure of significance to the innocuous (ring-pulls have changed so often that they will be able to assist in the accurate dating of our own age).

In spite of the fact that MacKinnon-Day's intervention, called 'Marking Time', was more ambitious than the original brief called for, it is balanced by a similar urge for restraint. Martin Lupton, director of BDP Lighting, knew at once that he could have lit the stonework to heighten the sense of drama inherent in ruined sites – but he didn't. 'We could have illuminated the whole site very dramatically and it would have looked fabulous. I'm sure we could have done an incredible job,' he says. The artistic programme was to tread lightly, to focus not so much on the building but on the lives and minor histories that the building contained. The outside of the ruins, therefore, is barely lit at all and Lupton contrived to arrange light sources that would lure visitors in.

Entries copied from archival records and inscribed into new stonework are illuminated, while inside the chapel is lit gently by a grid of fibre optics.

The textures, edges and depths of walls are only selectively lit, leaving the glass monuments to old doorways, with all the symbolism that doorways attract to themselves,[1] to speak the loudest and provide what MacKinnon-Day calls 'traces of past journeys'. These 'doors' are a celebration of what artists call negative space, which makes manifest what wasn't there in the first place – the space between things.

Above: The glass 'doors' double as display cabinets containing historic debris: Roman pottery, medieval earthenware and molten beer bottles.

---

1 In his classic book *The Poetics of Space*, Gaston Bachelard begins chapter 1 with a quote from author Pierre Albert-Birot: 'A la porte de la maison qui viendra frapper?' ('At the door of the house, who will come knocking?').

St John-at-Hackney and St Barnabas

Hackney, London

David Littlefield

St John-at-Hackney, London, designed by James Spiller and completed 1797
St Barnabas church, Hackney, London, designed by CH Reilly, 1909–10
Matthew Lloyd Architects has been asked to draw up proposals for both churches

Top: St Barnabas. The church is completely landlocked, stranded so far from the pavement, that many local residents have forgotten it is even there.

Opposite: St Barnabas. The view from the organ loft, looking through the screen – on which stands an elegant crucifix (above) – towards the nave.

St Barnabas, a Byzantine-style church which is being strangled by its neighbours in London's Hackney, is one of the city's hidden and forgotten buildings. It is abandoned but in perfect working order: choir robes hang in vestry wardrobes and music lies by the organ ready to be played, but gossamer cobwebs thread their way between the pews. A cupboard at the rear of the church contains leaflets printed in celebration of an event in 1953; a stack of colourful booklets, *The Children's Worship*, dates back to 1938. There are even hymn books in Braille. The congregation appears to have become disembodied – its moods, rituals and style of service are plain to see. The building is the manifestation of a cultural memory, a social mausoleum.

The church is not, in fact, entirely abandoned – each week the parish priest and curate hold a service in a small side chapel for no one but themselves. It is a brave act of devotion to what is still a consecrated place, but their worship takes place out of sight of the main body of the building, which can seat 400 people. Architect Matthew Lloyd, a Christian whose faith in the profundities of his religion outweighs his faith in the doctrines of the Church, struggles to know how to respond to this place. It is a battle between architectural rationality, the respect of a believer beset by doubt and a sensitivity to the uncanny.

'This place was made in the name of God as a real entity. The people who made this building were doing it for a profoundly real, believable, palpable God. What's happened to our religion? This building now has no function,' says Lloyd, who feels a heavy sense of responsibility for the building and what it stands for.

If buildings can accumulate a voice, places of worship are probably the most susceptible to this process. In almost any sense of architectural voice (stylistic, historical, imaginary, atmospheric) churches and other holy places resonate powerfully. To the Christian mind, the presence of a cross, a simple intersection of two lines, is enough to transform an otherwise ordinary space into one of some significance. St Barnabas is particularly multivalent. From an architectural perspective, it is well crafted and slightly daring, employing arched lintels of concrete at a time when concrete had purely industrial associations; Lloyd is struck with admiration for 'the love that has been lavished on this building'. Historically, it is a fine example of a missionary church, a sort of outpost in the East End enabling the rich to minister to the poor. It is a forgotten place, but shows not the slightest evidence of vandalism. It is, too, big enough to hint at the sublime, which is often the case when you find yourself alone in a large, empty space. Lloyd talks of the 'personality' of St Barnabas rather than just its voice. It is an observation prompted by the peculiar state of the church's abandonment. It suffers from such an abandonment of purpose that it has become a curiosity. It fits into the same category of unpeopled places as the *Marie Celeste* and David Rodinsky's room.

Rodinsky was a Jew who lived above a synagogue in Princelet Street in London's Whitechapel. Little is known about the man other than that he left his absurdly cluttered room in the 1960s and never returned. The room – full of books, diaries and arcane paperwork, as well as mundane items such as beer bottles – left nothing but a trail of clues about Rodinsky and his state of mind. The place became an obsession for artist Rachel Lichtenstein, who later collaborated with writer Iain Sinclair to record her investigations into its contents and the man who had inhabited it. The room began to take on a life of its own. More than

ARCHITECTURAL VOICES

ARCHITECTURAL VOICES

representative of Rodinsky – in many ways the room *was* Rodinsky. 'My sense, at that time, climbing the rickety stairs, poking about the shuttered chamber, was the sense I still have: of a man who had become a room,' wrote Sinclair.[1] 'The man remains, it is the room itself that vanishes.'

Sinclair's poetic observation certainly has an application for St Barnabas. In examining the accoutrements of the church – the books, the robes, the orders of service, the memorial plaques – one touches the missing congregation. In both a social and a cultural sense, the congregation is still palpably there, or at least not very far away. It has all the unreal reality of an old photograph, which captures the likeness of a person without being lifelike. The congregation of St Barnabas has about the same presence as the image of the Reverend W Armstrong Buck, whose photograph hangs in the vestry. It shows a young man whose gaze is so unfocused that he appears lifeless; his portrait, which emerges through the sepia, illustrates his status rather than his character. It is an image of a man devoted to Christian service, whose missionary role takes precedence over any personal ambition other than his work for the glory of God. The picture reveals nothing of Buck himself, because Buck himself does not matter, and the same is true of his congregation. It is a haunting presence – Lloyd calls it 'spooky'.

Equally, in its intactness, St Barnabas provides the perfect surface on which to project one's own metaphorical voice – especially for someone alert to, and slightly sad about, the decline of Christianity. This building, owned by the Church of England but

Above: St Barnabas. The liturgical robes, forgotten and hanging in wardrobes along with extraneous clutter and vacuum cleaners.

---

1   Rachel Lichtenstein and Iain Sinclair, *Rodinsky's Room*, Granta, London, 2000.

Above: St Barnabas is squeezed in among surrounding buildings. Outside space is rationed and the base of the church is rarely warmed by the sun.

Left: St Barnabas. Much of the interior of the church, erected in 1909–10, is simple and spartan – including the unembellished yellow cross in its principal window.

Above: St Barnabas. A cob-
webbed crucifix. 'This place was
made in the name of God as a
real entity. The people who made
this building were doing it for a
profoundly real, believable, God.
The building now has no function,'
says architect Matthew Lloyd.

traditional enough to appear almost Catholic, appears to be saddened by its own demise; the prints and statues of Christ and the Virgin, whose faces depict their despair over the Crucifixion, symbolise just as much a lament for the unused church. But this is a projected reading. Bob Tavernor, Professor of Architecture and Urban Design at the London School of Economics, describes in the Introduction to this book how the architectural voice emerges through a circular process – the building prompts memories and emotional responses in the viewer who, with a head full of personal and cultural memories, is waiting to be prompted. 'It's the inner voice that, ultimately, you're hearing,' says Tavernor. In much the same way, Lloyd describes St Barnabas as an amplifier: 'This building is amplifying our questions of it. It's a speaker for our own experience.'

Lloyd, who runs a practice elsewhere in the borough, is almost the architect of choice for the modernisation of Hackney's churches and other local institutions. He gained a certain notoriety for his reinvention of St Paul's Church in nearby Bow, in which

Lloyd slotted a large timber-clad, multi-purpose volume into the nave of a Victorian church, reducing the space for worship but introducing social amenities which now bring considerably more people through the door. That project, a meticulously planned interplay between the new and the old, brought Lloyd to the attention of another church, St John-at-Hackney, an immense Georgian volume built to accommodate more than 2000 worshippers, but now patronised by around 70 regulars. St Barnabas, which has actually been forgotten by the local community, is the end of the line and it presents Lloyd with a problem which spans architecture, history and personal morality. 'I just don't know what on earth we're going to do with this. If we get rid of it, we get rid of a piece of history and that is very painful,' he says.

One of the problems for the church is that it is land-locked, surrounded by buildings and with virtually no street presence and therefore little attraction for developers. Not only does the building have no function, it appears to have no value. St Barnabas is a conundrum.

Right: St Paul's Church in Bow. Section of the redeveloped church, by Matthew Lloyd Archi-tects. The timber-clad insertion, containing community facilities, is raised above ground level, leaving most of the church's floorspace free for worship.

Above: St Barnabas. *The Children's Worship*, dating back to 1938. Dozens of these little booklets are still stacked in a cupboard, unused and unread, at the rear of the church.

St Barnabas was built in 1909–10 and consecrated in 1929. Designed by CH Reilly, a proto-Modernist who advocated a return to late 18th century classicism, the church is Byzantine in form with a barrel-vaulted nave and round-headed windows. Built of brick and concrete and finely crafted, the church was a missionary project by the Merchant Taylors' School. Its vestry was added in 1937 but there is little evidence of more recent building work, apart from replacement windows and a badly located water tank in the organ loft. Set back from Shacklewell Row, the church has little street presence and is surrounded by a community hall and social housing.

St John-at-Hackney, a classical church designed by James Spiller, replaced a medieval church which, as well as requiring repair, could not accommodate the increasing population of the expanding parish. The new church was consecrated in 1797, although the spire was not completed until 1814. A centre of the 'Hackney Phalanx', a highly active group of influential churchmen and politicians, St John's experienced a very slow decline. The church received substantial repairs in 1929 and underwent a more comprehensive reconstruction programme in 1954. The building work was scheduled for completion on 19 May 1955 but, on 18 May, a serious fire broke out among builders' materials. The rebuilt church was reconsecrated in 1958. Since the 1980s church authorities have explored alternative uses for the building, including conversion to flats or even a swimming pool.

In 1991, according to a church booklet, Andrew Saint of English Heritage described St John-at-Hackney as 'this august church which … is the kind of vast hulk which gives modern inner-city incumbents a headache. In essence a plain, centralised auditorium, it has just enough shallow gallery space at the sides and back and enough eastward projection to qualify as a Greek cross. But the central space, with its bare ribbed vault, is dominant. It could be as splendid as the exterior, but poverty, liturgical change and, worst of all, a disastrous fire of 1955 followed by a necessarily cheap restoration, have left the church too much of a shell … Spiller's large scale treatment cries out for rich, Regency colour.' (David Mander, St John-at-Hackney: the Story of a Church, *Parish of Hackney, London, 1993.]*

Above: St Barnabas. The Reverend W Armstrong Buck, whose photograph hangs in the vestry. The image is as unfocused as the gaze of the man himself.

Right: St Paul's Church in Bow. Drawing by Matthew Lloyd Architects illustrating how the architects slotted a new structure into the volume of St Paul's Church in Bow, not far from St Barnabas and St John-at-Hackney.

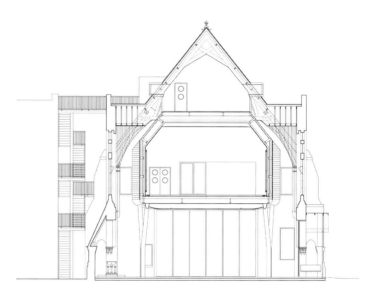

Left: St Barnabas. Designed by CH Reilly, the barrel-vaulted nave and round-headed windows suggest Byzantine influences.

Below: St Barnabas. Members of Merchant Taylors' School Mission Cricket Club. Undated photograph.

ARCHITECTURAL VOICES

St John-at-Hackney provides a more straightforward canvas because a prolonged period of decline, not helped by a savage fire in the 1950s, has caused the fabric of the building to deteriorate in line with its dwindling congregation. The church was built to accommodate 2,000 people but it often contained more than that; indeed, 300 baptisms were conducted in the course of just three days in the summer of 1837. By 1903 around 750 people were attending Sunday services, and today just one-tenth of that number worships there regularly. Unlike St Barnabas, whose 400-strong congregation appears simply to have vanished leaving behind a facsimile of itself, St John's has been in decline for too long – any sense of its humanity disappeared in the fire of 1955 and the church was rebuilt as a simpler place. Since the 1980s, church authorities have been considering alternative uses for the building and, apart from converting an ancilliary wing into a day-care centre for the homeless, they are still looking for an answer.

Matthew Lloyd is slowly working towards a solution. 'You have to attack. You have to lose the history. This makes me sad, but any spiritual qualities of a building like this one have long since disappeared. For a building that has been so substantially changed, I need to look for evidence of a human presence, evidence of people's lives. But there's not a lot here.' Once again, there are old photographs hanging in the vestry, including one from 1910 showing Rector Algernon Lawley and his six supporting clerics. Unlike the image of the Reverend Buck of St Barnabas, this photograph depicts lifelike individuals, relaxed, confident, even cocky. All gaze at the camera bar Rector Lawley, who looks intensely elsewhere, adopting the clichéd pose of eyeing the future.

Above: St John-at Hackney. This cavernous church is a place of light and dark, of empty volumes and heavy structure. Here, even the church's porch is vast, dwarfing individual churchgoers but perhaps appropriate for the some 2,000 people who assembled in this building in the late 18th century.

Opposite: St John-at-Hackney. Now with a congregation of around 75, the church dwarfs the people who worship here. Instead of symbolising the immensity of God, the building merely serves as a reminder of falling attendance.

Above: St John-at Hackney. 'This august church … is the kind of vast hulk which gives modern inner-city incumbents a headache.' (David Mander)

Below: St John-at-Hackney. Upper-level seating – finely crafted and simple pews created for what were once large congregations.

'This is where the voices are,' says Lloyd. The vestry is lined with images, depicting the Oxbridge graduates who passed through Hackney on their way to somewhere else. But these images are not mere artefacts; there is more life in them than in the church itself. The building and the photographs have an almost Dorian Gray-like relationship with each other – the washed-out emptiness of the declining church juxta-posed with the crispness of its youthful and ever-young curates. At St John's there is a spell waiting to be broken.

Right: St John-at-Hackney. The war memorial, tucked into what was once a side chapel.

ARCHITECTURAL VOICES

The Power of Absence

interview with Gerry Judah

David Littlefield

Gerry Judah was born in Calcutta, India, and lives in London. He studied Fine Art at Goldsmiths College and postgraduate Sculpture at the Slade School of Fine Art, University College London. His work has been exhibited at London's Whitechapel Art Gallery, Camden Arts Centre and Yorkshire Sculpture Park. Since the 1980s he has been designing for film, television, theatre, museums and public installations for clients including the Royal Shakespeare Company, Royal Opera House and BBC. Latterly he has returned to his fine art roots with exhibitions Frontiers at the Timber Yard, London in 2005 and Angels at the Royal Institute of British Architects, London in 2006. His new work is held in public and private collections internationally including the Saatchi Collection, the Imperial War Museum and the Goodwood Sculpture Park.

Gerry Judah is an artist for whom absence – in the sense of what was once there but is there no longer – is a generator for something positive. A ruin, the remains of signage which indicate a long-closed

Right: *Angels*, 2006. The paintings are large-scale works depicting clusters of savaged buildings set within featureless plains.

enterprise, an empty room … all prompt in Judah a heavy sense of what *ought* to be there, what *could* be there. His is not a mourning for what is past, and neither is it a sentimental position; instead, it is a reaching out towards what might have been the present. In Judah's work, absence is depicted so strongly that it begins to make what is actually there almost a secondary consideration. Judah creates circular, self-reflexive arguments which chase themselves through layers of metaphor and reach no conclusion other than the fact that a question ought to be asked.

Judah's work *Angels* (2006), a series of paintings which encroach upon the realm of relief and sculpture, depict buildings and settlements which have been subjected to sudden, apocalyptic attack. There is no suggestion of gradual decay; instead, buildings have been violently stripped of both purpose and inhabitants. The imagery is that of war or the vagaries of nature, and human habitation is reduced to one of texture, a desolate and oddly picturesque event which interrupts an otherwise flat and absurdly featureless landscape. These are mesmerising objects, spanning the spectrum of one's understanding of what is real and unreal. These depictions of modern ruins, the obliteration of the ordinary and unremarkable, contain enough satellite dishes and water tanks to suggest, say, the wreckage of very real, bulldozer-led incursions; but the amount of cabling stretched between these broken buildings, indicative of electricity and telephony, is too contrived and subjective a composition to be mistaken for faithful reproduction. Instead, the cabling provides a gossamer-like directionality to what, from a distance, appears to be a delicate affair.

This work has been boiling away since the 1970s, when Judah graduated from Goldsmiths College

Above: Joseph Gandy's 1830 portrayal of Soane's Bank of England as a ruin: London is imagined as a future Rome, the centre of a lost but once-glorious empire. Equally, the painting acts as an architect's axonometric, showing the building as a diagram.

with a degree in fine art. It is a dangerous cliché to record the influences which bear upon the work of artists, as far too often these influences are either contrived or post-rationalised, but Judah had already developed a sensitivity to semi-ruinous buildings which permitted passers-by a glimpse into what were once private worlds. The physical remains (pictures hanging on walls, doorways opening onto spaces that are no longer there, fireplaces stranded high above the streetscape) became to Judah manifestations of stories, remnants of memory which could either be discovered or imagined. And then, in the 1980s, he was forced to vacate a studio in London's Islington; the studio was demolished and, for a while, an interior wall covered in Judah's notes and drawings was exposed to public view. 'I was looking at myself,' he says.

To Judah, a man who challenges people to overlay artworks with their own prejudices and imaginings, buildings tell us little on their own. 'What

makes a building's voice is not what it tells you, it's what you can tell from it. You project, and you've got to make room for that.' The distinction is a crucial one. For Judah, a visitor is never an observer of a building, submitting to its signals and signs; visitors are, instead, participants in the life of a building and they have to do a little work if they are to 'hear' anything at all. Brecht-like, Judah expects us to engage in an active sort of listening, one that goes beyond mere *hearing*. And that listening is one which is loaded with the weight of people's personal and collective memories. Moreover, Judah describes a way of listening that must be handled responsibly, otherwise one might encounter only what one expects to hear.

Judah has conducted a number of studies of Nazi concentration camps, notably as research for the scale model of Auschwitz-Birkenau he created for the Imperial War Museum in 2000, and he has therefore spent a considerable amount of time measuring,

ARCHITECTURAL VOICES

Above: *Angels*, 2006. This series of paintings encroaches upon the realms of relief and sculpture, depicting buildings and settlements which have been subjected to sudden, apocalyptic attack. Shown at the Royal Institute of British Architects in 2006.

Left: *Angels*, 2006. Decay, abandonment and destruction settle evenly across the landscape. The iconic building suffers the same fate as the commonplace.

Below: *Angels*, 2006. The paintings are stripped of colour and humanity; they are visions of a monochromatic world. Their neutrality begs interpretation and the application of meaning.

Opposite: *Angels*, 2006. Judah's *Angels* are not facsimiles of real ruins – they show, instead, how one might imagine ruins.

looking, listening and 'feeling' his way through these emotionally charged spaces. To Judah, however, these places do not speak powerfully; simply being present at the location of the Holocaust provides no experiential trace of the event itself. After his visits, he wrote the following: 'While I expected to be overwhelmed with horror, I was simply numbed. There is little resonance of evil in what has been left behind. The place was not designed to express its purpose – like a church or a bank – but, on the contrary, to conceal it. The scatter of shoddy buildings that survive does not make a setting for extreme evil. If you passed the place you probably wouldn't notice it. Even the gatehouse, one of the icons of 20th-century terror, is a rather small utilitarian brick building.'

'I felt numb – but not unmoved,' says Judah, who was, however, most emotional in the empty synagogues of Cracow; where there should have been bustle and noise and life, there was quiet. 'This lack of voices, this absence, was very profound.'

Judah's work is an exploration of the chain reaction of metaphor ('Everything is a metaphor for something else') and nothing represents itself. Absence suggests presence, and what is present is open to interpretation. His work is an enquiry into the possibilities of ambiguity; his paintings in the *Angels* series present ruined spaces as textures and the images are not named. He has been accused of beautifying war, especially with regard to his similar collection *Frontiers* (2005), which tackled comparable ground but was inspired more overtly by the remnants of conflict; there is something in this, but any beauty in these works is purely the invention of the spectator. The paintings in *Angels* are stripped of colour and humanity, they are either black or white. If there is a predetermined view-

Right: *Angels*, 2006. The title *Angels* was arrived at through the composition of these pieces. Surveyed as a whole, these paintings offer filigree structures suggestive of flight, vaguely symmetrical forms pivoting around a central point. Close inspection reveals nothing but destruction.

Above: *Angels*, 2006. Although *Angels* is primarily a series of white artworks, Judah produced a handful of black pieces. The colour change is dramatic. The sense of absence is more palpable; the apocalypse which has befallen these places appears more recent.

point at all, it is one of a spy-plane or a GoogleEarth depiction and, as such, these objects are open to interpretation; they beg that meaning be applied to them.

In 1830 Sir John Soane commissioned Joseph Gandy to paint an image of the Bank of England (one of Soane's architectural masterpieces) as a ruin. The resulting image is an ambiguous one – it is simultaneously a Romantic vision of London as the future Rome (where people may come to wonder at the achievements of a lost civilisation) and a technical drawing, illustrating the spatial arrangements and construction of the building. Like an architectural model, this image shows more clearly than any set of plans and sections how this building actually worked. It is both poetry and technical information. Judah's *Angels* have much the same ambiguity. They do not show what ruins look like – instead, they show how one might imagine ruins. Gandy does the same thing – he depicts walls that are evidently strong enough to withstand calamity, but he also populates the site with arches of unlikely slenderness. It is as if the site has been unpicked, not ravaged, and it is difficult to know quite how to respond. This is the ambiguity that lies at the heart of *Angels* – these sites, too, have been unpicked, and it was a selective havoc which befell these places. Load-bearing walls have been swept away, but satellite dishes remain.

Like absurd buildings which have lost their facades, leaving doors and wallpaper and plumbing hanging in mid-air; like the Holocaust sites, Judah's *Angels* are diagrams, emblems, of a state. And what is that state? What exactly are these places? What is their status, these non-buildings? What do they want and what do they want us to think of them? They stare blankly and say nothing. One has to work very hard to find a response and apply a meaning

Above: *Angels*, 2006. A selective havoc befell the places depicted in *Angels*. Load-bearing walls lie in pieces while satellite dishes are left intact.

Above: *Angels*, 2006. In Judah's work, absence is depicted so strongly that it makes the visible a secondary consideration. The viewer is invited to fill in the gaps and invent histories to suit the evidence.

Clock House

Coleshill, Oxfordshire

Saskia Lewis

It was indeed curious that the Burneys were to have signed their lease the following day. So curious that one cannot but wonder if the house did not want to have other occupants. For indeed, it seems to me – but I am queer about houses – it would not have liked strangers, and I doubt if strangers would have felt at home in it. It could never live – in the full sense of the world – under modern conditions, even had your family been able to stay in it. Perhaps it preferred to die – and it died with magnificence and dignity.

Extract of a letter from Ray Cochrane to Doris Pleydell-Bouverie, 30 September 1952, Fresden, nr. Highworth, Wiltshire.

Maybe Coleshill House not only had a voice but also a will of its own. It knew it had been a spectacular specimen, that had been the intention. The house, designed by Roger Pratt (1620–84), was built around 1650. It had been an exercise, on Pratt's return to England, in interpreting the identity of the English country house by way of Palladio and all that he had witnessed in his travels across mid-17th-century Europe. He had consulted Inigo Jones on the design that was to be lauded by Pevsner in 1966 as 'the best Jonesian mid c17 house in England. It had nine bays and two storeys, and a big hipped roof, a top balustrade, and a belvedere cupola.' The golden orb at the top of the cupola could be seen from miles away. Those miles could in turn be surveyed from the flat leaded roof that acted as a promenade. It was a beacon, a focal point for the local community.

George Pratt (Roger's cousin) had commissioned and built Coleshill House. Later his daughter married Thomas Pleydell whose family had owned the Coleshill

Above: View north to Clock House from between the wings of the single-storey kitchen extension to Coleshill House.

estate in the 15th century. House and estate were handed down in the family from generation to generation until the mid-20th century, gathering the Stuarts and the Bouveries through marriage along the way. The last of the line to live there were Molly and Bina Pleydell-Bouverie, neither married or had children themselves although they did bring up their niece and nephew Doris and Bertrand Pleydell-Bouverie in the family home. During the Second World War the house was requisitioned by the military and the golden orb on the roof was wrapped in rugs to prevent it reflecting in the moonlight during the blackout. The Pleydell-Bouverie sisters continued to live there during this time, but were unaware that their house had become the headquarters of auxiliary units training an army of resistance under top-secret conditions. There was a lot of practice with explosives, during which part of the kitchen extension was demolished by accident and the resident dogs had to be tranquillised with a regimen of aspirin and brandy.

Bertrand Pleydell-Bouverie who lived there with his aunts remembers that 'from one end of the roof it was possible to look down into the rooks' nests in the

Above: The front facade of Clock House looking north. The wash-room was housed in the wing to the west; the laundry, paint shop and lumber room were located in the body of the building under the clock tower and the brewery was situated in the wing to the east.

Opposite: View from the old Coleshill House roof over Clock House and subsidiary buildings, stables and piggery. This image gives some indication of the height of the original country house.

elms and see their eggs, whilst at the other end one looked down into the laundry'. There is a photograph of this, the humble and rather stark courtyard of the subsidiary buildings; the laundry, washhouse, paint shop, lumber-room and brewery, now known collect-ively as Clock House, with the stables and piggery beyond. This subservient collection of buildings had a functional sense of order in contrast to the grandeur of the main house with its raised ground floor, eight huge chimneys, restrained formal gardens, extensive lawn, gravel drive and dramatic views over parkland towards the Ridgeway. The tables have turned.

Coleshill House perished in a dramatic fire on 23 September 1952. The next day Swindon's *Evening Advertiser* reported that molten lead had poured from the roof like 'silver rain'. The house had been undergoing minor repairs to prepare it for renting out to tenants. A beehive, resident in the cupola for two decades, was dripping honey through the ceiling and finally was being removed and, in addition, all the wood-work was being stripped and repainted. Sparks from a blowtorch used on paintwork to the dormer windows in the roof had initiated the fire that had smouldered undetected for some time until it was wildly out of control. Clock House, sitting perpendicular and north of the main house, from which it was separated by a lane at a distance of about 15 metres, had escaped any trauma but had witnessed the destruction of the country house that it had serviced for its entire life.

This is a tale of the dialogue between two buildings both belonging to the same era but of different statures. Many magnificent buildings failed to survive

Right: The interior of Coleshill House after being damaged by fire on 23 September 1952. Some of the plaster busts that decorated the hall survive in niches surrounded by a chaos of debris.

Below: Parkland surrounding the grounds of Coleshill House looking south-west towards the Ridgeway.

the 20th century for one reason or another, mainly through the crippling cost of their upkeep and the daunting prospect of introducing modern living to their bulk. It is curiously reassuring to think of a building that had stood for some three centuries flatly refusing to accommodate the ways of the modern age. Legally this estate could not be broken down into smaller lots while the repeated losses through inheritance and death duties had severely depleted family funds, leaving the sisters unable to maintain the house and its grounds. This was a common problem in the mid-20th century and resulted in many country homes being demolished. To avoid this the sisters sold the estate to Ernest Cook for a modest sum on condition that he provide an endowment to the property and thus allow it to pass to the National Trust on his death. Cook flattened the site after the fire and on his death the estate did pass into the care of the National Trust. For nearly a decade the wrecked site stood absolutely still, abandoned.

It was in the early 1960s that Clock House took on the gravitas of becoming the 'main house'. Michael Wickham, artist, carpenter and photographer and Kit Evans, an architect, secured the lease from the National Trust. They began using it as a weekend retreat from London with their families. Clock House is a single cell thick and wraps around three sides of a courtyard facing south towards its now absent master. It sat just across the lane from the main house with a little acknowledged extension in-between; two single-storey wings flush to the east and west facades of Coleshill House separated by an open corridor. This contained all the fuel and food stores, the kitchen and the servants' hall. It was in part destroyed during its wartime military requisition and finally demolished along with the rest of Coleshill House after the fire.

Right: The two statues that stand at the entrance to Clock House – one open-mouthed and surprised, as though looking on as the house burned down, and the second with a stern and military air.

Soon the Wickhams were living there permanently. They made the interiors livable on a tight budget, planning, designing and building the conversions themselves. Michael, Cynthia and their children Gemma and Polly lived in what had been the washroom and laundry, the west and north elements of the building. Cynthia remembers how, on the first night, they had 'slept in a row in sleeping bags on the living room floor',[1] in what had been the westerly end of the laundry, a double-height room originally for hanging washing – huge sheets and long drapes – from the rafters. The washroom became the kitchen, and the heart of their home. Michael made a huge circular table that could seat at least a dozen, and frequently did. Oil stoves heated the space and there was an Aga to cook on. A bathroom and bedroom were located above the kitchen. The bedroom looks south over the site where the original house had stood and the bathroom has a sliver of a window low to the floor that overlooks a paved walled garden to the west that would have been the drying yard; now it is full of plants, a greenhouse, a couple of chairs and a table, all beautifully informal. The walls of

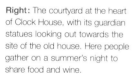

Right: The courtyard at the heart of Clock House, with its guardian statues looking out towards the site of the old house. Here people gather on a summer's night to share food and wine.

ARCHITECTURAL VOICES

Above: Originally the drying yard to the west of Clock House, this paved walled yard is now used and nurtured by Denny Wickham.

3-foot-thick rubble-stone enclose spaces that are slow to heat in winter but easy to keep cool during the summer. From the ground floor, windows are high and their sills filled with plants and objects – sit nearby and your gaze is directed towards the trees and sky.

The Evans family, Kit, Marsha, Toby and Dan, settled in the old brewery and the first floor of what had been the lumber room, the easterly wing of the block. This they converted rather differently. The outside drifts into the ground floor of the old brewery. It is full of boots and coats and, during the autumn, baskets of apples, windfalls collected from the garden. In fact full of anything that needs to be kept sheltered for the moment. A simple timber stair on the eastern elevation of the interior takes you to the first floor, to a timber deck suspended within the stone envelope. Their living room sits within the walls of the brewery and the kitchen at the apex between that and the lumber room, and marks the separation between the living and sleeping spaces. Toby and Dan spent their youth running wild in the old park and exploring the dark and dungeon-like cellars of the old house that despite being filled with the rubble of the house are still in part accessible. Dan now lives here full time with his family and runs his architecture office from home.

Cynthia moved away and Michael married Denny. Gemma had a family of her own and so the west and north elements of the building were partitioned off from one another to provide for a third family. The Fox family live under the clock tower. The double-height living room was floored over to provide more space.

1   Gemma Fox, *Coleshill 2000 – Memories of Coleshill*, privately published by Adrian Buratta, p 120.

Right: Pinned to the notice-board, an aerial photograph of Coleshill Garden.

Below: The stair to the first floor is rich with paintings and drawings, plants, mirrors and curios.

The kitchen that had been the easterly end of the laundry sits on raised timber, leaving existing surfaces with memories of the past; drainage channels and gratings in the old stone-flagged laundry floor slip underneath the new domestic deck. But the building is still used as a whole. There are always people wandering from one home to another, casting an eye over things, welcome in each other's space.

Clock House has flourished, not in a prissy or pretentious way but rather organically. These buildings have not been overly tamed; the spaces are vertical, even with the insertion of upper floors. Small interventions have been made to accommodate living rather than trying to convert the feel of the building wholesale. Boundaries have been negotiable. Over the years the interiors have been opened up and sealed as necessary. If not magnificent in the same way as the big house, this collection of buildings might be called handsome and much loved. They are packed with the clutter of living. They are homes.

The courtyard that had been so bare and functional in the old days has become the animated heart of this community. A scattering of tables and chairs fills the space – the natural place for informal gatherings, especially on a warm summer's evening, to drink a glass of wine and catch up, a legacy perhaps of the days when the brewery did duty as the unofficial pub for workers on the estate. Two classical sculptural figures in military dress flank the entrance to this courtyard. One has a look of open-mouthed, wide-eyed surprise; the features of the other are fixed in a stern frown; they are looking in the direction of the house that is now gone.

In one of his texts, Michael Wickham described how, on his arrival in 1961, the lawn to the original

Above: Collection of objects on the window sill of the first-floor extension over what was the laundry room.

Right: The kitchen in the old washroom. Michael Wickham made this beautiful circular dining table for family and friends to gather around – it is the heart of the kitchen.

Above: The box hedge marking the envelope of the old country house – trimmed lower to indicate the position of the original windows – can be seen through the foliage of the original avenue of limes.

Right: The box hedge marking the walls of Coleshill House. The treads of the main staircase are marked with slabs of slate which have shifted slightly over time, giving the garden a liberated air.

ARCHITECTURAL VOICES

Left: The new lime avenue, laid out in the 1960s, helped shift the orientation of the site to acknow-ledge the new status of Clock House as the main house.

house had become 'a great weedy field'. Even after it was mowed, it gave no indication of what had once stood there save for the fact that the lawn did not lie completely flat and had some of the qualities of a slightly rucked cloth about it. Until 1989 it lay, still the scene for flamboyant parties, as it must always have been, but giving little of its history away. With Clock House now occupied, there was a shift in axis with relation to the site. Planting an avenue of lime trees in 1965 across what would have been the west facade of the original building reinforced this transition and redirected the view southwards. This avenue mimics the language of the older, original, established avenue of limes that lines the north edge of the front lawn to the house that is no longer there. They sit perpendicular to one another.

These families have now become the informal guardians of the immediate estate. The demise of a large country house in the middle of the 20th century is a familiar story, but there is something unique about Coleshill – the decision to mark the site where Coleshill House once stood. There was talk of drawing the plan in white lines used for marking out tennis courts, but this was superseded by a decision to lay out a garden

Right: Door leading into the old washroom and laundry in the west-ern wing of the building. This is where Denny Wickham lives and works, commissioning richly colour-ed garments from India and selling them from Clock House under her own brand name.

laid out in box hedge that was grown from cuttings and cut down in height at points where the windows of the house would have been. Now home to nesting birds, it becomes less wall-like during the summer and is only cut back once the nests are abandoned.

All steps were translated into slabs of Delabole slate that marked the position of the original steps and terraces as if in an architectural drawing. The slate has since been displaced over the years by visitors who have walked through the garden and has taken on a more liberated, scattered identity. As the ground floor was raised there had been external steps to the front and rear of the house marking a path across the building from east to west. Jean Simmons was shown running across the lawn to the front steps in the film *Uncle Silas* (1947). Anyone familiar with the building would have imagined her then running up the steps and into the hall flanked on both sides by a dramatic sweeping stair.

An unusual central corridor that ran the full length of the building north to south, dividing the front from the back of the house on each floor, has been planted with lavender, home to bees and butterflies and creating a direct promenade with the courtyard of Clock House. This was the first English example of this type of plan, something which had been more common in Europe at the time. Some of the interior wall divisions are marked in lengths of timber that have been shifted by the growing of the plants and so alter the rigidity of the original room layout.

The success of the garden lies in its sense of freedom. If this is the representation of a house then it is a house that is really lived in. It is almost as if the ash from the disaster now feeds the frenzy of self-seeding plants that occupy the depictions of the ground floor

according to the ground-floor plan of the old house. It is now from the upper floors of Clock House that one looks south over lawns, parkland and an extensive garden that lays out the site of where Coleshill House once stood. Michael and Denny Wickham designed the layout, raised the sponsorship and set to work.

This is not a garden that is precious about its boundaries, not a garden that demands endless clipping. The footprint of the building was cleared of turf and covered with a plastic (to discourage weeds) and then laid with gravel. The external walls of the house were

Left: Entrance to the Evans home – the old brewery. The ground floor is full of boots and bikes, baskets and drying clothes.

Right: The central corridor of Coleshill House is now marked by an avenue of lavender bushes set on a direct axis with the courtyard of Clock House. The bushes attract bees and butterflies that now animate the reincarnated site.

Below: View over the old drying yard from the bathroom at first floor above what was once the washroom and laundry.

divisions of the original. The carpets that occupy each room vary from soft spongy thyme to a covering of wild strawberries or winter savoury. There is a constant shift in emphasis in the garden. Walking on the carpet in bare feet sends scent into the air. The Clock House and the garden have both relaxed. They have retained all of their dignity but with less of the pomp and have maintained a sense of identity that keeps the heart of the community beating.

There is a heritage of endeavour and creativity that belongs to Coleshill and its occupants in a collaborative relationship. The buildings and gardens still host regular gatherings of local people and visitors from afar and inspire a deep affection for the place among those who live here and visit alike. It is fitting that following the Pleydell family's occupation of the main house for the duration of its existence, it is now the Wickham, Evans and Fox families that are resident and nurturing new generations within the walls of Clock House. Others have moved to the area more recently and share the sense of community. Here, different generations spend time with one another in a way that, on the whole, seems lost in contemporary society.

Occasionally, it is the myth and spoken knowledge of the recent past that keeps the voice of a building alive, albeit in translation. There are few places where time really seems to slow right down but Coleshill is such a place. The remaining buildings feel as if they hold onto their occupants, who in turn take care of them. There is an intimacy here, a serenity, a stillness. The residents have inherited a legacy and relationship with the estate and village that is based both on the buildings and the personalities of the people who have spent their lives here. The past is treasured and integrated into the present.

Above: The aperture to the drying yard is littered with pencil marks that bear witness to the shifting heights of family and friends over the years.

Above: View from the corridor to the bathroom. Daylight seeps in through the aperture but otherwise the interior is softly lit.

Right: The living room at the Evans home. Another entrance leads you directly to the stables on the east elevation of the building.

Below: These days the roles are reversed – now when you look out of the first-floor bedroom, in what was once the washroom and laundry, you look down onto the garden that marks the plan of where Coleshill House once stood.

Battersea Power Station

Battersea, London

David Littlefield

Designed by Sir Giles Gilbert Scott. Commissioned 1933, closed 1983
Currently the subject of proposed redevelopment discussions

Battersea Power Station was built in two sections: the A side, which opened in 1933, and the B side, which was commissioned in 1944 and opened 11 years later. Each side was equipped with a chimney at either end. The site has been in limbo since the power station closed in 1983. Developer Parkview International, a Hong Kong-based family firm which bought the power station in 1993, secured planning consent for the reinvention of both the building and the entire estate, but sold the site to Irish group Real Estates Opportunities for £400 million towards the end of 2006. Before the sale, it was feared that the building's four iconic chimneys would have to be dismantled, due to their poor condition, and re-erected.

John Collingwood started work at Battersea Power Station in 1969, when he was 18. He was an electrician, a job he kept for five years until the shiftwork caused him to leave and drive a London bus. Now retired, and latterly having found the time to study Fine Art at Central St Martins College of Art and Design, Collingwood has returned to Battersea to photograph what has become an empty hulk. These visits have turned into an exploration of both spaces and his own memories, and the photographs convey a certain disappointment.

Collingwood remembers the power station (which continues, even in its ruined state, to weigh heavily on the landscape of London) as a place of contrasts. It was a hot/cold building, spotless and impossibly filthy, dry/humid, deafening and rather quiet. As an instrument engineer, Collingwood would routinely examine intricate little mechanisms within spaces of incredible vastness. Today, roofless and stripped out, its contrasts have evaporated and the building offers little by way of variation or surprise, other than the fact it is still standing.

Battersea Power Station is a place of secrets and myth. According to Collingwood, the US Army regularly arrived (armed) with sackfuls of state documents to burn in the building's boilers. Locals believe the Bank of England, too, burned banknotes here, many of which (due to a suspiciously fortuitious combination of temperature and pressure settings) fell unburned into the ash pile; legend suggests the Bank never knew how many notes, having disappeared, re-emerged to find their way back into circulation. And there is a further myth, that during the Second World War German aircraft crews deliberately refrained from bombing the building in spite of its strategic significance; the belief is that the power station's iconic chimneys served as orientation points, and its continued existence meant that damaged planes with instrument failure could steer themselves home.

It is painfully ironic that a building which may, conceivably, have served as a navigation aid for the German air force is now so difficult to navigate on the ground. Collingwood, who in his day had an 'access all areas' occupation, became lost in the building on his return visits in 1999 and 2002. 'It was as though I was seeing it for the first time. I just couldn't figure out where things had been. It was hugely disappointing. I almost had to give up on exploring what I had mapped out.'

Collingwood's photographic method depends on the slow exposure. In an attempt to capture all the tricks of light and shade, and the 'history' of a space, he leaves his aperture open for many minutes ('over time, things burn into the film you never knew were there'). But at Battersea his minders were not so patient: 'What I really wanted was to just stand there for a very long

Below: Battersea Power Station was built in two halves, each with two chimneys. The 'A side' was completed in 1933; but the iconic four-chimney building did not appear until the 1950s. The station quickly became a London landmark and did the work of dozens of smaller power generators until it closed in 1983.

time and take it all in, which I was never allowed to do.' Here, the shutter was left open for only around 90 seconds. In taking these pictures, Collingwood photographs spaces he tries to remember; they are pictures of otherwise innocuous doorways, empty spaces and curious details. They are the photographs of someone repopulating the building in his imagination: of someone conjuring up the deafening clatter of the steel bearings that forced workers to lip-read and crushed coal into pulverised fuel ash before it was pressure-fed into the boiler system; of someone reimagining the colour-coded boiler suits (brown, green, white, blue) that signified the varying status and occupation of the people who served the building; of someone recalling the Flash Gordon verve of the Art Deco emergency control room and the 'gorgeous' Italian marble of the turbine hall.

Collingwood describes the power station in terms of a living entity, an 'inhuman' force requiring the ministrations of attentive servants – it was populated by watchful machine-minders, including many ex-Navy engineers resourceful enough 'to conjure something out of nothing'. It was a finely tuned place, constructed not as a large shed into which machinery was placed, but as an integrated whole. Collingwood remembers a boiler being removed: it was a long-term act of surgery, one of careful incisions that took more than three years to complete. 'This building was alive,' he says. 'Entering was like stepping outside of normal society. Every time you walked in, it took your breath away.'

Today, what particularly disturbs Collingwood is that the building has been so comprehensively abandoned (indeed, wilfully neglected) that there are not even clues to the very human oddities that softened the labyrinths of this machine. The fact that parts of it were, in winter, so cold that employees wore submariners' socks, while other parts were so hot and humid that men made their own vests out of muslin. Also, for reasons of which he cannot be sure, Collingwood remembers female cleaning staff wearing wooden clogs. The power station was, in many ways, a strange place. Parts were 'all steam and flashing lights' while the quieter, colder, less populated and more elevated spaces, like the Fan Floor at the top of the building, were 'moonscapes' of undisturbed grey dust and repeated forms. 'It was just a collision of shapes and light, no colour. It was like looking at a Sol LeWitt painting. When I first saw the work of Sol LeWitt I thought "I've seen that before".'

In spite of its present condition, Collingwood feels Battersea Power Station retains an elemental strength, a sort of potency derived both from its sheer bulk and from the fact that it has managed to survive, roofless, stubbornly, the corporate vandalism that has been visited upon it. It is a lovable brute, like the subject of the delightfully ambiguous piece of graffiti on the perimeter wall: 'Vern is doing 10 years for GBH. Don't turn your back on him.'

Right: Most of the internal floors have been demolished or have simply dropped away. The inside of the building's massive walls now bears only scars indicating the position of former stairs and floors.

Interview with Eric Parry

Saskia Lewis

'What I'm really trying to understand is whether a building can acquire a voice through having witnessed the lives that it has contained. There is a symbiotic relationship between buildings and people; they leave their mark on each other. I imagine that St Martin-in-the-Fields and the Cathar site of the Château de Paulin must have had rich evidence of past lives. I am interested in how you relate to an existing building and describe the fine line between whether you allow the histories and the enigmatic qualities of a place to enter into a dialogue or whether you stamp your mark regardless ...'

Eric Parry sits at dusk in a room in Clerkenwell and considers my point. In the 40 minutes between the end of a working day and a lecture that he is due to attend at the Royal Academy he talks of Nash, Gibbs, Wren, London, ruins, rural France and aspirations to country living.

'There is very little that is raw and natural when working in this country – or London in particular. It is all so layered, and consequently many of the projects have a strong socio-historical background that means that, when working with buildings, one becomes something of an amateur historian by osmosis. A conservation architect would start by doing all the historical analysis first, like a pathologist or a barrister with a case history, and would submerge themselves in it until they knew all the detail and could answer all the questions about the history of the building or place. From my perspective it's never worked like that. When thrust in to a competition or invited to respond to a potential project, I find that one is essentially working with imaginative intuition. Initial basic judgements or

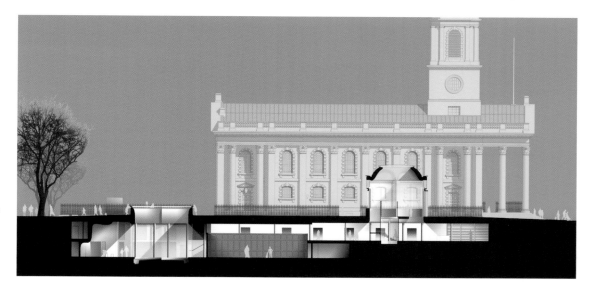

Right: St Martin-in-the-Fields. Section through the pavilion which gives access to a single-storey space that then drops into a double-height volume with a lightwell penetrating the reinstated ground plane.

　　　　　　　　ARCHITECTURAL VOICES

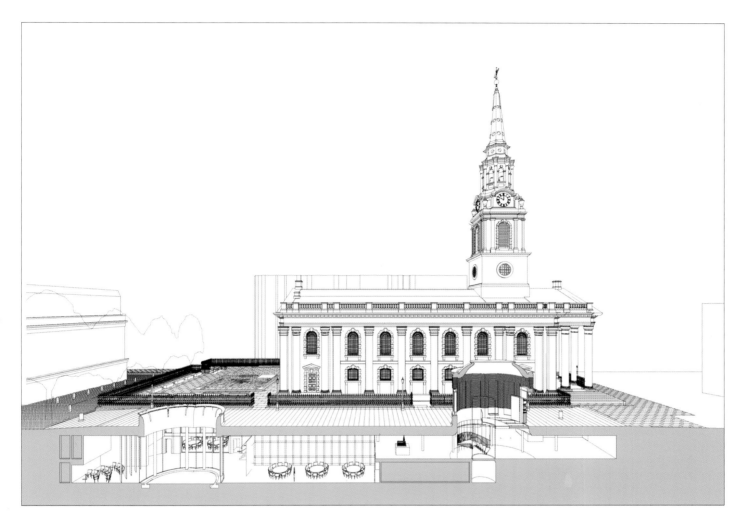

Above: St Martin-in-the-Fields. Sectional perspective looking south, showing the sequence of spaces below the ground plane against the northern elevation of the church.

decisions that are fast, furious and intuitive get challenged all the way through the development and manifestation of the project and they either crumble or get stronger. Any interference in the environment of any scale is very powerful and I think that retaining a certain sense of innocence in these things is probably important. If you had stage fright it wouldn't work. That's what's good about architectural education. There's a freedom in speculation but you always have to defend yourself don't you, and discuss your ideas.'

He opens a file documenting the ongoing process of the restoration and expansion of St Martin-in-the-Fields. It is a well-known Central London church that sits to the north-east of Trafalgar Square and is renowned both for its work with the home-less and for candlelit concerts. The project was won by competition about four years ago and has been on site for roughly a year.

'St Martin-in-the-Fields offers an opportunity to work with and between both Gibbs and Nash. Walking around that site there are two things that struck me. Firstly, the labyrinth of Nash's vaults and all the people that worked in there – green rooms for musicians, a Chinese community, loos and the intense atmosphere of the night shelter and work with youth and the homeless. Secondly, the immediate realisation that light and orientation were going to be the key design problems and as soon as one goes underground one has a tendency to lose both. The theme of light at a more philosophical level

Below: St Martin-in-the-Fields. Sectional perspective looking west through the body of the church, the remodelled crypt, the newly excavated volumes and the renovations to the Nash Range. The drawing illustrates clearly the full extent of the new works and how the spaces relate to one another.

ARCHITECTURAL VOICES

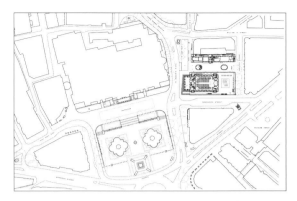

was interesting in terms of the way that the church was organised architecturally and the iconography of light in the church from the west to the east, inside and outside. The drawings made at competition stage were based on these immediate responses, and the structure of those has been a really good skeleton that has retained its integrity throughout. You see, there have been several different stages in the life of St Martin-in-the-Fields. One needs to understand the critical elements without perhaps all of the detail in order to make some leaps of faith in terms of design.

'Between 1721 and 1726 James Gibbs was designing and building the church amongst medieval fabric – the old church before Gibbs gets to it is clearly an Anglo-Saxon site of some significance. His adaptation of the church is remarkable – it's almost a surreal juxtaposition of a temple with a spire thrust through it. It has become the most iconic image of Anglican parish church architecture, now endlessly repeated in smaller parishes both here and abroad. Nash then appears in the early 19th century with his vision of Trafalgar Square and strips away everything around the church, treating it almost as an object in a landscape. In the 20th century we see the reuse of redundant burial vaults and this is the third rebuild to make sense of the site.

'And this site absolutely speaks through each of its transformations. I am very aware of the hands that have been there before – the way that the buildings have been constructed and understood. Some things are being erased of course. There was a market place around the church that has gone and so have the burial vaults. In the process of taking away Nash we found certain areas that had not been

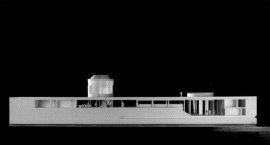

Left: St Martin-in-the-Fields. View of the church as seen from a crane at the north-east edge of the site looking west, with Trafalgar Square and Nelson's Column visible in the background.

Left: St Martin-in-the-Fields. The crypt of the church was used as a central London location for night shelter and work with young people and the homeless.

Below: St Martin-in-the-Fields. Plan view of excavation work around the base of the church.

disturbed with his redevelopment. There were 28 skeletons discovered, many of them Anglo-Saxon burials using Roman sarcophagi, and a 4th-century Roman brick kiln. Now there is the almost anatomical moment of the church and its Georgian crypt being exposed for the first time.'

He fetches a contact sheet of images that show the church stripped beyond the ground plane standing on a plinth made up of its own crypt and foundations. The idea of the church being an object in a landscape has been reinforced, it now sits, almost floating, free of any anchor – momentarily – while the earth around it is removed.

'St Martin's speaks to you for all its historical past and all the people involved in it. It is an extraordinary place. It's where the anti-apartheid campaign centred itself next to South Africa House, where Amnesty International was born, where Shelter was conceived and is right next to all the angst that Trafalgar Square has hosted in terms of national grievance, demonstrations and riots. It is open to everyone. You'll find people taking shelter during the day or attending one of the 27 services a week or going to one of the concerts – in terms of concerts, there are more people that go to St Martin-in-the-Fields than go to the Wigmore Hall. It's the parish church to Downing Street and Buckingham Palace; huge memorial services take place here. It's the most extraordinary concoction of identities.

'As it's next to Trafalgar Square it's very much part of World Squares and all that cultural identity – this is the spiritual part, a non-avaricious place – a sense of goodness in the navel of London. It speaks at so many levels and obviously, without its history it

Above: St Martin-in-the-Fields. Looking west towards Trafalgar Square and down onto the excavations around the church, which is temporarily suspended from its ground plane.

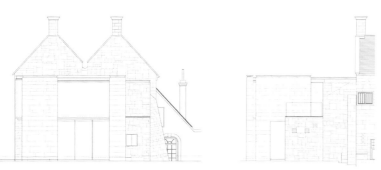

Left: Old Wardour House. The elevations show how the fabric of the old and new building is stitched together, acknowledging and articulating the join between the two.

Above: Old Wardour House. The extension provides a new kitchen, dining room and bedroom above. It is designed to suffuse the interior with light and afford framed views out to the gardens.

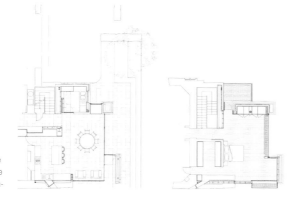

Right: Old Wardour House. Ground and first-floor plans of the extension. The ground floor can be opened up to allow a fluid relationship between inside and out.

wouldn't do that. We've dug around the church creating new public spaces above and below ground level. Underground the space is huge, about 60 metres by 16. This surrounds the church, single storey in some areas becoming double storey in the church hall. At ground level the scheme consists of a pavilion and a lightwell that sit against the northern facade of the church, the positive and the negative. The pavilion is a glass structure that echoes in its proportions something of the world between Nash and Gibbs. In a sense the architect's voice in this case will be the least heard; I mean you have space and you have the rooms, it's not bombastic, it's quite a discreet underground space.'

Once complete, the pavilion and the roof light will be the markers that indicate the presence of this project. The full extent of works, though, is enormous. The excavation around the church is understandable and anticipated but the work that has been done inside the Nash Range, the building to the north of the site, is phenomenal. All of these spaces are being tied together below ground and that, when the project is complete, will be a very discreet marker of success and a huge alteration to the historical way in which these buildings have previously related to one another. He opens a book, *Country Houses Today* **by Jeremy Melvin.**

'Old Wardour House on the other hand is a small project, an extension to a house at the base of a ruin, but you could describe it as a sort of palimpsest of living or the aspirations to living in the English countryside. It's in Wiltshire, in what was a hunting park that had a castle constructed in it in 1385. The plan of the old castle was very rare, hexagonal with

Above Old Wardour House. The extension is made up of what look like freestanding solid walls that evoke the nature of the ruins; these hold double-height glass panels between them, trapping dramatic views between slabs of stone.

a beautiful big room celebrating the landscape. It's not very defensive but feels much more of a sort of strange confection that's been put there. During the 16th century it was worked on by Smythson who put these lancet windows in, then during the Civil War it was blown up by Arundell himself (the owner) after it had become occupied by Cromwellian troops – a large part of it was destroyed. The next century the Arundell family built New Wardour Castle (1770 – 1776), a huge Neoclassical pile designed by James Paine. The ruined Old Wardour Castle became the folly decorating the view from the new building. At

the base of the Old Castle there are fragments of 17th-century buildings. There are some examples of beautiful masonry in these fragments. At one point it was a Jesuit centre of some sort, full of priests' escape routes and tunnels. Old Wardour House was built in the 19th century in amongst this historic debris and was the estate bailiff's house. In the 1960s it was bought by a judge who brought his library and cook down here. The kitchen had no aspect originally so the plan was to create a kitchen with a dining space at one end of the building. It evokes with a very simple strategy of walls, the walls of the ruin but is all about how to inhabit, for a family in more democratic circumstances, a bit of the English landscape.'

---

1   Jeremy Melvin, *Country Houses Today*, Wiley-Academy, London, p 184.

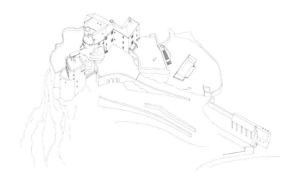

Right: Château de Paulin. An axonometric drawing of the route up to the château and the building's relationship to its site on the edge of a precipitous drop into the valley. The geology of the site informed the nature of the existing architecture.

The extension sits at one end of a mass of buildings that get roughly younger from one end to the other. Melvin comments that Parry's use of stone 'weaves a skein of connections between past and present'. When building against and into an existing structure the texture of the stone is designed to bear some resemblance one to another although the join between the two is designed to be readable. 'Where new stonework is detached from the old,' writes Melvin, 'it is smooth and refined – as if imitating the characteristic of glass ... and inviting the striations of history that will themselves become history.'[1]

'The Château de Paulin in the Tarn, France is all about the section. It's perched on the edge of a precipice, there's a whole geological tale here. Originally it was one of the most northern of the Cathar strongholds, a little fortified hillock. I stayed there when I was surveying, in that room there on the first floor.'

He gestures towards an image taken from the valley, the château on the edge of a precipice with a drop of 200 metres. He points to a room on the corner of the first floor on the edge of the void and,

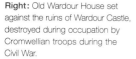

Right: Old Wardour House set against the ruins of Wardour Castle, destroyed during occupation by Cromwellian troops during the Civil War.

ARCHITECTURAL VOICES

caught up for a moment in the past, gestures to the right and the left indicating windows on elevations perpendicular with one another.

'I had that window open, and that window, and from [my] bed I watched the cloud run through the room. This space is placed entirely in the sky, it can disappear, be completely enveloped in cloud. The sound there was extraordinary too. The client had been complaining of hearing things – water running – so we had the spaces tested acoustically and found that it was the quietest ambient noise level ever registered. You could literally hear plants grow. It was something like an acoustic chamber where you could hear absolutely everything, you could become overly aware of any noise you made yourself. You were amplified. There were a lot of legends attached to the place, it was such an intensely isolated and beautiful site. One of the most powerful things made visible was time and erosion. We had geologists look at the structure of the rock to anticipate its collapse and incorporate the erosion into our plan for the future of the building.'

ARCHITECTURAL VOICES

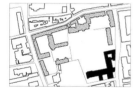

Above: A sequence of plans illustrating how the grounds of Pembroke College have been developed over its 650-year existence.

We have now turned to look through a sequence of plans of Pembroke College, Cambridge dating from 1592 to 1997. They show the chronological development of the site and the surrounding area. Parry's scheme has made more articulate the possibility for future projects to complete the court around gardens.

'To be honest, all projects have a reading of the past even if they're completely new buildings. I could safely say that there's something to do with continuity that is intriguing. It doesn't mean that things have to be architecturally of a style that is anything like continuous, but the sense in which the place has been inhabited is incredibly important when you're thinking about how things develop towards the future. Pembroke College, for instance, has continuously occupied this site in Cambridge for 650 years. This scheme required a more analytical approach because it developed out of a masterplan that was about how the college could expand. It involved the destruction of a single isolated master's lodge to create 100 student rooms, a new master's lodge and a new court. There will be further versions of this overall plan. People will always be working on it. I can quite see that having done this there are going to be plans for further building work, so this will be part of a continuous development.'

Later, Parry spoke about going back through old sketchbooks – he was surprised to have found pages and pages of sketches of people, not buildings, as one might have imagined. And this was really what it was about – creating the environment for life to play out. Physical moments to act as a backdrop to a living narrative.

Above: Pembroke College. The new buildings from the street.

Milky Voids – the reinterpretation of a mining building

Botallack, Cornwall

David Littlefield

19th-century mining engine building – architect unknown
Installation, *Milky Voids*, by artist Ken Wilder, 2004

'Devoid of their machinery and ancillary struc-
tures, the buildings take on an unselfconscious
monumentality that belies their diminutive stature.
This ambiguity of scale is most keenly felt in the
interiors: stripped of their functional imperative,
they take on a Tarkovskian [1] ambience of an inter-
nalised landscape. It is a quality enhanced by the
fact that neither building can be entered easily.
While the upper building is readily accessible from
the footpath, a deep recess in the granite floor
prevents ingress beyond the high "entrance door".
The approach to the lower building involves
clambering down a steep incline, only to discover
that there are no openings at ground level. These
are structures that are seemingly protective of
their hidden secrets, reluctant to reveal what lurks
behind their punctured facades.'

Ken Wilder, in a booklet accompanying his *Milky
Voids* installation.

Cornish mining engines are peculiar things. The remnants of a voracious, even rapacious, extraction industry, these buildings are now largely in a state of disrepair. Many are on the verge of collapse and close inspection is something to be undertaken with extreme caution. The stubborn relics of what was once a significant industrial centre (producing tin, copper, arsenic, clay, wool), these buildings sit within rural emptiness. The landscape is so post-industrial it is difficult to imagine it was ever industrial.

These largely granite buildings, which appear to grow out of the landscape rather than sit as an imposition upon it, are three-dimensional puzzles. Because they once housed giant steam-powered machinery and massive moving parts, they now appear irrational and slightly enigmatic structures. Pierced by odd slots and openings that have no relation to the scale of the human figure, these structures are obscured under a series of poetic veils. Isolated objects within an often desolate and rugged landscape, they are ruins, with all the appeal that ruins have to the Romantic mind; to the unenlightened, their form does not suggest function; they also have a way of playing tricks with scale, and can appear to be simultaneously very large and rather constrained.

Cornwall has been subjected to mining since Roman times, when seams of copper and tin could be spotted in cliff faces from boats. Dedicated mining engines began to be constructed in the 18th century and, at the industry's height in the mid-19th century, more than 600 mines were at work in the county. Essentially, all these buildings operated in the same way – a massive 'bob wall', typically up to 1 metre thick, would act as a pivot for the rocking beam (or 'bob') which plunged up and down, driven by a steam-powered engine situated inside the building. The cast-iron beam was attached to gear which could do a number of things – pump water out of the mine, lower people down the shaft, and bring the mined material to the surface. Opposite the bob wall there was often a huge vertical slot through which the massive machinery was brought into the building. The doorway itself was often far above the ground, like the entrance to the White Tower within the Tower of London, and accessed via a timber stair. Other practical requirements of the machinery forced the creation of a building with deep

---

1   After Russian film-maker Andrei Tarkovsky, director of (among others) *Stalker* and *Solaris*.

recesses in its base (inside and out) which were often carved into the granite on which these buildings stand. There is no floor as such, rather a series of plinths and platforms. They were technological wonders, and even attracted Royal visitors.

Today, stripped of all timber, machinery and temporary outbuildings, these structures stand as exoskeletons, bereft of anything (bar a deep and dangerous hole nearby) that allows the casual observer to make any sense of them. These are buildings which encourage guesswork and reinvention, that stimulate the visitor to work his or her imagination hard and overlay the stonework with possibilities. Although the brute industrial strength of these buildings is clear, it is harder to imagine the appalling noise, pollution and environmental degradation they used to generate. Because they are constructed from the material on which they sit and they have a comfortable relationship with their setting, they occupy the landscape in much the same way as do Greek temples. For this reason, and because of their verticality and the trouble that obviously went into making them, it is easy to attach a spiritual, even monastic, air to these ruined spaces. Visitors generally adopt an attitude of reverence when approaching and entering these buildings, and images of hermits such as St Jerome or Simeon Stylites quickly suggest themselves.

But, in spite of first impressions, it is obvious that these buildings are not religious structures. They are barely habitable and were designed at the scale of machinery rather than people. Without coming forearmed with a knowledge of 19th-century mining practice, you are faced, inevitably, with questions: What happened here? How did these buildings work? What were these buildings for?

It is these enigmatic and ambiguous qualities that bring Chelsea College of Art and Design's Ken Wilder to Cornwall. For a number of years, Wilder has been using these mining engines as sites for design students to reimagine, and in 2004 he used one of a pair of buildings at Botallack as the setting for an extraordinary art installation. Perched on a steep cliff-face 6 miles north of St Just, facing directly west into the Atlantic, these buildings are exemplars of their type. Isolated and weatherbeaten, Botallack sets out clearly the reality of the Cornish mining industry – dangerous, desperate and a testbed for human ingenuity and courage. Visited by Queen Victoria in 1846, and the Prince and Princess of Wales two decades later, the building used by Wilder once housed a winding engine that serviced a mine which extended more than 2,500 feet from the cliffs and reached a depth of 1,360 feet below sea level. On 18 April 1863 the chain to a wagon hauling miners to the surface broke – the safety mechanism failed and eight men and a boy of 12 died when they were sent to the bottom of this diagonal shaft.

Wilder, who runs the MA programme in Interior and Spatial Design at Chelsea, believes buildings accumulate a psychological status through the way that people project on to them their own mental states and imagined narratives. Of course, some buildings are designed to elicit particular responses but Wilder says that here the combination of the buildings' setting, their state of ruination, the ambiguities of scale and their architectonic forms make them especially rich in imagined possibilities. In particular, Wilder identifies a sense of loss at Botallack – engendered partly through the violence of its history and the decline of an industry, partly through the vulnerability of these decaying structures, and partly, even, through the sound of wind and wave.

The mechanism by which the voices of a space can be imagined depends, therefore, on an interplay between an individual's internalised response and sensibilities, and the external realities of the space itself. The one aspect reinforces the other, much in the way that the setting of a Gothic tale simultaneously moulds and reflects the protagonist's state of mind. 'We project our inner world on to a place. My feeling is that any resonance is a result of what we project on to a

Below: *'Devoid of their machinery and ancillary structures, the buildings take on an unselfconscious monumentality that belies their diminutive stature.'* Ken Wilder

Above: Wilder's installation appears to erase whole areas of the mining building. The whiteness and flatness of the trays of milk contrast so completely with the texture of granite that rectilinear patches appear to melt into light.

building,' says Wilder. 'But there was something about the buildings which spoke to me about loss, and I can't quite pin that down.'

Entering the buildings at Botallack is easier said than done. A footpath leads to the uppermost building but a deep recess cut into the granite provides an obstacle to the most obvious entry point; approaching the lower building involves negotiating a steep incline, but once down, there are no ground-level openings. This is a building whose internal space cannot be experienced, only seen from above. Oddly, once inside the upper building (called Pearce's Whim), there is little sense of internal space – rather, the interior of this structure feels like a constrained exterior, a claustrophobic landscape. These buildings are smaller within than they appear – the walls are thick and the buildings' fractured groundscapes make it almost impossible to pace out their extent. What does happen, though, is that the combination of modest proportions and massive incisions through the walls focuses attention on the texture of the surfaces and the landscape beyond. The building becomes a space of just two textures – there are the roughness and visual weight of the granite, and then there is the insubstantiality of the panels of light. Wilder says this duality emphasises the 'graniteness of granite' and 'the lightness of light' – which provides the starting point for his installation *Milky Voids*.

Wilder's installation in Pearce's Whim consists of shallow trays of milk set into depressions in the granite floor. Set up to replicate the intensity of the light which appears almost solid in photographs of the building, the panels provide a foil from which to read the roughness and rudeness of the stonework; their white-ness, and the whiteness of the sky, have a presence (through the absence of colour and texture) that rivals that of the

more substantial granite. Moreover, with their straight edges, the trays provide a clarity that the buildings lack. It is an exercise in contrasts, in showing the substance of insubstantiality, the insubstantiality of substance.

Importantly, Wilder never intended the installation to be the completed artwork. Instead, the photographs and video footage of the installation, rather than being a record of the work, *are* the work. The film shows the panels of milk to be liquid with subtle ripples running across their surfaces, a tentative physical reminder of the power of the wind which blows through the mining engines constantly. The photographs, however, reveal in a very subtle way the reflectivity and depth of milk; traces of the surrounding building can be glimpsed in it, while the milk is also perceived as a presence with depth rather than just a flat surface. The result is very different from an image created by electronically selecting an area and deleting its content in Photoshop – these white panels have a definite three-dimensional presence. The panels provide the site with a similar mechanism to that provided by Richard Wilson's *20:50* installation, in which an observer is taken into a room filled with sump oil. But Wilson's oil, for all its presence, has a disappearing quality – its high reflectivity and utter blackness turn in on itself and become void. Wilder's milk, however, partly because it is used sparingly in contrast to the oil of *20:50*, has a presence greater than it deserves. Oddly for something so white, these panels absorb light rather than reflect it.

The photographs of Wilder's *Milky Voids* also emphasise the absence of predictable scale in the mining engines. There is little in these images that indicates size and, if you were to guess at it, the reality would probably not bear you out. What appears to be a doorway is, in fact, 4 metres high. Many of the photo-

Right: Interior of the engine building. Without the machinery that gave these buildings their form, they appear as three-dimensional puzzles. With the shallow trays of milk installed by artist Ken Wilder, images of the building become curiouser still – what is up and what is down becomes uncertain.

graphs also defy orientation and would make just as much 'sense' turned through 90 degrees. Thus, the three-dimensional puzzle that is these buildings is pushed to an extreme – not only is it impossible to fathom their function just by looking, but their orientation is also something to be guessed at.

In spite of the possibilities revealed by the photographs, however, the most profound impact of this piece of work lies in its physical presence – and the actual experience of being in these spaces. These buildings/puzzles invite exploration and deciphering. Like many pieces of redundant analogue technology – typewriters, cameras or record players – these are buildings which can be pieced together. Without any prior knowledge one can imagine, like the fantasies of Erich von Däniken, inventing fanciful uses for these

places. Wilder's students have reimagined these engine houses as anything from crematoria to performance venues. But what is encouraging about Wilder's work is that detailed prior knowledge of a site does not inhibit the process of reimagining – indeed, the opposite seems to be the case. A combination of careful observation, a sensitivity to context and a working knowledge of the social and architectural history of a place can trigger highly creative thought processes. Wilder even talks about the 'temporal anamorphosis', a stretching of time, that seemed to characterise Pearce's Whim while his pieces were present.

'It did have a strange atmosphere. There was something very calm about it. There's this tumult of activity outside but, within the building itself, a sense of calmness, of loss and even a sense of death.'

Left: The sorting rooms are over-looked by watchtowers, reminiscent of the bridges of small ships. Now empty, they embody the idea of watchfulness so completely that they appear frozen in a fixed stare.

Royal Mail Sorting Office

Victoria, London

David Littlefield

Built 1894–1912 by Sir Henry Tanner and Royal Mail Office of Works
Remodelled by Squire and Partners 2006–7

Above: Stripped of virtually all the hardware that made this building work, the former sorting office still preserves a sense of itself in the scratches, knocks, scuff marks and loose parquet flooring. Glass has all but lost its transparency thanks to dirt, grime, smudges, and stickers, and windows admit only partial views out.

The South Western District Office, an ex-Royal Mail sorting centre built to handle the post for London's 'SW' area, is built on one of those sites that never seem to sit still. It's a place for which old maps indicate the presence of buildings that have not only vanished but been forgotten, along with roads that have changed both course and name. Sites like these (like the 'Indian burial grounds' of American horror movies) provide even new buildings with instant histories.

This building, which occupies a triangular plot at the junction of Howick Place and Francis Street in London's Victoria, marks the north-eastern edge of a site which once contained the Middlesex House of Correction, a prison for female inmates which closed in 1883. Completed in 1894, the sorting office was built to help manage the rapidly increasing volume of post that was flooding in and out of London towards the end of the 19th century, but it quickly proved inadequate for the job. An extra storey was added in 1902, but just a decade later Post Office officials began eyeing a disused fire station, which sat on an island in front of the building, with a view to further expansion.

The idea was to connect the fire station with the Post Office building by infilling the road which separated them. Westminster Council objected and demanded that, if the Post Office wanted to convert public space for its own use, then it should create public space elsewhere in the borough. Protracted wrangling resulted in the decision to demolish the fire station, rather than adapt it, and to replace it with a building that drew back from the old facade line and left more space on its north-eastern edge. It was a utilitarian decision, and the principal facade of the ruggedly simple 1884 building disappeared with the construction of the more elaborate post-Edwardian extension of 1912. But the

road is still vaguely present: the combined assembly is, internally, very much two buildings; externally, the join of new and old manifests itself in two deep notches.

The Royal Mail vacated this complex in August 2005, consolidating its services south of the Thames at Vauxhall. The building now occupies a slightly ambiguous position in heritage terms: although it falls within the Borough of Westminster's conservation area, it is not listed, which means that while demolition is unlikely, there is nothing on the statute books to prevent radical change. In fact, applications for the building's demolition were turned down in the early 1990s but later the Royal Mail did succeed in securing consent to all but demolish the building and insert 120 apartments behind retained facades. Architects Squire and Partners, however, found a new client and proposed an alternative – to retain the building and use its vast, open spaces as design studios and exhibition halls. Just nine apartments would be built.

Westminster Council officials were excited by the idea of attracting creative businesses to the borough, but council policy specified that office developments should be matched with housing schemes of the same magnitude. This pledge, if enforced, would have made the scheme instantly unviable. The architects and their client argued that they were not creating offices, and that design studios fell into a category of their own. It was also an argument that gave the building the best chance of surviving relatively intact, and planning consent was duly granted.

The Howick Place sorting office is not a building of architectural distinction. Even Squire and Partners, which raced to the building's defence, does not pretend that either its facades or interiors offer anything unique or of historic interest. It is a robust, very typical, rather

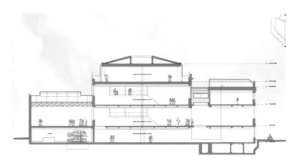

Left: Cross-section through the main building. The large, open floor-plates were ideal for conversion to any number of uses.

Above: A dirt-encrusted helter-skelter down which mailbags once slid. The structure is now merely a curiosity, an industrial sculpture.

confusing and even awkward place; it was clearly built as, and used as, a purely functional space and it bears the scars of a century of hard work. Its basement contains a bulky steel structure that was designed to prevent total collapse in the event of Second World War bombing. Howick Place sorting office is rather a graceless building.

But the building is large, light and full of oddities. There are vast, rivetted helter-skelters, down which mail bags would have been thrown; there are peculiar colour schemes of pink, orange, green and pale blue; smashed clocks; and windows that have all but lost their transparency under the sheer number of smudges, stickers and Post-it notes on the reinforced glass. David Beckham, flashing his Number 7 shirt in the 2002 World Cup, still screams from a tabloid newspaper glued irreverently to a wall; the ghosts of snooker tables show on the carpet of the top-floor social club as dark rectangles; six months after the mail sorters moved out, the canteen still retained the odour of cooking oil.

Stripped of virtually all the hardware that made this building work, it still preserves a sense of itself in the scratches, knocks, scuff marks and loose parquet flooring. It is a 'behind-the-scenes' building, a tired workhorse that provided the muscle implied by the fragility of a postage stamp. In a practical sense, the sorting office's high ceilings, large floorplates, generous windows and intimate office spaces make it ideal for exhibition/studio use. Poetically, the building is a conduit for stories, the medium for messages, a sort of constructed synapse through which human communication is routed.

Emotionally, the whispers of this building – especially in its smaller, darker, more discreet spaces (corridors, counters, cubbyholes) – powerfully evoke a

bureaucratic institution characterised by surveillance and suspicion. The grubby office used to process the mail from Buckingham Palace, although stripped of virtually everything else, still contains a suite of CCTV units suspended from the ceiling in gleaming black spheres. Indeed, the two large sorting floors (one blue, one pink) are punctuated by the 19th-century equivalent of these cameras: observation platforms, little sealed offices accessible only by vertical ladder, provided eyries from which supervisors could scrutinise those handling mail below.

Perhaps none of that is surprising. This corner of London has always been a place of watchfulness and noise. Before the sorting office, it was home to a prison and fire station; before the prison, there was a bull-

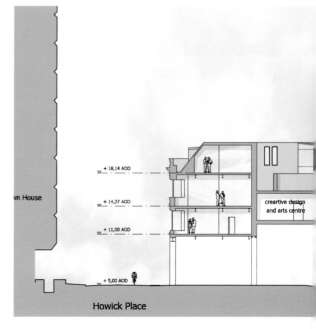

+ 18,14 AOD

+ 14,27 AOD

+ 11,00 AOD

+ 5,00 AOD

vn House

creartive design and arts centre

Howick Place

ARCHITECTURAL VOICES

Right and below: Architect's views of the redeveloped sorting office, reinvented as apartments with broad spaces for designers' studios and exhibitions.

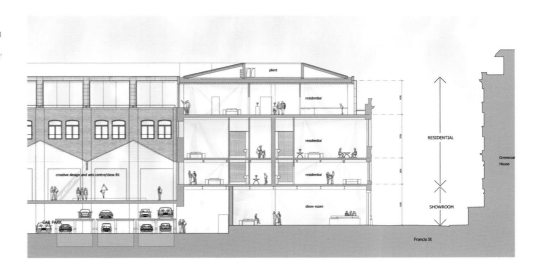

baiting ring; before that, a marketplace. It is fitting, therefore, that once the Royal Mail had vacated the building, retailer Marks & Spencer moved in with a temporary fashion show. The site has always been a place for observing and being observed, for containing activity and framing views. The functions have changed, but the course of human behaviour has remained remarkably consistent. Perhaps it was inevitable that the plan to replace the building with apartments didn't last as an architectural proposition; that would have been too much of a rupture with historical continuity.

This sort of analysis (what novelist Will Self has called 'psycho-geography') enters the realms of Peter Ackroyd's *London: The Biography*, a book in which he traces physical, emotional and symbolic relationships throughout the city. In a conversation between the authors of this book and Ackroyd, he proposed that people impose an identity on a place that becomes an indelible part of the built fabric.

'The sense of place … may have something to do with the history of the building. The past can be a very powerful presence,' wrote Ackroyd. '[Buildings] are not simply assemblies of dull stones but are powerfully

affected by human inhabitation and human practice. Certain buildings have a moral value, for example as a token of human will and human idealism. Other buildings are moulded by a sense of the sacred. Others are dedicated to the pursuit of profit. Each of them then acquires an identity which, through the years, becomes as integral a part of the structure as the bricks and stones.'

Architects at Squire and Partners also talk about a sense of place. After all, this is a practice that acquired a small Victorian building in central London with permission to replace it with a four-storey residential block. In spite of the financial consequences, the directors decided against demolition and, instead, converted the former workshop into a bar.

'We just couldn't do it, even though it wasn't commercially justifiable [to retain it]. That type of decision is taken by having a feeling for a building. We wanted to keep it from Day One. It was an emotional thing, an emotional response to what this building could be for us,' says Mark Way, a partner at Squire and Partners who left in 2005 to set up his own practice.

'Your initial response as an architect has to be a sense of place, a sensibility for light and spatial

awareness. People talk about voices in different ways. When we talk about it, it's about respecting the architecture. If you're talking about voices, you're talking about a level of respect. Having said that, you don't do much by listening – you have to bring something to make it a conversation.'

In both the workshop and the sorting office a conversation is brought about by approaching these spaces in a spirit of architectural humility. It is a quiet, tentative dialogue of hints and mild gestures; it is one of careful and active listening. Fortunately, Squire and Partners now has a client who is willing to sponsor such a restrained approach. Project architect Bettina Brehler talks about 'doing the least we can to make it work'.

However, there are still likely to be interventions of considerable magnitude. For example, mezzanine levels will almost certainly have to be introduced where floor to ceiling heights allow to increase the floor area available for letting, and the replacement of windows and lifts is unavoidable. There is also a question mark over how to handle a triangular void that cuts right through the building (it could remain a void, or be roofed over to create a winter garden).

And there is a further question – what is to be done with those supervisors' watchtowers? In practical terms, they are clearly redundant and lack the ambiguity which might suggest viable alternative uses. But in their regimented blankness, and in their intrusive human scale (lacking in security cameras), they have a very real, disturbing presence. No doubt they were designed to have this effect and the strength of these little boxes, with their metal-runged, naval-style ladders, is not diminished by the absence of people. With nobody to watch, and nobody watching, they remain part of the voice of this building.

Above: The basement, a place of brightly coloured walls illuminated by dim fluorescent lighting. A partially deflated balloon hangs from a ventilation duct.

Of All We Survey
Drawing out Stories of Place

Carolyn Butterworth

Carolyn Butterworth is an architect and a tutor at the School of Architecture at the University of Sheffield. In generating architecture Butterworth takes an oblique view – to get to the real meaning of architecture (its psychology, its hidden lives, its poetry) Butterworth has formed collaborations with artists and taken risks. Below, she explains why the conventional architectural 'site survey' is not enough; that a genuine understanding of a place entails making a personal commitment.

The music of the mariachi could just be heard over the noise from the buses and the hot-dog stand. Claudia Amico stepped up onto a makeshift stage in front of the grand Market Hall in Accrington. Tentatively at first, she started to step and sway and then, picking up confidence and speed, she twirled her bright orange skirt faster and faster, her stamps and handclaps becoming louder and more insistent. People reacted in many ways – some barely noticed, some averted their eyes, some stopped and watched, two little girls started their own silly, giggly dance. As Amico danced, their memories prompted by the spectacle, onlookers recalled other dances and performances in Accrington, how there used to be more dancing and how people don't dance so much in public any more.

How do architects get to know a site? Their education and professional practice provide a long-established methodology which architects apply anywhere and which provides them with the 'site survey'. Their tools are the camera, the architectural drawing, and physical, historical and social data. The application of these tools results in a survey which stands as evidence of an understanding of the site. Once back at the office the site survey becomes source material which is reduced until it can sit in a folder; through this process of reduction the map becomes the territory. The site survey becomes the actual site for design to take place. This transformation of the actual site into site-as-site-survey promotes a particular attitude towards the place for which architects are designing. The site is abstracted from reality and appraised at a conceptual distance.

The information which results from a conventional survey is useful to describe many tangible aspects of a site but it is not able, nor is it intended, to record the temporal, the immaterial, the personal and the poetic. The conventional survey speaks of what a site is rather than what it could be, of how the site looks rather than how it feels and of what is present rather than what is absent. The qualities of a site that are not captured by normative practice are important and material to sited architectural design. They cannot be integrated within the design unless the distance between the architect and the site (created by the conventional site survey) is removed.

Within my studio at the University of Sheffield's School of Architecture we have developed a methodology which closes the gap between architect and site. This method promotes an active engagement with the site and expands our readings of what already exists and what is possible. The studio uses conceptual art practice to provide us with tools to work directly not only with a site but also with the people who use it. We learn from the work of Sophie Calle, Adrian Piper and Mierle Laderman Ukeles, artists who place themselves at the heart of their explorations of place and, in so doing, invite users to reconsider their own relationships with a place. By adopting this form of art practice the architect becomes an active player in the survey of the

site; the survey becomes an event and the event becomes a conduit for unexpected readings which can go on to shape an architectural proposal. Techniques inspired by conceptual art practice such as story-telling, game-playing, performance and conversation allow survey material to emerge that is useful because it is subjective rather than objective, propositional rather than merely reactive.

The Victorian Market Hall in Accrington, built in 1868, is the oldest market hall in Lancashire. It still

Above: The Market Hall, a symbol of Accrington's glorious and affluent past, is now mute, stifled, a ghost of itself.

Right: Architecture student Richard Gaete-Holmes fishing in the Victorian Arcade, Accrington, 2006. Intrigued by the fact that the arcade covered the River Hyndburn, Gaete-Holmes went through the motions of fishing the river through a drain as part of his study of the site.

houses an indoor market, although most of the shopping in Accrington now goes on in the nearby Arndale Centre. The Market Hall retains its civic grandeur externally, but internally it is under-used and has fallen into disrepair. With its neighbour, the Town Hall, the building forms the centre of a once prosperous mill town; now the old town square is empty and forlorn while the pedestrianised shopping precinct behind is where most people are to be found. The Market Hall stands as a symbol of Accrington's glorious and affluent past and, as a result, it has become a ghost of itself. The building is mute.

In 2005 my students explored the possibilities for public space in Accrington and many were drawn to the Market Hall. Several alternative site surveys were carried out of which Amico's Mexican dance was one. Amico's site survey revealed stories about performance and dance that no amount of conventional surveying would have uncovered. Her dance transformed a place that passers-by thought they knew into a place that surprised them. This alternative form of site survey does not claim to discover the authentic voice or the essence

of a place (should such a thing exist). However, it does provide access to the stories immanent within a particular place.

A year later, a further group of students returned to Accrington. Kirstin Aitken and Richard Gaete-Holmes, conducting their own alternative site survey, explored the possibilities of the culverted River Hyndburn which runs beneath the town centre. As the 'Gutter Fishermen' they spent a day fishing down drains and gullies which connected directly with the river. One such site was the Victorian Arcade, a curved run of shops which bisects a town block across from the Market Hall. The arcade is a listed building and many original features remain but, overall, the atmosphere is one of neglect. The sight of a person patiently sitting by a gulley, waiting for a bite on a line, having apparently already caught a couple of fish, aroused great interest. Passers-by stopped and stared, trying to make sense of what had appeared in a space they knew so well. The ground beneath them had become transformed into a thin surface under which was rushing water teeming with fish. Some told of how the river occasionally bubbled up through the floors, and how it was called the 'River Stink' before it was culverted. The playfulness and simplicity of the idea of the Gutter Fishermen sparked their imaginations and a dialogue developed between architect and user, student and local, fisherman and shopper.

Architects are not the experts in understanding a place; to approach any level of expertise, they themselves have to become users. In contrast to the information gathered by conventional survey techniques, the stories told by people uncover hidden possibilities, speaking of the imagination and the metaphorical, and not just the measurable.

Right: Fish, apparently caught through a drain from the River Hyndburn which runs beneath the streets of Accrington. The architectural site survey as installation and performance art.

Park Farm / River Cottage HQ

near Axminster, Devon

Saskia Lewis

Above: View south through the interior of the farmhouse to the kitchen garden beyond. This doorway was the entrance most used by Eli Collier and his predecessors between the farmyard and the house – in the summer the two doors can be left open to create a cross-breeze.

The 20th century witnessed the slow decline of farming in the UK. It is in crisis still and the population of Britain, seduced by image and convenience, has fallen into a supermarket coma of ready meals and forgetfulness. The River Cottage identity emerged when Hugh Fearnley-Whittingstall left London in the mid-1990s to live in a cottage in Dorset and test his skill at rural self-sufficiency. In a climate of sedentary inertia, this was a near anarchic move. He filmed his efforts, experiments and frustrations, relationships with neighbours, the buying, rearing and slaughter of livestock (including regret and sentimental attachment), mistakes, humiliations and the eventual satisfaction of preparing, cooking and consuming the results. His television series *Escape to River Cottage*, broadcast by Channel 4, touched the nation and began to rekindle an interest in some basic truths about the production and consumption of food.

Fearnley-Whittingstall is now a well-known author, journalist and advocate of real food. He and the River Cottage team are still producing and recording for television, questioning and examining how we relate to food. But they have expanded their organisation to provide the opportunity for people to attend workshops and experience first-hand the results of living a little more closely to the land. River Cottage cookbooks are in production as well as a line of foodstuffs that include organic yoghurt and River Cottage Stinger beer made from handpicked organic nettles from Dorset. In 2005

Right: North elevation of the farmhouse and the working farmyard. The interior of the house is used as a backdrop to the filming, while the administrative hub of River Cottage is housed in timber sheds. The yard is levelled with the debris of the two 20th-century buildings that have been demolished.

they secured the ownership of Park Farm in east Devon, 3 miles south of Axminster and 5 miles north of Seaton on the south coast. This will now become the new head-quarters for River Cottage.

An aerial view of Park Farm is deceptive especially when taken around noon on a clear summer's day. From above you can see what appears as a delicate web of paths made by the animals over decades that fans out from each gateway through pastureland, to converge again by an aperture at another boundary. You see how hedgerows and woods divide the land. You can pinpoint the roofscape of a group of buildings but this tells you nothing of its topography or the experience of the site by foot. The road sits on the ridge of the hill at a height of 182 metres above sea level, from here the landscape tumbles into a ruckled valley. The stony track meanders steeply, first to the south and then doubling back on itself, aiming north-west. The farm buildings shift in and out of view between the trees, they sit at the point where the land

begins to level out a little, a drop of 50 metres from the road. Finally, you approach the farm from the east like the morning sun.

Eli Collier was the last resident at Park Farm. The last man to make hay in the meadows, scything by hand. The last to raise, nurture and export meat fattened in these pastures. There is a picture of him sitting by the fire in the late 1980s. He would have known the prevailing wind from the south, the kink in the valley that drops swiftly to the sea, the dramatic sunsets that light up the long horizon to the west. He will have savoured the sweet warmth of a summer's hay-making to the drone of insects, the chill of a winter wind, the bitter savage air of a bleak day and the pale cool light that is quick to dull. In the summer the doors to the house would have stood open, both front and back, creating a cross-breeze, and in the winter the thick rubble walls and roaring fire would have provided refuge against the force of the wind and the deep dark of the night. For some time now the front of the house

Above: Aerial view of the site. Paths worn bare by herds of animals exist as a fine web in the meadows.

Right: Eli Collier scything the meadow by hand, land he worked for decades. The land here is not particularly fertile but is suitable for raising small herds of animals.

has not been used as the entrance; people have entered from the courtyard for decades. The front is for show, for best, an image and an idyll; the back is about work, industry, reality, the day to day.

The farm was bought in November 2005. In early 2006 Malcolm Seal, the head gardener, laid out a formal kitchen garden to the south of the farmhouse along the lines of a 16th-century model. He divided the vegetable garden into four manageable plots surrounded by gravel paths in a cruciform arrangement centred on the front door of the house. The ground had to be turned over, prepared and planted to provide the necessary crop of vegetables for the beginning of filming in late summer. For the first time in several decades this soil was broken up, the solid crust that had formed through years of compacting was systematically eased apart and enriched with organic nutrients.

Malcolm Seal, along with a couple of others, camped in the derelict farmhouse from February and made tending the garden their daily task. They would cook homemade soup on an open fire and feel the presence of the frugal farmer Eli, who had been the last person to spend the night in the place. Through the ritual of those early, basic days Seal felt a growing sense of responsibility to honour the farm, the man and the sense of tradition and seasonal knowledge that were embedded here. Each field, for example, once had an ancient name describing its use, names that had been lost until Seal rediscovered them. He looked at soil type and drainage, prevailing winds and the route of the sun and married these to plants and species. He started to plan the layout of the landscape paying close attention to site and season, as if he were writing theatre directions for a play that would define an annual ritual of repeated tasks.

Right: Photomontage of the western elevation to Park Farm. A crudely made 20th-century concrete shed has been dismantled and pulverised on site, its debris used to level the courtyard.

Above: The farmhouse kitchen where Eli Collier sat two decades ago remains little changed. Guests will gather around the table to prepare and eat the food that they have harvested and cooked, while the room itself – as the main backdrop to the television series – will become an iconic image of rural wholesome living.

Left: Eli Collier in his armchair next to the fire in the farmhouse kitchen at Park Farm.

Left: The front door before and after its hasty restoration in time for filming during summer 2006. The rendering was repaired and the door quickly repainted, with a temporary panel masking the damaged lower section, itself painted with a *trompe l'oeil* image that repeats the moulding above.

Below: Night view of the south elevation of the threshing barn during conversion.

Left: Squash harvested from the restored kitchen garden sit on the window sill.

Meanwhile Stewart Dodd, director of Satellite Architects in London, was preparing to transform this traditional mixed Devon farm into a venue that would be the synthesis of a working organic farm, a permanent set for filming and photo shoots and accommodation for workshops and courses anticipating around 20,000 visitors a year. In addition, there would be permanent offices for the running of River Cottage HQ, the media hub of the organisation. Park Farm had been one of 40 farms which they had looked at as possible sites for this project over a period of several years. They were looking for a venue that felt truly remote but was nevertheless easy to reach by public transport, and this farm is exactly that. It sits in its own valley enclosed in a self-contained world.

As you walk down to the farm you feel as if you are walking away from contemporary life, moving into a space where time is measured, doesn't race, isn't forced. The courtyard to the rear of the farmhouse made sense programmatically – the existing buildings provided a clear model of how the proposed spaces could sit in relation to one another. The farmhouse would continue to be home to the farm, and the yard to the rear would still be its working heart. In addition to the traditional products associated with farming, Park Farm would now be producing experience and sharing knowledge. In effect, the farm was being brought back to life subsidised by the media and other events that would take place there. The first elements to be transformed were the garden and Eli's kitchen. These needed to be fully operational and recognisable within months – they would be the first areas to be completed and would provide the tone to reintroduce a television audience to values and knowledge that had been increasingly lost as the 20th century had drawn to a close.

Right: View north towards the yard through the interior of the house. Bags of potatoes stand in sacks next to the door, the remains of a photo shoot for the *Observer* magazine.

Left: Fragment of the 17th-century chert wall retained and extended using traditional building techniques to provide the external wall to River Cottage HQ offices.

Above: Proposed site plan.

Below: Drawing of the proposed
west wing to Park Farm. The new
green oak timber structure is highly glazed to afford uninterrupted
views over the rolling landscape
to the west.

The farmhouse provides the intimate set for the television series. This will remain a private space and yet, peculiarly, it will be the image of River Cottage that will be broadcast on television. It will represent the home with which the viewers associate the ethics and values of the River Cottage brand. It is the public face of River Cottage, but it will not be open to the public. The set or image of the farm had to be complete in advance of the building work that is expected to continue until March 2008. The 17th-century front door has been 'repaired' with a trompe l'oeil painting sitting over its battered base and the concrete floor temporarily covered with blue linas, the traditional stone that will eventually be laid properly throughout the ground floor of the house. Upstairs will provide living accommodation for a farm manager and his family, while downstairs will exist as the set for filming as well as the venue for dinners and courses with Fearnley-Whittingstall.

In October and November 2006 a group dedicated to eating only pre-prepared food spent two weeks with Fearnley-Whittingstall. Having shot their own pigeons they were taken through the stages of preparing them for cooking. They pulled away the feathers, slit the bellies of the birds and slipped in a hand to strip away the entrails, sifting through them to identify the organs and putting them aside for a subsidiary dish. They sliced away the breast from the carcasses and gently laid them out to grill and eat warm with salad gathered from the kitchen garden. Gradually, around the worn kitchen table laden with produce which they had caught and gathered themselves, they began to overcome their aversion to handling food.

With guidance and encouragement from Hugh – a kindly and understanding connoisseur and keen enthusiast – they began to appreciate the taste of their dishes and learn something that was common currency for earlier generations, namely what it is like to eat food

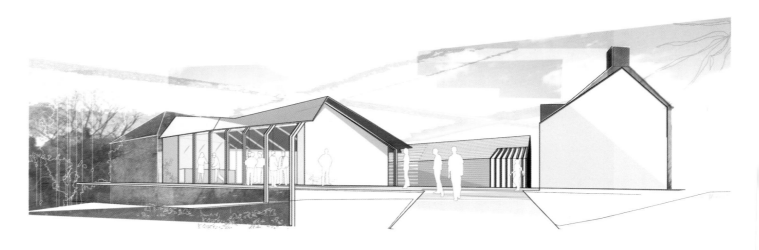

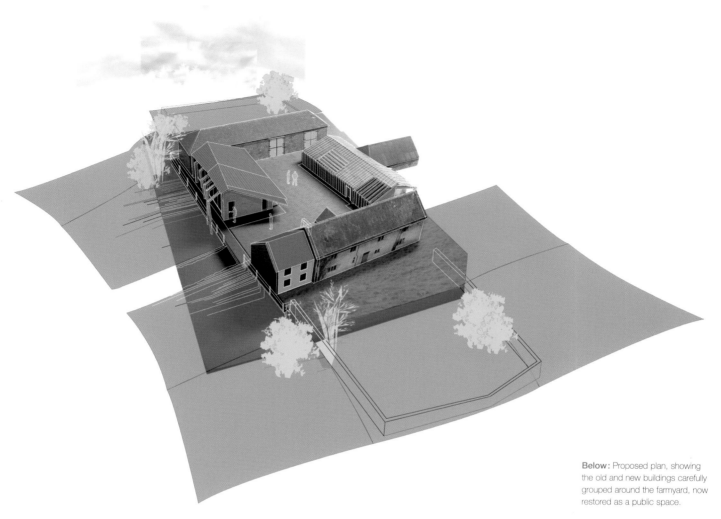

Below: Proposed plan, showing the old and new buildings carefully grouped around the farmyard, now restored as a public space.

produced with knowledge, dignity and care. And all the while, behind them is the wall of the hearth, touched with soot from the fires that Eli and his predecessors had built and burnt, fires that had long been absent but had now been rekindled into a new type of life.

The buildings to the north of the farmhouse that formed the hub of the farm some 20 years ago will be licked into shape to provide the event spaces for the paying public around a generous gravel courtyard. Two of the original buildings will be retained and converted. At its eastern end, the 18th-century threshing barn to the north of the courtyard will provide space for the cutting room, meat storage and a cold store. This is where those who have subscribed to the Pig in a Day course will learn how to butcher and joint a whole pig.

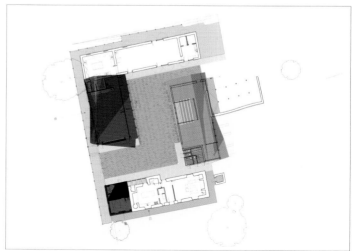

Ray Smith will have slaughtered the pig, most likely, with his 40 years' experience, in the kindest way possible, with all the respect due to an animal that is giving its future for food. He will have drained the blood from its body and the life from its eyes.

Although the animal can no longer be slaughtered on site the carcass will be fresh, the blood will colour the white tiles as the systematic precision of jointing takes place. People who have both actively and passively kept themselves remote from this knowledge will, for the first time, feel the resistance of a large mass of flesh against a sharp knife and the pride of having separated parts of the animal into cuts of meat. At lunch they will eat a selection of dried and cured hams and at supper they will regroup to taste another pork dish, a roast or a stew.

At the western end of the old threshing barn there is now a substantial working kitchen which can be used both for demonstrations and for cooking for large groups of people. Between the main areas handling the preparation and the cooking of food is a space to gather, talk, lecture, eat, drink and discuss. The floor has been levelled and the interior opened up to the roof trusses. Doorways have been lined with timber and fitted with

glazed doors. All the repairs and installations have been carefully considered so that they remain clearly readable against the fabric of the original building. Outside, the rickyard to the north of the old threshing barn will become a rambling, informal garden of watercress and herbs, with espalier cherry trees trained across the northern facade. After a day of tasting and cooking, watching and discussing, the audience will spill out among the herbs for a walk, to look and ponder, to pick a leaf and crush it between forefinger and thumb and release its scent.

The old cart shed to the south of the entrance also dates from the 18th century. This will see only the most necessary repairs and is intended to house more modern carts – golf buggies – that will ferry people from the top of the site down to the farm and back again. These will run on electricity generated from sustainable means on site, and will give the whole process something of the surrealism of a 1960s cult TV show. There is a clear effort to avoid the farm becoming clogged with cars and losing its rural, isolated atmosphere. Visitors will literally be suspended from their day to day, the convenience of cars will be removed from site, the comings and goings of people will be kept to a

minimum – this farm is to act as a model, a place to re-engage with old knowledge and slow the pace of life.

Two other buildings have been demolished, their carcasses crushed on site and used as rubble to fill and level the courtyard before dressing it with pale gravel. These were both 20th-century concrete structures built in the 1930s or 1940s. Each of them was out of true, drunken DIY sheds squatting on the foundations of their forebears. They sat opposite each other to the east and west of the courtyard and their removal has left clear scars by which to locate the new proposed buildings. The dairy shed to the east had stood against a very early chert wall which dates back to the 17th century, an example of early traditional Devon vernacular. While the concrete structure has now been removed, the chert wall has been retained and will be extended with the same material and technique used hundreds of years ago. The management offices of River Cottage HQ will be wrapped in this low-tech ancient skin. The skin will be pierced with glazing to allow staff to monitor the comings and goings from site, but the roof will overhang to avoid views into the interior, screening the computers and technical equipment from those outside. From the courtyard the building will appear contemporary and utilitarian, discreet and functional, timber clad and louvred, allowing light to penetrate but denying views in.

By contrast, the western edge of the yard looks out over the most magnificent valley. Fields roll down to the River Axe that in turn flows south towards the sea. The floor and easterly wall of the second event space will be built of rammed earth using traditional construction methods and locally sourced material, the rest will be built of green oak timber frame highly glazed to frame the spectacular views. Designed to be honest; you will be able to see how the building has been made, how each element slots or sits next to the other, a series of articulate junctions. Pushed flush against the western facade of the old threshing barn, the industrial kitchen is the pin or pivot that joins these buildings together. Huge doors open directly from the kitchen into their large volumes. This new structure sits on very old buttressed foundations that create a retaining wall for the courtyard allowing the land to drop away to the west.

Both new buildings to east and west are strangely, literally, twisted – their roofs overhang the walls, appearing to slip from their ridges. This is a direct and affectionate reference to their ungainly 20th-century ghosts, a hint of humour, a clear marker that the new builds are not trying to fit in with their solid dignified neighbours but are fresh, liberated and quirky. Both are lined with cedar, a timber with a complex and mystical history – its aromatic scent will mingle in the heat with the smell of cooking. At sunset, light will flood the

courtyard trapping the glow of the golden hour – the day will end with a drink on the balcony facing the valley and the setting sun.

Dodd creates a further series of buildings which have chameleon-like qualities, restlessly shifting from site to site. This strategy is intended to produce well-made temporary buildings that will provide necessary interim accommodation during the construction of River Cottage HQ. One of the sheds was originally built as a portable kitchen for River Cottage at the Architecture Biennale festival in London, June 2006. Nothing is wasted in this project so the roving pavilion has come back to HQ to settle for a few months and, with a new timber cladding, has become the greeting building at the top of the hill. Similarly, the temporary toilet shed, with a woodpile for a back elevation supplying a brazier in the courtyard, will be stripped later in 2007 to be reborn as a fruit and vegetable stall. The stall will join the greeting shed at the entrance from the road and will sell any surplus seasonal produce from River Cottage. At the main entrance, another shed will act both as a reception and as a large agricultural barn to house the

herd of ruby red cattle being reared on the farm that need protection from the wind. Parking spaces are laid out just off the main road although participants on the courses will be encouraged to use public transport and can be collected by the team instead of driving.

The aim, says Dodd, is to be as carbon neutral as possible. He has been instrumental in employing an ethical and honourable method of building, in tune with the River Cottage ethos. All materials have been locally sourced and finishes have been chosen to adhere to as near a non-toxic profile as possible. Old traditional building techniques have been used alongside cutting-edge technology. He is creating an optimal synthesis of both to enhance whatever is available. Energy is to be provided by wind, sun and renewable energy boilers burning locally sourced wood-chip. A wind turbine will sit 11 metres tall at the road entrance on the ridge and will double as a marker for point of entry. A smaller turbine to the south of the farmhouse will catch the prevailing wind and look more like something out of an American Western. A large solar panel will be situated to the north of the outcrop of buildings on a slope facing south; it is a plane 1.8 metres square connected to a GPS tracking system. Like a sunflower, it will follow the sun, trapping and absorbing any available energy. Rainwater will be harvested and collected in a tank located just west of the farmhouse, naturally draining there via gravity, then pumped back to provide flushing water for the toilets. The soiled water will then be pumped to reed and willow beds that break down the waste, cleansing the water before it is fed into the River Axe.

Embedded in the renovation of this site is the history of the buildings and the surrounding pastureland. The ecological and organic ideology that River Cottage embraces is essential to our modern day – we must harness this knowledge before it is lost to us; we have become careless with our production and consumption of food and here is one model that will strive to address that mistake. The buildings enclose a space that will become the public heart of the River Cottage endeavour. They in turn will witness a wealth of experience that is both intensely personal and televised, broadcast periodically to a loyal audience. This is the recreation of a farm and a rural way of life both as ideal and as educational tool. Surrounding the buildings are the gardens and the pastures that will provide River Cottage with the ingredients used and the subject matter to be discussed. Occasionally the sea mist will roll in and become trapped in the valley. The farm will appear to be totally cut off from modern life and its ancient secrets and enforced calm will slow everyone down. The voices here are soft spoken but knowing and they have been given an environment in which to survive with dignity.

Below: A shed with character. One of the River Cottage toilet blocks in the yard – a galvanised facade faces the prevailing wind.

Right: Photomontage looking east – the buildings housing the offices to River Cottage HQ are disguised as simple utilitarian sheds.

The Royal Military Asylum

Chelsea, London

David Littlefield

Architect: John Sanders, completed 1803
Remodelled by Paul Davis and Partners for Charles Saatchi, 2006–7

Above: Originally built as the Royal Military Asylum in 1803, the building was designed by John Sanders, one of Sir John Soane's first pupils. An austere, uncompromising place, it also has the robustness of design and construction to sustain two centuries of change without being visibly altered externally.

The Royal Military Asylum was built in 1803 to educate and discipline the children of soldiers. One thousand boys and girls, strictly segregated and provided with either military training or the skills required for domestic service, were drilled in vast 'classrooms' 250 at a time. The building, constructed of brick with Portland stone trimmings, is practical, highly formal and, internally at least, simple. As a piece of solid, no-nonsense architecture the asylum neatly expresses the rational and uncompromising values of its age. A State-sponsored institution, it is a pared-down palace, an intimidating barrack block of some grandeur. The building is fronted by a running track on which, it is said, Roger Bannister trained for the 4-minute mile. It is here, in 2008, that art collector Charles Saatchi will relocate his collection after withdrawing it from London's County Hall.

Contained within the area defined by a curving boundary wall, the 19th-century cadets lived a highly disciplined existence within vast spaces. Apart from the north and south wings, each of which contained five dormitories, the building contains not much more than eight rooms measuring 86 feet by 34 feet – four at

Right: In what was once a classroom, the positions of the tiered seating and mezzanine staircase are clearly visible. With the plaster removed, the building reveals its past uses and configurations.

ground level, with matching spaces above. The ground-level spaces were dining rooms (two on each side of the central vestibule and a pair of stairways which separated the boys from the girls); the classrooms on the first floor were double-height spaces with mezzanines/balconies. This would have been a building with an abundance of natural light, but it would have been cold; each of those eight vast rooms contained just two domestic-sized fireplaces.

Over two centuries, the asylum (later renamed the Duke of York's Headquarters) has suffered more than its fair share of repairs, adjustments, modifications and indignities, although its essential robustness has allowed the building to survive with only superficial scars. The most significant intervention was the 19th-century removal of the classroom mezzanines and the construction of a second floor in their place. Less intrusive, although quite ridiculous, was the more recent partitioning and dry-lining of the building to create a new set of interiors for the Territorial Army and a variety of other military occupants: the original fireplaces disappeared behind plasterboard while their ersatz equivalent appeared elsewhere, in no relation to the chimneys, throughout a labyrinth of cubby-holes and wardrooms. The rigid internal geometry of the building was obliterated. And the second floor, home to an intelligence and communication element of the SAS, became virtually closed to the rest of the world – cages, access keypads and high security locks made entry an awkward process and imprisoned its occupants. (In the 19th century, when functioning as a school, occupants were educated under a strict monitorial system devised by the Reverend Andrew Bell, in which talented pupils would teach others; these 'sergeant monitors' were empowered to order cadets who were paying

Above: One of the dining rooms during the stripping out works in August 2006. The floor bears marks showing how the space had been subdivided in the 20th century.

insufficient attention into an iron cage which would be suspended from the ceiling.)

During 2006 the military vacated the building and it became the subject of yet another reinvention. Under the direction of Paul Davis and Partners, working for the Cadogan Estate, the entire complex was stripped back to its essential self. For a brief moment, one could glimpse simultaneously both the workman-like mass of the original building and the broken inner skin of more recent times which purported to lend the building some sort of respectability; the heavy doors of that SAS comms unit swung open easily and rooms were piled with builders' junk. The architectural team also discovered that the parapet gutters in the dormitory wings had, for two centuries, been too small to cope with sudden downpours, and frequent inundations had caused the ends of many joists to rot dangerously.

The asylum, originally a confident expression of the ambition and reach of the State, had become merely a container for government employees. Apart from the historic value of its imposing facade, the building itself had become almost irrelevant. Part of the job of the architects was to look for any residual value in the building itself, to rediscover the rigour of its geometry and volumes.

'Everything you can think of in an old building, we've found it,' said project architect Alec Howard. 'But as we start to strip away its old clothes, I think we start to get back something of the building's dignity.'

Paul Davis, founder of the practice, talks about the 'energy' of buildings – they acquire it, he says, and energy can subsequently fade. Davis is an interesting man. His practice has established a strong reputation for restoring and reusing elderly and listed buildings, often for the Grosvenor and Cadogan Estates in central

London. But Davis is far from a sentimentalist and his primary interest is neither historical nor conservation-led. Instead, Davis is sensitive to 'the trace of human use' and the 'spirit' of a place. That being the case, his rationale is often hard to pin down and his responses to any site have much to do with how a building lodges itself in Davis's imagination through subtle suggestion. 'I always like to go into a building for the first time, trying to feel its past, and what it might be,' says Davis, who some years back walked into the Victorian interior of 15 Sloane Square and decided on a programme of uncompromising 'facadism' because the building had become, he felt, 'dead, spiritually'.

'It felt so depressed. That's one of the ones I've felt the strongest about,' says Davis. 'It's incredibly important to feel open to a building and to be able to take your lead from it. Sometimes I can feel it immediately; occasionally it takes longer to get a feeling for a place. It's about letting a building talk to you and not walking inside with a lot of preconceptions.'

In many ways, Davis has the temperament of a Romantic artist. His approach is intensely personal, one based on subjective judgements rather than established systems; he is more comfortable quoting sources and influences than discussing methods. He will discover what moves him and then try to establish what it was that made the difference – it might be the quality of light, a geometric purity or the embodied energy of a culture or era that is implicit within a building. The mosques of Isfahan, Granada's Alhambra, the San Miniato church in Florence, the skyscrapers of 1930s Manhattan, the churches of Wren and troglodyte community buildings of medieval Tunisia … all feature prominently in Davis's architectural mythology.

'These are all buildings which have very powerful voices when you're in them. I don't think you can help but feel the energy of the civilisations that created them,' says Davis, who has a sneering contempt for the component-based, efficiency-led contemporary construction industry that is championed by manufacturers and followers of Sir John Egan. 'The architect has become merely a developer's commodity. The building is just a product. Buildings get more and more component based and that is just another example of the decline of our civilisation. We've lost the plot.'

It is important to Davis, then, that his office occupies a Victorian school built on what was once an orchard adjacent to the house that was home to an 8-year-old Mozart, who lived at 180 Ebury Street from 1764 to 1765. This is where Mozart composed his first two symphonies. Davis is not so literal that he hears music, but he is poetic enough to believe that places

Right: Royal visitors assemble under the central portico. By 1908, the asylum had been renamed the Duke of York's Royal Military School.

Above: The ground floor of the building contained four large dining rooms, each measuring 86 feet by 34 feet. Boys and girls ate in separate rooms until the 1840s, when the asylum became a boys-only institution.

The Duke of York's Headquarters, close to London's Sloane Square, was designed in the late 1790s by John Sanders, one of Sir John Soane's first pupils, who went on to design the Royal Military College at Sandhurst. Completed in 1803, the building is certainly Soanian in terms of its proportioning, but it also owes something to the work of Sir Christopher Wren – the building is similar in general layout, and in certain details, to Wren's Royal Hospital elsewhere in Chelsea.

Nikolaus Pevsner described the building as containing a combination of 'austerity and dignity', which is perhaps apt, given the terms in which the building was described in 1869 by G Bryan in his book Chelsea in the Olden and Present Times: 'The motives which gave rise to the establishment, and the principles upon which it is founded, are alike honorable to the present age, and congenial with the soundest maxims of policy, humanity and benevolence.'

The building was designed as the Royal Military Asylum for the children of soldiers – orphans, the children of soldiers serving abroad and those from families where poverty was especially acute. Originally, the asylum provided for both boys and girls (700 boys and 300 girls), although girls were no longer admitted after

1841 and it gradually became a boys-only establishment.

In 1909, however, a new Duke of York's College was founded in Dover and the building was renamed the Duke of York's Headquarters and reconfigured as the London centre for what was to become the Territorial Army. The building also provided accommodation for a number of regular army units, including the 10th Battalion, the Parachute Regiment and the Special Air Service, which occupied a high-security space at the top of the complex.

The roof of the building was rebuilt after destruction by a Second World War incendiary bomb; restoration work was undertaken by Donald Insall Associates in 1978; and further rebuilding and remodelling work was completed in the 1990s, including the lowering of the basement and the underpinning of the building with concrete. The military vacated the building in 2005 and it was purchased by Cadogan Estates, which commissioned Paul Davis and Partners to undertake a programme of 'creative reuse'. The building opens as the new gallery for collector Charles Saatchi in 2008. Paul Davis and Partners continues to work for Cadogan Estates; Allford Hall Monaghan Morris Architects are working for Saatchi.

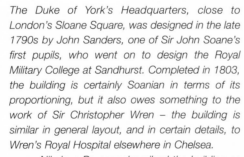

Right: By the late 20th century, an intelligence and communication division of the SAS inhabited the upper part of the building. In a setting characterised by locks, cages and security keypads, occupants became virtual prisoners.

Below: During the 20th century, the interior of the building was entirely remade. Genuine fireplaces were covered up while their artificial equivalents were situated wherever seemed appropriate. Resting in the corner of a stripped-out room, a fire surround of no historic value has unaccountably avoided being thrown in a skip.

capture some of the energy of their inhabitants, and that places that have been inhabited for long enough can be lent some special quality. 'It's something one senses. You might be walking through the woods and actually, palpably, feel a route. If you feel that, you're probably going in the right direction.'

All of which philosophy conspires to underpin the practice's approach to the Royal Military Asylum. Quite apart from the obvious geometric rigour of this building, which preserves a certain inner strength and discipline within the place, Davis is looking forward to re-establishing the original circulation routes and rediscovering the immensity of its internal spaces. When built, the vestibule inside the central front door opened in three directions: left, right and straight ahead. At some point during the 20th century the doors leading to left and right, through which boys and girls were filtered into their segregated dining rooms, were filled in, channelling all visitors straight ahead to a pair of staircases. Reversing this change will go a long way to restoring the rationale of the building – a place of two halves, a single structure providing for, but separating, the two sexes. Simultaneously, this move will have the effect of transforming the vestibule into a genuine filter, a point at which visitors can proceed in almost any direction, rather than functioning as a corridor, a waystation between door and stair. Elsewhere, a maze of corridors, offices, kitchens and toilet facilities is being swept away and the building will be restored, essentially, to its starting point of eight vast rooms linked by a central circulation space. The principal deviation from this plan is the demolition of the officers' club now situated in a wing at the rear of the building and its replacement with a block of similar size attached to the main building via a glazed link.

Davis talks about 'doing what is right for the building' and keeping something of the memory of the place alive. Which is why he was unexcited by the original plans for this building, the floorplates of which are so large that conversion for commercial office use was almost a foregone conclusion. Eventually, however, Davis was asked to draw up a scheme for a large auction house, which he felt opened up a better opportunity for a more faithful creative reuse – the spaces and circulation routes of the original building would lend themselves to this purpose almost effortlessly. Indeed, there is something about the celebration of tradition, the respect for due process and the bang of the hammer that makes even an auction house the natural successor to the military occupancy of this building. But this scheme, too, slipped away, providing

Above: New second-storey accommodation, this space (identified by the square windows) was once at mezzanine level, looking down on to the classrooms.

Right: In 2006 the polite 20th-century interior was stripped out, laying bare the raw fabric of the building.

an opportunity for Charles Saatchi to relocate his collection of contemporary art.

This latter incarnation embodies a significant irony which will, perhaps, suitably amplify the spirit of Saatchi's artworks. Almost as soon as the building has been stripped of its inner lining of plasterboard fakery, it will be reapplied to satisfy the collection's requirement for simple white spaces. But where recent uses at least allowed the windows to function, the Saatchi Gallery will close them off and admit natural light into just one small space at the top of the building. 'It's like somebody closing their eyes,' says Davis, who compares the

abstracted building to the whiteness of George Lucas's 1971 dystopian science fiction film *THX 1138*. 'I feel slightly sad for the building. Its spaces and volumes will be blank.'

The only comforts are that the building has always been knocked about, and the total denial of the quality of its interiors is likely to be just temporary – the plasterboard coverings can be easily removed. But after just a year or two of its completion, cast iron columns had to be inserted to strengthen a sub-standard structure. There's something of the idiotic victim about this building.

The building will stand mute. Probably, it always has. If it ever had a voice, the echoes faded to nothingness long ago. A photograph once hung in the building showing 20 or so of its occupants (boys and one adult) dressed in white vests and trousers, all of whom are frozen into curious athletic poses – bar the adult, who stands to attention facing the camera. The boys are performing handstands, swinging weights, hanging from parallel bars, thrusting forward in classic fencing poses and interlocked in a bout of boxing (the right glove of one meets the face of the other, who counters with a left). The dateless image must have taken an age to compose and hold, and it stands as a fine commentary on the building. The boys, in spite of their exertions and awkward poses, are expressionless; they are wrapped in pressed whites and represent nothing but an abstract choreography. What these boys have to say, and what their names and fates are, is irrelevant. The building is no different. For 200 years it has been largely hidden behind a strong wall, its interior surfaces covered, its occupants engaged in secrets, and now its windows are to be concealed from within. Outwardly, the building appears unchanged; inside, it is just space.

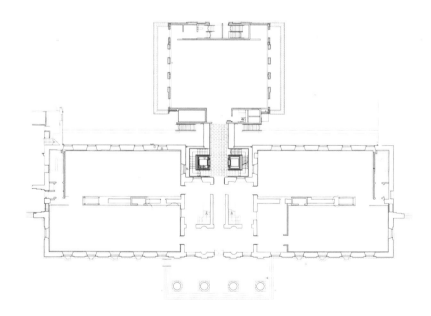

Above: Proposed plan. The building is to be stripped of its recent partitioning and its principal spaces will regain something of their 19th-century dimensions.

The USA and Mexico

Through the Eyes of Funda Willetts

David Littlefield

Funda Kemal Willetts is a senior urban designer and architect at Bath and North East Somerset Council. Having worked with Feilden Clegg Bradley and Julian Harrap Architects, both of which feature elsewhere in this book (see p 184 and p 198), Willetts occupies a singular position within her profession. In spite of the fact that it is her job to comment on and facilitate new architecture within a World Heritage City, and that she has worked on a considerable number of elderly and listed buildings when in practice, she is not a conservation architect. She is, indeed, fiercely critical of (and rather sad about) much that is done in the name of conservation, especially in the United States. She is a champion of new architecture and sustainability, as well as of appropriateness and a consideration for the demands of a site.

More particularly, Willetts's approach to architecture as a social art has much to do with the non-architectural – the subtle, even invisible, presence of people whether actually there or not. Often, Willetts is drawn to sites which have been abandoned and are defined by the pathos of lost and forgotten lives. But she is also moved by buildings which continue to have a relevance after many centuries of occupation. Indeed, the power of architecture to cause people to look up, or to rest their hands on a particular spot, has a magical quality for Willetts; that a rose window in a church may move people to stop and gaze is interesting, but more interesting is the idea that the same window has had the same power over people for many centuries.

In 2005 Willetts won funding from the Winston Churchill Memorial Trust to travel to Mexico, the USA, Canada and Germany to study the role of heritage as a regenerative tool. Her subsequent study examined the ways that a community can form an identity based on its perceptions of heritage and group memory. The scholarship exposed Willetts to communal responses which ranged from neglect and the perversely eccentric to over-zealous re-creations which saw any subtle trace of humanity blotted out in a craving for meticulous 'authenticity'.

What is interesting about Willetts's tour was that she found the presence of an architectural voice in the most unexpected places – the immense and largely empty grain elevators of Buffalo in New York State, an unseen city beneath the streets of Seattle and a submerged town in Mexico that is now re-emerging as the water level of a reservoir recedes. These are places of loss and abandonment, but which somehow retain a humanity beyond the simple fact that they are there. The quality of their construction is an important part of our understanding of these places, especially of Old Guerrero which disappeared under the Falcon Reservoir in 1953 and which has temporarily reappeared, most of it surprisingly intact. 'You can almost see the hands which built these places,' says Willetts.

Willetts looks for the subtleties, the vulnerabilities, an essence which clings to a site and which is easily overlooked – soot, smells, detritus, an industrial latency. 'That's where the voices are, in the things that are left behind and that are of no use any more.' The grain elevators of Buffalo, most of which are now superfluous (some of which even have rusting cargo ships tied up alongside, equally redundant) retain an energy in spite of their condition. They are structures composed of a function-driven architecture and their logic is still compelling. Elsewhere in the US, Willetts visited colonial towns which prized their elderly buildings so highly that they took them to pieces and corralled them into conservation ghettos. It appears to

Above: Old Guerrero's inhabitants in 1953, standing on the roof of the bandstand as the new reservoir's water levels rose.

Right: An old colour photograph showing the church of Old Guerrero surrounded by water following the creation of the Falcon Reservoir in 1953.

have been a misguided effort because any sense that these buildings were located on a particular site, in a particular orientation, had evaporated. It became an exercise in what buildings looked like. They had been cared for too well and any authentic voice had somehow been lost in translation. And that, perhaps, highlights a characteristic of an architectural voice – it is unplanned, unpredictable and unquantifiable; it is in the detail; it is in an integrity of construction that survives decline or reuse.

Below, Funda Willetts describes the architectural voices which cling to places in spite of decline and abandonment. In Mexico's Villa Nueva and Guerrero Viejo, and the USA's Buffalo, she looks for clues about what might have been and creates narratives from slowly dissolving evidence.

When a place is deserted, abandoned, there is an element to its spatial quality that is no longer apparent because there is no occupant to demonstrate it. These places are not used as they were planned to be, so people, wildlife and the elements encounter the place in a different way. But there remains evidence of what has passed, and this is inevitably a human trace. Buildings in ruin or no longer in use often provide an insight into the communities that built them. The choice of stone, the use of ornament, the scale of buildings can be seen, even if only in fragments, and this allows one to discover at least a fraction about a former way of life without speaking to the people who lived it. Often, the nature of these places allows us to see further into the built environment than would be possible if the place was still occupied or even new. They allow some insight into what has been, what was important and how life has changed. Interpretation is secondary because there is evidence – actual proof. That is what the three places described below have to offer.

In a practical sense, this information can serve as a measure of the successes and failures of construction methods, the weathering of materials and the ability of buildings and settlements to adapt to changes in society or even climate. The way people relate to remnants of the past teaches us what communities hold dear and, in declining communities, this may provide an indication of what is missing. References can be used by designers as tools to reconnect people to their surroundings – whether one is retaining a building that embodies memories or community identity (like the church in Guerrero) or recognising the need for a new

Old Guerrero church behind piles of rubble and trees that have grown since the reservoir waters began to dry up.

building relevant to the current culture of a particular neighbourhood. Probing and questioning what is evident in sites like those described below allows an understanding of the historic and contemporary links between society and the built environment. This inevitably serves as a key tool in the aspiration to achieve successful sustainable regeneration.

Guerrero Viejo, Mexico

The Falcon Dam serves as a USA-Mexico border crossing. It is an immense structure, forcing the Rio Grande into an artificial lake which, in turn, forced the evacuation of Ciudad Guerrero's 2,500 inhabitants. This 250-year-old Mexican town, discarded to make way for President Eisenhower's development plans but never fully flooded, has begun to return to life. Extreme drought coupled with population growth has caused

the water to recede. Many of Ciudad Guerrero's displaced people (who have refused to suffix their former home with the word 'old' to distinguish it from Guerrero Nuevo, the functional replacement city 35 miles away) are returning. No one can live there, though – the revival planned for this town is for the tourist trade only.

Arriving at Ciudad Guerrero Viejo, located at the end of a very long dusty road through an arid and bleak landscape, summons alien sensibilities. The buildings that remain are skeletal, stripped back to bare stone. Their render skin has vanished, no doubt cracked by the harsh sun before being washed away by the rain. The stone is exposed, revealing the labour of builders of a different time, and all buildings are accorded the same status. Those that were on the edge of the lake are marked where the water lapped repeatedly over the stone, carving lips and sills. Some structures have

collapsed, and it is these piles of stone that are most resonant. The discovery of a beautifully carved cornice stone compels one to touch it, tracing the chisel-made pattern the water did not reach. Other blocks are smooth and rounded, weathered over time. Elsewhere remains a doorway, with carved capitals and imposts from where the trace of an arch springs. Arches predominate among these ruins, proving the resilience of these structures that have withstood neglect more effectively than other designs.

Everywhere are traces of the people who lived here and there is the suggestion of hasty abandonment. There are the remnants of internal decorations, like blocks of colour and a picture of the Pope; old kitchens retain a dusting of soot and the stains of wood smoke, visible through missing walls. Timber lintels, joists and frames survive in places, and the occasional outdoor WC stands in isolation.

The cobbled streets remain as defined routes and it is still possible to find one's way around the city using makeshift landmarks. The town is quiet and stark, with little vegetation other than cacti and bare mesquite trees. There is, however, one small plant with red flowers located outside the house of the city's last resident who refused to move, a woman whose funeral was held in the newly restored church that had spent the best part of 50 years submerged in the lake. Former inhabitants campaigned to repair the building, but the patched-up walls and gleaming orange timbers look disappointingly out of place. Another former resident points to the rubble that embodies his childhood memories: his home, schools and the butcher's shop selling *chicharrones* (pork crackling) whose smell wafted across the plaza to his classroom. Guerrero, in spite of its almost complete abandonment, remains a

Above: Now in retreat, the waters have left their mark at the base of those buildings of Old Guerrero still standing.

place of compressed memory. Its physicality continues to be powerful enough to conjure up intense personal recollections in those who knew it as a living place while, for those who know it as a ruin only, it performs well as a prompt to the past. But it is an intermittent prompt – the town will, no doubt, come and go with the arrival and retreat of the Rio Grande's waters.

The Grain Elevators of Buffalo, USA

Located in Erie County, Buffalo is a unique city. At the northernmost tip of New York State, it is often called Buffalo Niagara due to its proximity to the falls. But without such a dominant natural feature as its neighbour it is a place rarely visited, in spite of being peppered with works by Louis Sullivan, Frank Lloyd Wright, Eliel and Eero Saarinen, and Central Park designer Frederick Law Olmsted. Buffalo is a city which has long suffered decline, leading to the deterioration of both suburbs and downtown areas.

Buffalo's industrial past as the grain distribution hub of the Midwest is still evident in a neighbourhood that is littered simultaneously with monumental industrial grain elevators and tiny Irish pubs. It is a spectacular streetscape that, despite widespread

Right: By 1900 Buffalo was the largest inland port in the USA. Today, many of the city's grain elevators stand empty. Even the ships which served them sit idly rusting.

ARCHITECTURAL VOICES

Right: This grain elevator, one of Buffalo's oldest, appears as a building on a building. It is as if the structure has spawned a smaller version of itself.

Above: The lines of Buffalo's more recent grain elevators give the concrete structures a sculptural quality.

dereliction and a lack of regeneration plans, still speaks clearly and intimately of how this city once worked. Grain elevators are a common site around the United States. Often they loom high like skyscrapers, alone in vast flat landscapes. A delight to see, they are beautiful although they were never meant to be. Nowhere is this more the case than in Buffalo where, uniquely, a whole district of these magnificent structures exists.

Branches of the canal drift around the grain elevators and other industrial buildings, one of which exudes the unexpected smell of the manufacture of a well-known brand of breakfast cereal. There is intermittent traffic from heavy trucks carrying loads of sawdust or cement from the few other buildings that remain in use, while a redundant railway line snakes through the suburb, linking the grain elevators and crossing the canals over claw-shaped bridges before disappearing into the sprawling community of timber clad houses and pubs that often host a star-spangled banner on the front porch.

The grain elevators retain potency due to their magnitude and the clues to their construction, use and operation. Rusting remnants of hoists and pulleys remain at the top of vast concrete silos that are moulded together without any sign of a seam. The eye is drawn to the top to witness graceful curves posing questions as to why they were constructed so elegantly, and how complex and painstaking a process it must have been for the men who used slipforms and jacks to pour and draw the concrete structures up bit by bit. It must have been a laborious and coordinated effort involving considerable numbers of people – construction on this scale would simply not have been possible otherwise.

The great northern elevator is the historic centrepiece, an immense brick structure built to house an array of steel storage drums. Constructed in 1897, it is the oldest grain elevator on the site and one of the few that does not outwardly reveal the form of its containers. The bulk of the building is emphasised by its tiny windows and steep upper storeys of corrugated metal which appear to have been added as a precarious afterthought. The remains of chimneys and pipes which protrude from every surface force the viewer to look up in awe.

ARCHITECTURAL VOICES

Below: Villa Nueva: '… a fascinating place that encourages wonderment at why it was abandoned in
favour of such bland constructions
nearby.' Funda Willetts.

Villa Nueva, Mexico

Villa Nueva is located near the Mexican city of Camargo, not far from the border with Texas. The town is a sudden discovery at the end of a dirt road that passes numerous impoverished suburbs with unkempt dwellings. Largely in ruins, Villa Nueva takes the dishevelled nature of its neighbourhood one step further. The place was abandoned slowly as its inhabitants chose to construct modern concrete homes closer to the town centre and these are visible as dull pastel-coloured blocks nearby. There remain only two isolated ranges of buildings that have fallen into disrepair, with walls, joinery and roofs collapsed and broken.

The sun has attacked surfaces harshly, drying out lime render and, in places, turning it to dust. Elsewhere the remains of a hand-made brick roof are visible through the debris of timber that once held it up. Walls above openings have given way as lintels have failed. Floors and ceilings are mostly rubble, while a large number of the timbers are missing altogether. Joist pockets, still filled with the broken ends of timber, reveal where floors were once located.

One building presents a series of thresholds which are emphasised by fine stone pilasters with matching quoins, topped with carefully carved capitals in a distinctive zigzag pattern. These forms are surprisingly primitive and unfamiliar, sitting proud of the unhewn stone walls. The building appears to lack an internal kitchen, although there is a large kiln or oven-like stone hemisphere in the backyard. Was this some sort of public building? Looking for such clues is an unavoidable part of the experience of being in Villa Nueva.

Villa Nueva is a fascinating place that encourages wonderment as to why it was abandoned in favour of such bland nearby constructions. Few people remain,

notably a friendly family that proudly shows off its living room roof that is a cleverly recycled upturned boat. The keel is not visible behind the parapet outside but inside each timber rib and foothold is plainly on view. It is a truly fantastic find.

Some of the other buildings have also gained noticeably new elements, like an additional storey or a dark grey cement render which is suffocating, and no doubt accelerating, the decay of the gentle construction underneath. The way the construction of these buildings is exposed, almost intimately so, contributes to the character of this place, providing both an insight into the physical structure and a glimpse into the lives of those who reside here as well as those who have moved on. The remnants of coloured plaster, the carved timber doors with their intact ironmongery and the elaborate thresholds provide clues to the former uses within, while nature is gradually reclaiming what it can.

Gibo and The Boathouse

Westminster and Ladbroke Grove, London

David Littlefield

Both reinvented by architect Cherie Yeo   2002–3

Above: The store closed in 2004. The signage has been taken down, but the name remains as a scar.

Some buildings have such robustness and brutish proportions that they shout at, and intimidate, those foolhardy enough to challenge them (North London's Victorian Round House – a brick circus tent of a building for steamtrains and, later, a venue for experimental theatre and rock performances – has been said to 'spit out what it doesn't like'). Others speak softly. Number 47 on London's Conduit Street makes quiet suggestions. This Edwardian-era shop has had a long association with the fashion industry and, like the clothes on display within, it is subject to rapid changes of appearance and ownership. For a long time a bridal shop, this store became Alexander McQueen's principal London outlet before he moved round the corner to Old Bond Street in 2002. Italian fashion firm Gibo was the next to move in, providing a showcase for designer Julie Verhoeven. Designed by architect Cherie Yeo, this particular incarnation lasted just two years and the space is now empty, awaiting a refit.

The transformation from Gibo to something else is regrettable because the store was arguably Cherie Yeo's finest piece of work; but, on the other hand, Yeo is particularly responsive to the layers of history found in elderly buildings and she is philosophical about witnessing her own work become just another piece of architectural stratum.

When Yeo and Verhoeven first visited the shop, they stepped into what was essentially a white cube, the interior of which was obviously an artificial screen that floated a few centimetres within the volume of this Grade 2 listed space. Once the plasterboard was removed, the shop revealed – apart from a welcome rooflight – a composition of smashed and missing mouldings, builders' pencil marks and workings-out, and little acts of playful grafitti like 'I want to go home'.

The unveiling of this hidden record of the building's life was an important design moment. 'At that point we got very excited by what the building revealed,' says Yeo. 'It started to tell us what to do.'

Verhoeven and Yeo are old friends whose work methodologies have evolved along similar lines – both have a whimsical and fluid approach to drawing which has a direct effect on their final design proposals, and both are particularly sensitive to ideas of personal and cultural memory. As soon as the 'smashed up' state of the site became apparent, Verhoeven and Yeo embarked on a scheme which was a direct response to the 'decaying grandeur' – to amplify it, contrast it, disguise it, reveal it and add to it. Along one side of this long thin site (28 metres deep and just 6 metres wide) a new concrete wall stopped just short of the ceiling, allowing the broken mouldings to be glimpsed; opposite, however, a 17 metre stretch was left as found.

'Initially, I and my husband, Fabio Almeida, shall draw directly on the wall in response to what is there,' said Verhoeven at the beginning of the project. 'And each season I should like to invite an artist to enhance this wall and so shall develop layers of drawings, so the wall will be a platform for improvisation and retain a sense of the shop's history.' And this, over four seasons, was exactly what happened. (A fashion season lasts six months, covering roughly autumn and summer.)

This wall – an ever-changing assemblage of sinuous, wandering lines, compositions of geometric exactness, scribbles and marks of indeterminate meaning – was the spiritual heart of the shop. It was a playful and puzzling surface, partly because it was there at all, and partly because of one's inability to discern new from old. Indeed, additions one would guess as being builders' graffiti (like the crest of

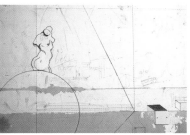

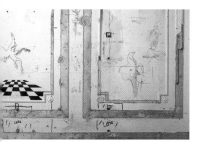

Portsmouth Football Club) turned out to have been added by Verhoeven herself.

At the time of writing, Yeo/Verhoeven's store was in the process of being redeveloped, and it was uncertain whether this graffiti wall would survive. Certainly it would be covered up, but Yeo was hopeful that it would be simply concealed with dry-lining rather than expensively replastered. That way the wall would survive for someone else to uncover, creating a richer seam of what Yeo calls 'alchemy' or the 'strength of voice' within the place. Yeo has a complex view of the psychological and metaphorical effects of buildings, and they speak with the full tonal range of people. Buildings can speak loudly and boisterously, she says; equally, they may speak quietly but, like people, often those with the quietest voices are the ones worth listening to. And like the human voice, buildings can take on accents and intonations that are by turns endearing, disconcerting, reassuring, irritating. Buildings can be 'manipulative', she says.

That said, Yeo also believes that buildings become vocal only insofar as we manipulate them and bend them to our needs. Once the trace of genuine habitation and use has passed, buildings become mute: 'I think it's fairly tough for a building to have a voice without it being used for anything. It has to have a function. Buildings have to be a slave to some sort of function or activity.' This observation struck Yeo especially powerfully in what began life as a Victorian school building in London's Ladbroke Grove. Called The Boathouse, for no obvious reason, this landlocked two-storey building, which now sits in the grounds of Middle Row Primary School, was probably used as a gymnastic, dance and musical training space before becoming a youth boxing club. When Yeo first visited the site in 2002, the boxers had left to make way for graphic design company Mode, but all their para-phernalia (work-out regimes, posters, a set of scales, photographs) remained. The building was, effectively, still a boxing club.

'The photos were so vital they seemed to add a noise to the place. There was the ghost of past uses somehow,' says Yeo. The most compelling artefact was a poster advertising an evening of boxing at the Albert Hall. Dated 31 January 1984, the poster celebrates 'future stars' and features a list of young, tough, forgotten hopefuls: light middleweights Jimmy Cable (Orpington) and Manning Galloway (Columbus, Ohio), welterweights Tony Adams (Brixton) and Dave Cox (Northampton). Even the main attraction, 10 three-minute rounds between Mark Kaylor of West Ham and Ralph Moncrief of Cleveland, Ohio, has become historically meaningless. But the intensity of these people, the virility and seriousness of their sport – indeed, the utilitarian, black and red, tabloid layout of the poster itself – filters out and energises the place. This poster performs a similar role to the portraits in the vestry of the church St John-at-Hackney (see p 86). In one image, taken in 1901, a group of clergy surround Rector Algernon Lawley; the seven participants strike a

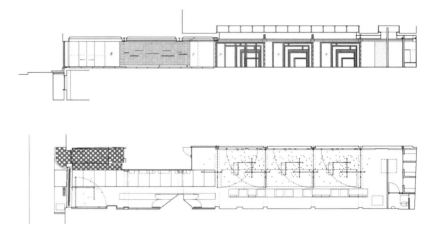

Below: Ground plan and section of Gibo, the store designed by architect Cherie Yeo and fashion designer Julie Verhoeven.

variety of poses and attitudes, ranging from the deliberately severe to the kindly, while the rector himself stares stiffly away from the lens of the camera. Photographic remnants like these populate a building powerfully, and they are hard to ignore.

Apart from its residual artefacts, the simple, unaffected architecture of The Boathouse itself became the starting point for Yeo's reuse. Its barrack-block regularity, the strength of the trusses, the hard-worked floor, the shadows and abstractions generated by the rooflights in this almost crude and spartan space became amplified in the conversion to a design studio. In effect, her design process became an exercise in what not to do, although this space has been scrubbed up and made presentable – here, any gymnastics and displays of power are likely to take place within an Intel chip, so the physical space has become more effete. But this doesn't trouble Yeo: 'I really do believe that if there's something very special and powerful about a place, it won't mind change very much.'

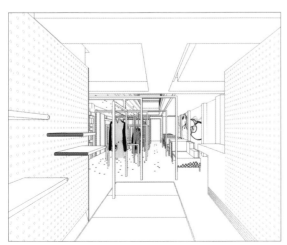

Left: Cherie Yeo's drawing, facing towards the rear of the shop. The corridor is flanked by 'shoe walls', where holes drilled into surfaces of Corian held pegs on which shoes were suspended.

Ditherington Flax Mill

Shrewsbury, Shropshire

David Littlefield

Designed by Charles Bage, 1797. Site vacated in 1987
Acquired by English Heritage 2005 and the subject of a masterplan by Feilden Clegg Bradley Architects

Above: For architects Feilden Clegg Bradley, almost every period of a building's history has a validity. At the flax mill, this philosophy puts them in a quandary because the building has had two legitimate (but completely different) lives. In rescuing this endangered structure, do the architects restore it to its 1790s state, its 1880s incarnation, or to something else entirely?

Opposite: The exterior. Two out of three windows were blocked when the mill was converted into a maltings, while the crown was added late to celebrate Queen Victoria's jubilee.

It is difficult to overstate the potency of Ditherington Flax Mill. Built towards the close of the 18th century, this empty and wounded building stands as a monument to the energy of the Industrial Revolution. Its iron-frame construction makes it the ancestor of the modern tower block but, unlike its modern incarnation, it carries the imprint of the hands that made it. It is a building which has been harshly treated, but in spite of being constructed as an almost lightweight structure, it has survived.

The building was born out of a kind of savagery – not just an entrepreneurial cut and thrust, but a very real, very physical series of incisions. The building itself has been cut and almost dissected in a nearly Gordon Matta-Clark-like manner. In 1793 Parliament approved the construction of a new canal, which was carved through the Shropshire landscape by 1797. The iron columns of the building have been eroded by teams of workers who filed deep notches into the structure in order to widen the capacity of the bays to accommodate machinery. Large holes were smashed through the floorplates when the building was converted into a maltings and at the same time the brick floor was torn up and those same bricks used to block the windows to create a darker interior. Even the vocabulary associated with the mill bears the hallmark of violence. In the production of flax the stems of this delicate flower need to be 'bruised and broken'; processes include 'hackling' and the fibres are beaten with a flat wooden sword called a 'scrutcher'.

There is an element of palliative care here also. Where the floorplates have been weakened, extra columns, also of iron, have been installed; other columns have been sheathed and strengthened. In the 1950s the canal was drained and filled (the flow of water

staunched) and, in the 1990s, many columns were wrapped in carbon fibre and epoxy resin. The Ditherington Flax Mill is a place of cuts and bandages, of closed wounds and scars.

And there is, consequently, a latent energy about this place. Partly, it is imaginary. These immense spaces, subdivided into bays by the strict grid of the columns' layout, can easily be repopulated with loud machinery and industrious people. Inside the building, in spite of being close to a busy road in what is now a relatively poor suburb of Shrewsbury, it is fantastically quiet. But it is the quiet of a battlefield long after the battle is over.

'The whole place has a voice. These were once green fields and market gardens. An army walked across these fields. It's even on record that the king's [the Lancastrian Henry IV] soldiers on the way to the battle of Shrewsbury [in 1403] walked across fields of peas,' says John Yates, of English Heritage. 'There are mysteries to this building. It is talking to us, but it's difficult to know what it's trying to say.'

The architects at Feilden Clegg Bradley's creative reuse team, which is drawing up a masterplan and rescue package for the site, are sympathetic to the idea that the flax mill embodies a set of subtle messages. And as well as employing the metaphor of voice, they talk about developing an emotional response to a building. Geoff Rich and Richard Collis consider the practice of architecture to be founded on a series of practical and emotional layers, like a professional geology. It is not enough to be versed in light and shade and volume; you need an understanding of craft and materials; you need to establish a sense of responsibility for, and a psychological response to, a place. 'Not only do we need to form an

Above: Upper storey. At this level the iron columns support just the roof. The space becomes more open, modulated by the rhythm of the ceiling, which follows the contours of the roof's ridges and valleys.

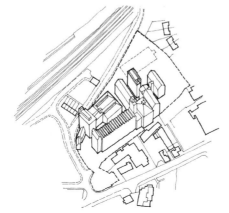

Right: Feilden Clegg Bradley drawing of the flax mill complex.

understanding of a building by rationally measuring it, we need to actually achieve a sort of empathy for a place. This is extremely important. But I think lots of young architects would think that is an extremely weird thing to want to do,' says Geoff Rich, who adds that reinvented buildings often remind him of clumsy taxidermy, conducted by people with little sense of the subtleties of the animal itself. 'Sometimes I see a building and I'm reminded of a badly stuffed cat.'

To Rich, empathy with a building extends to being open to the idea of the super-sensitivity of people. There is a latency in elderly places, whether it be of a smell or even merely an idea, that is difficult to quantify but is nevertheless powerful enough to guide the architect's hand. 'It is essential to be open-minded about it. It's important to listen to the building rather than be blinded by the information you've been given in advance – you could end up prejudicing your own opinion,' he says.

None of which adds up to conservation or restoration. Rich and his team are exploring the idea of 'living heritage', a concept that acknowledges the passing of time and attempts to identify the moment at which an architect engages with a historic building as merely a point of moving history. A neglected building will return to the earth, says Rich, but that is no excuse to restore it to an earlier version of itself. To Rich, almost every period of a building's history has a validity. At the flax mill, this puts the architects in a quandary because the building has had at least two legitimate (but completely different) lives – 80 years in the production of flax, followed by a century as a maltings. Indeed, two decades as an empty and dilapidated monument to Shrewsbury's former status as a world-class industrial centre has contrived to reinvent the building's profile

'Ditherington Flax Mill is sleeping now. In fact, she is quite poorly and awaiting surgery. She talks to us in her sleep. Like every old building – and, indeed, every old place – she regales us with stories from her past, stories from a foreign land that is at once exotic and familiar. She tells us tales of how we lived, how we thought and how we built.

'She speaks particularly clearly of how we lived, how a now sleepy Shropshire was once a centre of the world's first industrial revolution. The sheer scale of the building speaks for itself – big confidence, big investment, big risks, big rewards. Here were three men in a new partnership for a new enterprise, and their voices, too, echo through that forest of slender iron columns and across more than two centuries. John Marshall was already Flax King of the north, Thomas Benyon brought in local finance from the long-established wool trade, and Charles Bage used Shropshire's leadership in cast iron to produce a building like no other. These were successful men, giants in an age of giants, and the building proclaims their confidence. Then another confident voice rings out from nearly a century later, when William Jones made the building the flagship of his malting empire, blocking windows, levelling floors and topping out his elaborate new hoist tower with a corona to celebrate Queen Victoria's Diamond Jubilee. Not for him the stark austerity of the 1797 flax mill.

'Listen hard and we can hear other voices, too, a gentle hubbub rather than individual declamation. Over 400 people once worked in this now silent place. The clatter of clogs at daybreak on those worn stone stairs, female and childish voices raised above the rattling machinery, the purposeful beat of the steam engines and the rumbling drive shafts. The whole building was a living organism, vibrating and alive, attended by its workers and controlling their lives. Can we hear a murmuring from all those apprentices, brought here by the wagonload to live out their youth in this ordered and segregated world? Then we can hear the more measured pace of the maltsters – back-breaking work to steep and spread the barley, then a pause while the grain comes to life, then more back-breaking work to get it to the kiln and beyond. Perhaps we can even hear them enjoying their well-earned free ration of beer.

'The original building is much less talkative on how we thought, on matters of taste and culture, but its near silence is eloquent in itself. The flax mill trio gave absolutely no conventional architectural display to their great investment – 'functionalism' arrived a century early. So can we hear a whisper of rationalism here, a dangerously revolutionary philosophy from France soon driven underground by patriotism and self-preservation? The later buildings are much more polite in form and detail; as early as 1811 Bage is using the Tuscan order on his iron columns to rebuild the Cross Mill. By the 1850s the Dye House is telling us of a hardening of the commercial arteries, with later generations of Marshalls spending lavishly on its virtuoso brickwork.

'The Flax Mill tells us loud and clear about how she was built. The iron frame and vaulted brick floors explain themselves so lucidly that we can almost hear Charles Bage describing them to us. But the old lady has kept some secrets. We knew there was cracking in the frames, where Bage had been just a little too daring in places, but we didn't know until very recently that there is timber buried in the walls, as in almost every other Georgian brick building. We had all listened to the 1797 publicity that this was a building without timber – 'spin' then as now. The Flax Mill is also still very coy about what she used to look like; no picture has been found showing her as a mill with her windows in place. The iron enthusiasts want to hear that the windows were iron framed. But her lips are still sealed.

'Now we listen to another voice from the Flax Mill. Is the building telling us of her new life, to be adopted when she wakes from this long sleep? She adds her voice to our own.'

John Yates
Inspector of Historic Buildings, English Heritage

Left: In a dark room, illuminated by a shaft of sunlight, lies a rare example of what once brought the building alive with movement. The former flax mill is sliced through with numerous openings and shafts for machinery and power sources – most long since removed.

ARCHITECTURAL VOICES

Below: During the building's long life notches have been cut into many of the columns to accommodate pipes, wiring or machinery. Impressions of various examples are combined here to show their inexact nature.

Below: When the building was converted from a flax mill to a maltings, large holes were cut into the floorplates to accommodate hoppers, through which the barley could be channelled.

within the town: it is symbolic of a certain decline. 'In a sense, the reality of the place – damp, neglected, mean – is an essential part of the conditions we have inherited,' says Rich.

In the project to reinvent the flax mill there are, therefore, fundamental questions to be asked about what the building actually is, let alone about how to treat it. There are no images, photographic or otherwise, of the building as a flax mill and there is no one alive who can recall how the building appeared with its windows unblocked. In fact, the building is known locally as the maltings. Perhaps the windows should remain blocked. Possibly, this ambiguous history and the approach of Feilden Clegg Bradley is a liberating one. In fact, the architects appear less impressed by the historical importance of the building than by the qualities of the building as found. The history of the site is certainly an interesting one, but the original flax building, bearing its scars of dramatic reinvention, is more arresting. It is the fabric of the building itself that provides the scent of authenticity.

This search for authenticity, rather than asking what the building once looked like, is more like imagining what the building would say if only it could speak. 'The building is screaming at us, metaphorically,' says architect Richard Collis. 'It's hard to ignore it.' And it is hard to imagine this place asking to be restored to its original condition, to be recreated as a museum piece. It would rather fall apart.

The original building is an imperfect one. For reasons that are unclear, its 18 bays are not spaced out evenly and it appears to be a building of two halves. Perhaps it was built from either end, by competing teams who aimed to meet in the middle. Perhaps the construction team, having slowly learnt the art of metal

framing, got better at it as the building progressed along its length. Whatever the truth, the columns are considerably closer together in the northern half of the building than they are in the south. At the northern end, columns are spaced out at roughly 3.05-metre intervals; at the southern end, these intervals vary between 3.2 and 3.6 metres; more peculiarly, the bay separating these two zones is just 1.5 metres wide. For an iron-framed building, it is strangely haphazard.

This variation cannot be put down to intent, as if the building were designed around the machinery it would contain, because many of the columns are scared by savage notches that can only have been carved out of the iron to accommodate something that was unplanned. And these notches themselves are subject to wild variation, ranging from numerous rect-angular cuts of similar dimension to gentle sweeps or semi-circular gouges. They are ragged and energetic affairs, these notches, and their inaccuracy clearly evokes moments of steady concentration, recorded in angular cuts, and longer periods of weariness, revealed in rounder depressions. It must have been a frenetic, almost desperate, activity. The building was designed to be only as strong as necessary and it carried little excess mass. Cutting often more than 2 centimetres from columns just 11 centimetres thick can have been no easy proposition, and it signifies anything from a devil-may-care ignorance of construction to a blind faith in the integrity and strength of iron.

Identifying the point at which these notches, these cuts into the fabric of the building, start is almost an impossibility. The cast-iron columns are not themselves machined to the smooth finish we would expect, today, of a metal structure. They are highly textured, more so than dressed stone. There are even notches which could, conceivably, be mere undulations rather than intentional incisions. Wrapped in countless layers of white gloss paint, sitting on a far from flat concrete floor installed in the 1880s, these columns resist accurate measurement. And that, in a sense, was the starting point for those notches.

More than anything else, though, these notches demonstrate the zeal and practical mindset of the Industrial Revolution, and the building continues to embody a certain energy. In part, the form of the columns themselves has something to do with this energy – cruciform in section, they adhere to a sort of double entasis in that they bulge in the middle, and taper towards the top and bottom. They appear almost compressed, like compacted springs. But the real energy of the building lies in the human marks on the place, the very obvious scarring inflicted on the building in the name of industry and progress. It has been knocked about, this building. It needs to be wrapped up a little more, as there are too many cracks and slippages for comfort. 'The patient is on the operating table,' says Richard Collis. But it would be denying the essential history of the place to stop knocking it about – it was made for rough treatment and any reinvention needn't be polite.

History

The Ditherington Flax Mill enjoys a reputation as the world's oldest iron-framed building (and therefore as the precursor of the steel-framed buildings that led to the skyscraper). Constructed in 1797, and considerably expanded over the following decade, the mill was a response to the rising demand for flax and signalled the adaptation of Shrewsbury's declining wool industry. Conceived by three businessmen, Shrewsbury brothers Thomas and Benjamin Benyon and John Marshall of Leeds, the building was designed by Charles Bage.

Prompted by the approval for the construction of a canal, as well as close proximity to the emerging industrial zone of the West Midlands and Coalbrookdale, the entrepreneurs commissioned Bage to design

Below: After the building was converted for use as a maltings (a damp, dark environment for the germination of barley), the floors were soaked in water, leading to corrosion of the iron structure.

Right: Iron roof structure of the Cross Mill element of the building. A serious fire in 1811 caused this building to be rebuilt in brick and iron, minimising the use of timber as a construction material.

ARCHITECTURAL VOICES

Below: A pair of notches cut into one of the iron columns, marks that emphasise the energy of the early industrial revolution – an age of inventiveness, trial and error, and intellectual and muscular effort.

Below: The capital of one of the cast-iron columns, configured (it is assumed) to allow a drive shaft to pass through.

Above: Further notches in the mill's structure. Some were up to 1 centimetre deep, and often cut into both sides of a column to help accommodate machinery that was otherwise too large for the building.

a building that stood the best possible chance of withstanding a fire. Because of the amount of dust produced in the production of textiles, and the convention of using timber as a flooring material, it was not unusual for a mill to burn down (according to English Heritage, five mills burned down in Leeds in 1791 alone). Constructing a five-storey building with an iron frame and floorplates of bricks (constructed as shallow jack arches, sprung between iron beams) minimised the risk of fire. A later extension to the building, known as the Cross Mill, was constructed with a timber floor as an economy measure; the building

suffered a serious fire in 1811 and the reconstructed building dispensed with timber altogether.

In spite of lasting for two centuries, this pioneering structure has not proved to be a total success. Bage's calculations relating to the performance of iron were broadly correct but, unfortunately, the brick facades of the building are sinking into the ground faster that the iron-work, which is causing the iron to crack. Furthermore, the post and beam lattice-work of the iron is tied into the brick facades via timber blocks – rotting of this timber has, of course, had a corrosive effect on the iron. Unusually for a building of

Above: Facade of the flax mill, more commonly known throughout Shrewsbury as 'the maltings'. The building functioned as a maltings for a century until the 1980s.

this age and type, it was not over-engineered in that it is about as strong as it needed to be. 'So elegant, so light, so daring – Bage was flying a bit close to the sun,' says John Yates, a senior historic buildings inspector at English Heritage. In spite of remedial work in the 1990s, the present work on the building, designed to safeguard its future and make a sound investment for reuse, is proving a headache.

The mill complex was gradually expanded throughout the 19th century. A warehouse, constructed in 1805, is the world's third oldest iron-framed building; the 1812 Cross Mill, which replaced the fire-damaged building, is the eighth oldest of this type. Gas lighting was introduced in 1808. By 1840, the mill employed approximately 800 people, around a third of whom were under the age of 16. Male and female employees were segregated.

Later in the 19th century, due to the arrival of cotton in abundance, the flax industry went into decline and in 1886 the 7-acre complex was sold to William Jones Maltsters, which converted the site into a maltings (an industry based on creating damp, dark conditions for the germination of barley for the brewing industry).

Two out of every three windows, essential for the drying of flax, were bricked up while the remainder were replaced by smaller windows with shutters, allowing employees to control the level of light and humidity in the building. Barley corns were spread over the floors and soaked in water, resulting in further damage to the iron structure. Large holes were cut through the floors to accommodate hoppers, weakening the building and necessitating the construction of extra columns.

By the 1930s, the canal which ran alongside the buildings had fallen into disuse and it was filled in during the 1950s. The railway sidings, built a century earlier, were removed in the 1960s. Malting production continued until 1987. The site has remained vacant for two decades, an isolated assembly of large buildings with little obvious development potential. English Heritage acquired the site in 2005 and engaged architects Feilden Clegg Bradley to survey the buildings and draw up a masterplan and development brief. At the time of writing, specific uses had not been determined, although the brief, agreed with the local council, specifies a range of conditions for future commercial developers including, for example, that some of the large expanses of space within the mill building be preserved, and that public access be guaranteed to part of the site.

The project has also thrown up a range of conservation questions. For instance, which is the authentic building – the flax mill or the maltings? What, then, should be the status of the windows? And because the building has been adapted so violently throughout its history, does that equate to a licence for further radical change? It is a set of questions to which the architects and English Heritage have no easy answers.

ARCHITECTURAL VOICES

Below: 'So elegant, so light, so
daring – Bage was flying a bit
close to the sun,' says John Yates
of English Heritage. Bage's original
iron structure – shown here with a
channel for a drive shaft – is being
dragged down at the edges by the
masonry walls, causing cracking.

Random Thoughts on Background Noise

Lawrence Pollard

Lawrence Pollard is a radio producer and BBC arts correspondent.

Above: An anechoic chamber – the sound of silence.

Once upon a time, the celebrated avant-garde composer John Cage – he of the 4 minutes and 33 seconds of silence – decided that he wanted to experience silence. So he went to Harvard University and asked to sit in their anechoic chamber, a soundproofed room designed to baffle and muffle all reflections of sound. A man with an interest in Taoism and Buddhism, as a musician Cage was intrigued to experience absolute silence, but to his surprise on sitting in his promised silent space he instead heard two sounds, one high in tone, the other low. When he told this to the engineer in charge of the chamber he was informed that the low sound was the noise of his blood circulating and the higher whine was the electricity of his nervous system. 'Until I die, there will be sounds,' he said, and went off to compose his famous *4.33*, the movement of nothing being played. In effect, what the piece does is force the audience to listen to themselves and the room in which they are. It is an atmospheric piece, which depends for its impact on the space in which it is 'performed'. What Cage had discovered in the anechoic chamber was how we animate and soundtrack space, and that even though we might be distracted from it by other ambient noise, this mysterious murmur is the immediate interaction of our bodies and our breathing with the space we're in. Glamorous glossy photographs of modern architecture appear silent and often still, and in doing so totemise the building as an object. Not to think about sound is to erase an immediate felt experience of architectural space.

Giorgio de Chirico's street and cityscapes are among the most silent paintings you could wish to see.

Opposite: The nave of Canterbury Cathedral, animated by 'the echoing footfall, the congregation's murmur, the hum of people'.

They are habitually described as 'haunting' in recognition of the odd feeling evoked by the corners you can't see round, but of which you, the observer, are made aware by a falling shadow, for example. The shadow implies a space you cannot see but which might, alarmingly, be the same space you are in. As in a nightmare or a child's game, you are linked to something you cannot see. This is the way that sound operates with space. De Chirico's silent emptiness invites us to hear an echo of arrival, the steps of another approaching from an unseen place. These noiseless 'metaphysical' pieces rely on silence and sound as much as they do on space and architecture. Crucially, sound gives a fourth dimension to perspective – it animates.

At the same time that artists in the West discover perspectival space, they fill that space with observed, detailed reality. The noise of background activity is what WH Auden pinpointed in his poem 'Musée des Beaux Arts' based partly on Pieter Breughel's *Fall of Icarus*. In it Auden points out how momentous activity in post-Renaissance art – crucifixion or miraculous birth – takes place against a backdrop of 'someone eating or opening a window or just walking dully along', while children skate and horses scratch their rumps. Here is the noise of street life fleshing out that simple vault burrowed into a wall by artistic perspective. It is this sense of depth that sound gives to art, to de Chirico and to architecture – and to its representations. It's rather amusing that Piero della Francesca's *Ideal City* is, a bit like de Chirico's, a silent city. That is rather how one feels architects might prefer to see their designs embodied, silent and pure in line and sound. Sound implies an extension of space into an unseen realm, which is represented by falling shadow from an unseen object and teeming detail.

Altman's *Nashville* features scene after scene where the audience can hear action on the soundtrack which can't be seen on the screen – a brilliant way to conjure the vastness of society around and behind the viewer.

In the same way, when you walk into a bank headquarters in the City [of London], your footfall will ring on hard marble floors. The sound carries your mind (whether you notice it or not) beyond the simple reception space you inhabit to implied potential grandeur, grandeur you cannot see necessarily but which is implicit in the travel of your sound. 'Other important things are going on,' you are expected to think. 'There's more to this than meets the eye.' Conversely, if you walk into a high-class clinic, your feet, your presence will be muffled. Just for comfort? Partly, but also because the

The 1944 film *A Canterbury Tale* has its climax in Canterbury Cathedral, where all the protagonists come together to find their temporary accommodation with war, love, loss and themselves. The soaring space of the cathedral forms a beautiful backdrop to their fates, but is in fact completely artificial, built partly out of wooden flats and plaster and partly by shooting scenes through a glass plate photograph of the interior. But accounts of the brilliance of the contrivance leave out the importance of sound to its success. The echoing footfall, the congregation's murmur, the hum of people in a space are what create a sense of place far beyond that which the pictures can achieve alone, and it is totally, astonishingly convincing.

Sound creates a wider space; it implies and excavates architectural space and makes us aware of the not-immediately-visible, of presences we can sometimes only intuit. Rarely will film directors make full use of the 'sound bleed' in a finished movie. Robert

ARCHITECTURAL VOICES

designer doesn't want you to echo into unseen spaces: you're not supposed to think of what goes on in those other rooms and cells – quite the opposite of the bank or business. Sound can carry you through architectural space, and so has to be controlled. Denys Lasdun's National Theatre is an odd example, where a building of iconic purpose and uncompromising aspect in fact sounds muffled and velvety, in complete contrast to what you might expect or how it ought to sound.

At the end of one of the several versions of Shakespeare's *Hamlet* there is the most haunting stage direction in the canon. The prince is dead, Fortinbras orders his body to be taken off stage, which it is. They exit. Normally this would mean clear stage, on with the clowns to do a masque dance, show's over. Then in one of the printed versions of the play there's a stage direction asking for a fanfare of trumpets, but specifically a fanfare offstage. A fanfare, therefore, in that other space which we know is just the dressing room or the wings but which seems also to be implying that the world of the play continues, out of sight, round the corner, which exists on in sound. And with that, what are we to make of the empty space before us? What is it? An empty stage? A bit of a fictional world which has temporarily been vacated but could be filled at a future point?

Empty space is animated not only by the play of light, but in just as important a way, it is animated by what can be implied by sound. Sound is the stage direction of space, the perspective of the fourth dimension.

Below: *View of an Ideal City* (after 1470) by Piero della Francesca. Is this the architect's dream – harmony in silence?

Taming the Monster
interview with Julian Harrap

David Littlefield

Above: The architect Julian Harrap.

Julian Harrap occupies a distinctive position. An architect brought up in the Modernist tradition and a former employee of architect James Stirling, Harrap has a highly practical, entirely unsentimental but deeply reverential relationship with elderly buildings. He is drawn to historic buildings and conservation as a doctor is drawn to the sick; it is a calling rather than a career choice, and one which Harrap regards as 'sometimes a more challenging path to tread' than that of new-build architecture. This challenging path has led Harrap to intervene in a large number of profoundly revered buildings including London's Sir John Soane's Museum, by John Soane, and Nicholas Hawksmoor's church of St Anne's Limehouse.

For Harrap the strength of a building's voice lies in its power to diminish its inhabitants, to physically move them. He admires the way the walls inside the lighthouse-form of London's Monument, which marks the heart of the fire that destroyed the city in 1666, become smoother and greasier the further up the spiral staircase one climbs – as they ascend, visitors hug the stone walls, leaving faint traces of themselves behind in exchange for microscopic elements of the building itself. Harrap gets up close to buildings and relishes the robust detail, and enjoys unpicking the construction to reveal how architects as talented as Hawksmoor and Soane got themselves 'stylistically entrapped' but had the skill to extricate themselves from the problems of their own (or their contractors') making. Harrap engages with buildings in much the same way as literary scholars tease the character of Shakespeare out of his texts; Hawksmoor was an angry man all his life, while Soane simply got angrier as he aged – just observe the clash of detail, says Harrap. He is a man who seeks any building's centre of gravity, its

resonance, often in a highly physical way like being in a church tower when the bells chime or by tracing the incisions of prisoners' graffiti in Portchester Castle. Buildings, to Harrap, are marvels to be savoured; haptic, experiential, handed down by the ages but always experienced in the here and now.

Which is why he has an awkward relationship with the conservation lobby. Harrap has a considerable degree of respect for the principles of, say, the Society for the Protection of Ancient Buildings (SPAB), but he prefers to use his own judgement about when to apply them. There is within the British architectural profession, a pair of unidentical twins, both of whom are somewhat anxious about the idea of authenticity. The instinct of one will be to conserve, or even to seek to restore, and perhaps to agonise over historical accuracy in the hope that any intervention might pass as original, or will at least defer to the original; the other believes historicism like this is a fool's errand and celebrates the difference between the old and new in as unambiguous a manner as possible.

Harrap, though, reserves the right to float (like James Stirling) between these poles and exercise his judgement as to what tools and methods are appropriate for the job. But, he insists, avoiding intervention is a dereliction of duty: 'People often ask why I work with old buildings. They are buildings that are in distress; the materials are in distress and, almost like a doctor, I go to help the patient – not just in a physical sense, but also in a cultural and spiritual sense. You have to try and capture the idea of a building and balance it with the building's decay and fortune. It is like taming a monster. Conservation is the most difficult design challenge there is – it's the manipulation of a work of art which is decaying in front of your eyes. We

have all seen a ruin translated into a dead box by putting a roof over it.'

To Harrap, then, the idea of a building's voice is a useful one: 'But the trouble is, a lot of architects are tone deaf. If you're not sensitive to the cultural ethos of the building, its materiality, the skill of the engineer or the initiative of the original designer, then you can completely miss the point. Most architectural conservation is, I have to say, completely pedestrian and is no more than a tart up job. I put it in such vulgar terms because that is all it deserves.'

Sadly, this is not a new phenomenon. Many 'medieval' churches are, in fact, Victorian fantasies and churches were remodelled, in the manner of Pygmalion, not by listening to what the buildings had to say but by imposing an acceptable voice on to them. Harrap calls this 'corruption by reproduction'. Instead, he says, architects should look for clues, respond to '*objets trouvés*' and create (in the manner of Norman Foster's Sackler extension to London's Royal Academy of Arts, for which Harrap did the conservation work) something both contextual and new, respectful and bold. While no

responsible architect would want to diminish the status of a monument or national treasure, any intervention must be 'intellectually complete'. Harrap is clear, though, that interventions can rarely escape the fashions of their age – nor should they. There would be little point, for example, in replacing ageing electrical cable in a manner so faithful that it becomes inefficient or unsafe. How, asks Harrap almost continuously, can the 'document' of a building be preserved while simultaneously making it accessible, meaningful, relevant and a piece of living history, rather than a frozen relic? 'The superficiality of much of the heritage lobby makes me frustrated,' says Harrap.

It is a question which the former Royal Aircraft Establishment, in England's Farnborough, poses particularly forcefully. The 73-acre RAE site was sold by the Ministry of Defence to a private developer in 1999, along with a priceless collection of historic aeronautical artefacts. This was the site where the Royal Air Force was inaugurated, where Spitfire and Hurricane aircraft were subjected to wind tunnel tests and where the aerodynamics of Concorde were fathomed. This site, now redeveloped as a private airfield and business park, is part of aviation history. Harrap, one of the architectural ensemble responsible for redeveloping the historic core of the site, considers many of the structures and test rigs found here to be almost megalithic in their psychological potency; as well as being large, conceived on a completely different scale to human beings, many are curiously sculptural and barely comprehensible without studying the historical records.

Contained within the structure of two separate buildings, and now retrieved and reassembled, were the components of a 22 metre high, 17 metre wide and 210 metre long hangar dating from 1911. Designed to

accommodate an airship and a spherical balloon, all but four of the steel elements of this once canvas-covered structure are original, the remaining pieces being grafted on from contemporary metal stock. Harrap talks about 'theatrical thresholds' – from some distance the structure appears homogeneous, a filigree structure of repeating elements; only when much closer will the viewer detect the presence of the rogue steelwork and rivets, but these details appear slowly, only once the 'idea' of the overall structure has been established. The presence of the new really does not matter.

The wind tunnels on the site present a very different kind of experience. These are inhabitable machines, the largest of which – a 24 foot diameter mahogany propellor encased in an immense, sculptural concrete block – operates on quite a different scale from normal experience. It does, in Harrap's phrase, diminish you. However, these blades are so finely balanced and tuned that they can be turned by hand; they represent an immensity that is sensible to the human touch. It was here that the landmark aircraft of the 1930s, the Spitfire and the Hurricane, were put

through their paces in an airstream of 112 miles an hour (low-speed performance is crucial in the design of aircraft). Torpedoes, too, were tested for their water dynamics, and other ancillary bits and pieces (conifers, radomes, aircraft components) have also been positioned in front of this awesome machine. Built in 1935, this assembly speaks of its age; although built for nothing but functionality, its curves and sculpted perforations, its materiality, whisper of other buildings of its era – Erich Mendelsohn and Serge Chermayeff's De La Warr Pavilion on England's South Coast, Mendelsohn's Einstein Tower in Potsdam, perhaps of the sinuous forms emerging in the mind of Finn Alvar Aalto. 'These people simply could not escape the style of their age,' says Harrap.

This 24 foot behemoth, housed in an unremarkable building of between-the-wars utilitarianism, is one of five wind tunnels on the site and may get a new lease of life with a university patron. The two transonic tunnels, though, await a more troubling fate. This structure, housed in a 42 metre long metal container called the Flask, can generate wind speeds of Mach 1.2 at a variety of atmospheric pressures. Built in 1942, and upgraded for transonic speeds in 1957, this is a machine which reverses the idea of scale – only a seasoned submariner would not feel the crushing claustrophobia of this small space, and its metallic hard edges and technical paraphernalia speak a language which is largely incomprehensible to the casual visitor. Where the 24 foot turbine conveys its power at an emotional level, the Flask (smaller, tougher, more brutal) is more muted. Its wind speeds are so shrill and searing they cannot be comprehended, while the much more modest output of its larger cousin is more meaningful at a fundamental human level.

The Flask, containing a wind tunnel 8 feet by 6 feet (2.44 metres by 1.93 metres) in section and a smaller sub-circuit tunnel, was where the aerodynamics of Concorde were tested. Scale models of this iconic machine were fixed to a vertical fin and the wind pattern created by the model's lines was recorded, in the pre-digital age of the 1960s, on a series of flat surfaces covered in fine powdered chalk. What remains of the chalk, also used in the testing of other aircraft, is now covered in plastic sheeting to prevent it from being completely erased as the occasional visitor brushes by. The Flask has been decommissioned, and its brine-filled cooling tanks emptied, leaving it a relic too expensive and energy hungry ever to power up

again. It is a curiosity and, because this perverse object was sealed and observed remotely when in operation, there are few photographs to suggest anything of the inventiveness or drama of what once went on here. This space, this small labyrinth of ducts of intense and deafening potency, is crushingly silent and thoroughly meaningless. Its only hope is to become some sort of exhibit, a rather pathetic circus act within the wider redevelopment.

Robert Harbison, observing the architectonic remnants of NASA's space programme, makes a similar point in his book *The Built, the Unbuilt and the Unbuildable*. The *Apollo* launch sites of Florida are 'the strangest one-use ruins of all', he writes. 'We are astonished that anything so advanced and so thoroughly un-worn-out can look so discarded, as if through some acceleration which left it circling in empty space outside all human memory … the most advanced technology always lies under threat of instantaneous ruin anyway, for it inhabits a spot where perfectionism and the litter-mentality meet' (pp 129–130).

The only chance of survival for bespoke and very particular structures is the imaginative leap. The transonic tunnels are perhaps beyond all help – items too freakish and lacking in any meaningful scale to be used for anything other than their original purpose. The 24 foot tunnel, though, embodies a certain potential and Harrap is already conjuring up ideas for 'Plan B' uses, should university expressions of interest come to nothing. The tunnel's acoustic properties have a particular value, says Harrap, who contemplates the structure as a site for opera and experimental music. Apart from being 'entirely reversible and non-damaging', this approach would allow the building to breathe again without having to wrestle with it. Together with architect

Opposite and above: A Bristol Bulldog single-seat fighter aircraft being tested in the 24 foot wind tunnel facility.

David Chipperfield, Harrap was part of a team shortlisted to transform London's Bankside Power Station into Tate Modern – a key element of the Harrap/Chipperfield proposal was to retain the turbines and allow the essence of the original building to mingle with the work of artists. This suggestion always met with resistance from the Tate, to Harrap's frustration: 'It was unfortunate they felt the turbines had to come out. The space is empty without them. However inventive the mind of the artist, all you ever see is an empty turbine hall.' For Harrap, the voices of the building and the artists should be heard simultaneously. Sometimes, he says, a building can be scrubbed up too much – it can

suffer from, and become reduced by, the good intentions of the 'tidy intellect' and the contents of an ego-driven manifesto. Without care, says Harrap, the manifesto becomes self-serving and idiotic; instead, the architect's unique approach to historic structures should be balanced with a sympathy for history, an understanding of architectural vocabulary and a willingness to ask what a building might want. Buildings do, of course, have to respond to commercial realities which can lead to the occasional incongruity (London's Sir John Soane's Museum, 'which is nothing if not a museum' says Harrap, often plays host to dinner parties). The key is to ask whether the building would mind too much.

Soundscape of 2 Marsham Street

Westminster, London

Mathew Emmett

Mathew Emmett is an architect and conceptual artist. He seeks to make the invisible visible. Emmett gives literary references built form and explores the role of touch, hearing and memory in generating architecture. London's 2 Marsham Street is now demolished but, before this post-war monolith disappeared, Emmett recorded its sounds in the hope of detecting a deeper resonance.

Does the sound of a lost building reside in the space that it once inhabited? Could a sonic recording reveal the spatial voice of both the past and present; and, if so, how or what would we hear? Can one perceive a 'voice', an energetic resonance of what was, as if signalling a code for the proportion, volume, materiality and mass of what has been there? Can this sonic recording be coloured by patterns of occupation and habits of use, textured through the grain of time? What happens to the space once the building and its sound is removed: is a void created, or does the surrounding sound seep into that uninhabited location, remaining as a hum or the faintest echo? When a new mass replaces the old architectural form, do pleats of surplus sound drape and fold around it, or does sound mutate to inhabit the recreated space? This is the subject of a silent dialogue.

London's Number 2 Marsham Street was a fascinating building. A monolithic scheme designed by Eric Bedford, completed in 1971 and known as the 'three ugly sisters', it was demolished in 2002–3 and replaced with a brighter and more polite building by Sir Terry Farrell. Built for the Department of the Environment, the colossal towers stood over a pair of massive Second World War bunkers which, in turn, occupied the site of two Victorian gasometers. The 5-acre site was visually imposing with its podium, rotundas and towers. But it was the building's sound that captured the imagination; it was the sound that gave it a resonance deeper than anything visual.

A greater consciousness for a building can grow by literally listening to a space. By holding an auditory mirror up to 2 Marsham Street before it was demolished, one could document the contextual sound-scape and classify the building's aural characteristics, deciphering the whispers and teasing apart their own distinct identities. The distant sounds of the city could be heard entwined with fragments of private gossip, office paraphernalia and microscopic tremors of vibrating dust. Marsham Street is situated in one of the richest audio environments of Westminster: Big Ben, the Thames, wind and rain, traffic, people, the white noise of the city and even the hum of the Underground

Below: Plan of the buildings and surrounding area indicating the scope of the sound recordings taken by architect Mathew Emmett.

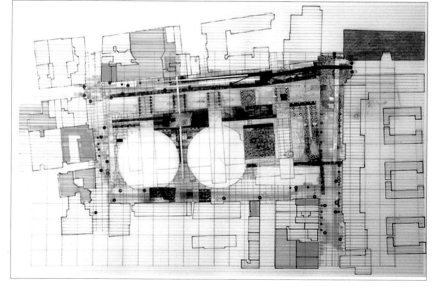

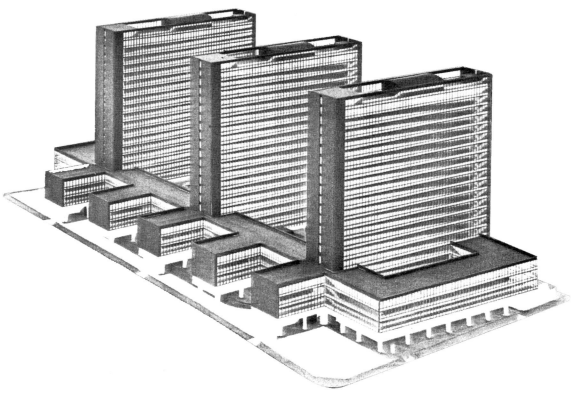

Right: Drawing of 2 Marsham Street. The row of imposing towers was dubbed the 'three ugly sisters'. Built in 1971, the complex was demolished three decades later.

Above: Part of the complex prior to demolition. Designed by Eric Bedford, the concrete building developed a patina typical of 1970s Brutalist structures.

are its setting. Often the geography of the site meant one could not see the source of the noise, the physical bodies dislocated from their voices; the infrastructure of the city was not always visibly present, but the imprint of its sounds was unarguably there. The sounds echoed and morphed into their own distinct language, coloured by the presence of the building's bulk. Atmospheric conditions and time played their part.

Historical maps, archived plans and mechanical/ electrical drawings reveal a fascinating lineage of successive histories for 2 Marsham Street and highlight the strategic importance of the site's role in the industrialisation of London. The plans document a syncopation of successive designs centralised around

the manufacture and storage of the city's heat, light and power. Historic routes connected by coal runs linked the site to the Thames, where barges docked at wharves before shedding their loads for the manufacture of gas. The two massive rotundas underscored this memory. Maps identified the past by showing the patterns of occupation, industry and manufacture. Acoustically, the place was ripe for microphonic exploration, to be plumbed like an archaeologist's trench to reveal the layers of accumulated sound. Here was the method: to record the soundscape every hour over a single day, to grid and plot the site into a temporal field, transforming sound into magnetic code as the space was traversed.

Below: The sound of a building is indicative of its volume, mass and materiality – its presence. It captures sound and rearranges it. Mathew Emmett's enquiry asks whether a building's low-level resonance can lodge itself in people's memory and in the fabric of the site.

The soundscape was made of a diverse texture. The 24-hour recordings revealed the building's presence and how, throughout the day, the richness and diversity of the city's noise threatened to obliterate and overwhelm the sound of the building itself – the building's 'sonic shape'. After 2am, the building's sonic imprint becomes most apparent, in spite of its vacated state; its aural presence becomes more real as material rubs against material, slowly decaying and oxidising. Its hulking mass had a silent presence one could hear and track and record.

The sound of a building portrays its volume, mass, materiality, function and design – its presence. It captures sound and reflects it, absorbs it, emits it. A building changes the sound of a place and that low-level resonance lodges itself in memory and in the fabric of the site. With more sensitive equipment can we hear the history of our buildings, the imprint of the past? The sound of a place never becomes extinct – it is absorbed by new structures, new memories. It metamorphoses.

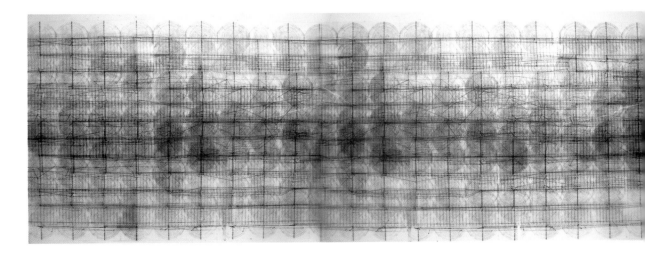

ARCHITECTURAL VOICES

Right: Mathew Emmett uses sound to study the characteristics of a place and to amass raw material from which to assemble new forms. As these three drawings show, through plotting, collaging and mapping in three dimensions, architectural forms emerge from the soundscape.

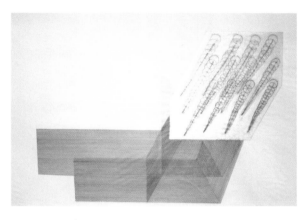

Below: One of Emmett's 'sonographic drawings' of the buildings. 'The drawings appear spatial as intensity of noise is plotted against time. The tonal qualities of the lines ascend, grow dense and fade.' Mathew Emmett.

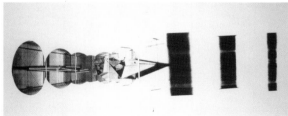

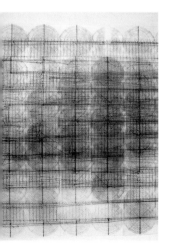

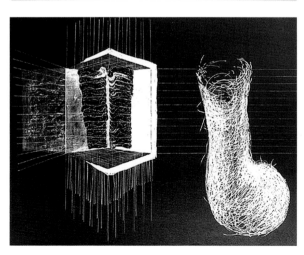

Mathew Emmett created a three-dimensional sonic map of 2 Marsham Street by locating the building within a grid and recording it at ground level with a microphone. Once the recordings had been made, the sounds were played through speakers on which were positioned graph papers on which were set coloured markers. As the sounds played, the vibration of the speakers, which varied according to the strength and pitch of the sound, caused the markers to move. Photographs were taken of this ensemble at 1-second intervals, capturing the intensity of vibration. Through these photographs, the trajectories of the markers were tracked and drawings could be made linking line with time into a sonographic drawing. The resulting 24 drawings represent each hour of the day, each of which describes the properties of the sonic space of 2 Marsham Street in an attempt to make this sonic presence more comprehensible.

'These specific features can be compared and classified, transcribing a dynamic perception into a system of codes and charts,' says Emmett. 'The drawings appear spatial as intensity of noise is plotted against time. The tonal qualities of the lines ascend, grow dense and fade. Oblique marks juxtapose a melody of repeated lines as the sounds are given a physical description. The drawings over the 24 hours vary considerably.'

David Littlefield

Hoxton Cinema

Hoxton, London

Saskia Lewis

It is late, say, 3am. The basement of the Great Eastern Bar and Grill is packed. There is probably a rolling stock of art cinema being projected on the wall. No one is sober enough to concentrate on it. The room is dense with smoke and sweat. People are talking loudly above the music, into each other's ears, their voices vibrating, full of sweet alcohol fumes, sticky, sickly. This is a night that no one will remember with any clarity (think Harvey Keitel in the bar scene of *Mean Streets*). Tomorrow, late morning, any memory will be more of a haze, any fact a hunch. Two guys of a similar age are standing by the bar waiting to be served – Tyrone and Andrew may never have met or spoken but one of them looks down and notices they are wearing identical shoes.

Tyrone Walker-Hebborn is a local roofer whose parents met at a cinema in Mile End. After a period of time that cinema shut and became derelict. He saw the same building up for sale more recently and bought it as a present for his parents' wedding anniversary. They worked together to turn it into a successful family enterprise. It is called the Genesis and creates a local community – it offers half-price entry for OAPs during

Right: Looking north up Pitfield Street. The derelict cinema is sandwiched between the mini supermarket on the corner and a small off-licence advertising 'Cheap Booze'.

Above: The elaborate front facade of the existing building evokes something of the idea of a stage set – a cut-out facade – a pop-up theatre.

the day and shows the films of local artists alongside Bangladeshi festivals; it prides itself on having an international profile. Tyrone judged the rake of the cinema by sitting his 5' 1" mum behind his 6' 7" cousin and jacking the seat up until she could see. She now runs the cinema herself. The enterprise is so direct, so DIY, and provides the perfect counterfoil for the commercial outfits that profess to being unable to make this size of project pay. Now he is ready for his next venture, another filmhouse. This time he has his eye on the desolate cinema in Pitfield Street. Pevsner locates it between the 'former Haberdashers' Almshouses' and the 'George and Vulture, with tall striped gable, c.1900'. He describes No 55 as 'the former Varieties Picture Palace of 1914–15, with light hearted classical detail'. It is in a state of limbo and has been derelict, without a dignified role in the community, for the past 50 years.

On Friday 12 October 1956, an announcement in *The Times* publicised a notice of execution for 55 Pitfield Steet: '9 Odeon and Gaumont Theatres are to be closed by the Rank organisation on 27 October it was announced last night. Part of the Rank organisation's plans to endeavour to rationalise the location of its theatres.' The cinema shut and Pitfield Street lost a valuable social venue. Local folk aged 60 and upwards remember it well. During the Second World War one man recalls watching a movie there when there was a bombing raid. When he got back to his address he found he no longer had a home or a mother – he was just a young kid at the time. The cinema, he felt in some way, had saved his life.

Andrew Waugh, a local architect, has been walking past this long-forgotten shell with its fancy facade, its redundant billboard, between home and

Above: A neon sign reading 'The Cinema' gives the first glimmer of life to the carcass of the building, a shudder, a flicker of future life.

work for 15 years. He says he feels as if he hears the building yell to be noticed, indignant at having been neglected for so long. The nearest operational cinema screens are some distance away at the Barbican or Whitechapel to the south, or the Rio further north in Hackney. The street does feel a little as if it lacks clear identity without the cinema – it is a mixed-up street, a crude junction between different eras, industries and expectations. It is a bit of a wasteland, an experiment in slum clearance and post-war infill. There is no feeling of a centre here. It is a street to move along, not a place to linger.

So it's appropriate that the commission for Waugh Thistleton to turn this building back into a cinema begins in a scene fit for the silver screen. Having met by chance in a bar, Waugh, director of Waugh Thistleton Architects, and Walker-Hebborn, the prospective leasehold client, are to collaborate on the redevelopment of the Hoxton Cinema. The Shoreditch Trust is the freeholder of the property and has been intimately involved in the realisation of the brief. Walker-

Right: The ticket booth has been locked up for the past 50 years – it has become a notice-board to the street hosting flyers and graffiti.

ARCHITECTURAL VOICES

Right: The columns and the recessed openings for ticket booths and the entrance to the foyer create a layering of public streetscape to cinema interior.

Hebborn is going to lease the cinema from them and operate it as a business. The trust is comprised of a charitable board of local residents and is part of a government incentive to regenerate inner-city areas. It is hard to imagine, as we are within a mile of the City, the financial heart of this capital, but this part of London is one of the ten most deprived areas in the country.

Since 1956 the building has stood empty or been home to transient trades. It is dogmatically symmetrical. Matching ticket booths flank the central entrance and once through to the foyer there are winding ascending stairs to both left and right that snake up to the balcony. From the screen and stalls there are single-storey fire escape routes that feed back

Right: The cinema in its prime.

ARCHITECTURAL VOICES

Right: At the back of the balcony an area is partitioned off from the terracing where the seating would once have been – most likely, this would have housed the projectionist, the film stock and the route onto the roof where the projection room was located.

Below: Entrance to the cinema from Buttesland Street. This area originally housed the lower stalls and screen but more recently has hosted a catering company that made sandwiches before operating temporarily as artists' studios.

directly to Pitfield Street bracketing the ticket booths on the front facade – now looking like a couple of lock-up garages. The projection room is situated on the roof of the building and only accessible externally by ladder in what was an initial solution to the dangers to the audience of projecting highly flammable celluloid with an arc light in such a small space. For the past 20 years the shell has been used as a storage depot. It has lost its function, its spirit.

Since the 1990s a full-height block wall has divided the front and back of house as part of a divorce settlement between the previous owners. This has exaggerated the building's sense of disjuncture as the separated spaces make no clear sense. The ex-wife used the entrance, foyer, top rake of cinema and balcony as a warehouse to store goods imported from Vietnam en route to smart retail outlets in Chelsea. The rake is caught at its genesis, running smack up against the whitewashed block-work interruption. A casual, poorly made stair sits against the wall, making a more direct route from stalls to balcony, avoiding the glamour of the winding journey made twofold from the foyer.

The balcony is stripped of seats but still has a series of slow steps that fall to the edge, to the balustrade. You can feel the majesty of cinema in its infancy. You can imagine the enormity of the space and the excitement of the audience. The ceiling is falling in and the paint peeling but the handrails are polished smooth and silken from the passing of audiences in their masses, in and out. The toilets directly off to either side of the auditorium are of a modest domestic scale, incongruous to the modern eye. We expect more – more space, more privacy, more facilities. You can imagine a queue forming here, polite and patient. There are small rooms partitioned off at the top, which must

Below: View from one of the freestanding insulated catering units built in the area that had been the lower stalls. The suspended ceiling and long preparation units mask most visual references to the building's original function.

Opposite: View from Pitfield Street down the length of what was once the fire escape to the original cinema.

have been to do with the running of the projector and storing of the celluloid. There seems to have been little separation between the audience and the people working in the cinema, facilitating the magic. The balcony has dignity and elegance which make it all the more poignant that it is severed so completely from its view over the stalls and down to the screen.

The ex-husband ran a bakery from the stalls, supplying the City with sandwiches and croissants with access from Buttesland Street. The screen has gone and the stalls house single-storey units for refrigeration and baking, and lengths of wipe-down preparation surfaces instead of seating. More recently artists have been using this industrial kitchen space as studios so there are drawn figures hanging from handles and drop-down ropes from holes high up. The false ceiling screens the makeshift kitchen from the full barn-like height of the building. It is severed from its past, has lost its dignity and any trace of resonance. It is a space that could be anywhere, there's not even a murmur in the stalls of the histories once enacted here. Pokey office spaces have been built against the screen and the fire escapes have become linear stores. The fire escapes alone give some indication of a curious division between interior and exterior; quickly and casually roofed over, originally they would have been open to the sky. The physical division and separate routes of entry to perpendicular streets are enough to give any building an identity crisis.

For Andrew Waugh this is a challenging project, not a refurbishment and not a straightforward rebuild. The original, single, massive auditorium accommodated 1,260 people in its day and ran a continuous performance from 10 in the morning until midnight. In essence it was a drop-in centre. The 'shed', as Waugh

Above: Internally the paint is peeling, revealing a unique patterning of layers of colour.

Above: The top of the stalls and ticket hall/entrance were used as storage for imports from Vietnam – the seats had already been stripped out but the rake of the floor and the decorative cornicing indicate the building's original purpose.

refers to it, is beyond mute; it is resigned, defunct, dead. 'There's nothing left; no seats, no patina, no feeling at all, just a shabby derelict shell that seems a bit awkward and useless. Even the auditorium has been cheaply divided in two, for storage purposes and is only recognisable as a cinema at all from the balcony.' The language the building speaks, if it speaks at all, is from another era and not easily comprehensible to contemporary society. In fact it speaks a language that is lost to us.

The facade is a different matter altogether and in a way this makes sense. It was designed, after all, to draw people in. Waugh describes how keeping and repairing the facade was the first main decision: 'There's no point in trying to recreate such an iconic image of cinema or theatre, an invitation to suspend your disbelief'. However it is due to be brought bang up to

date with a colour scheme by Gary Hume, a local artist of world renown, a scheme which Waugh anticipates will veer towards that of a Battenberg cake.

The shed to the rear, the auditorium, is to be demolished and replaced with a modern version. 'Efficient sheds behind a Wild-West cardboard cut-out facade is what I'm thinking. This building is just a memory in the local consciousness at the moment and needs to be given its function back.' These days with smaller audiences a single large auditorium and screen is not an option so the brief is to include four. A larger screen will seat 300 and should suit the regular popular 'blockbuster' patrons while the three smaller screens will serve niche audiences for less mainstream films.

The proposal includes a cafe and restaurant that will look out over the street from the first floor, inviting people to use the building as a meeting point

Above: The slow, measured terracing and decorative mouldings to the interior elevation of the balcony provoke a nostalgia for the era when the building enjoyed its original use as a cinema, a venue that was once at the cutting edge of its day. Sparse fluorescent lights illuminate the balcony – the ceiling appears to be caught in slow-motion free-fall as it disintegrates.

Right: At some point in the recent past the width of the balcony has been used for target practice.

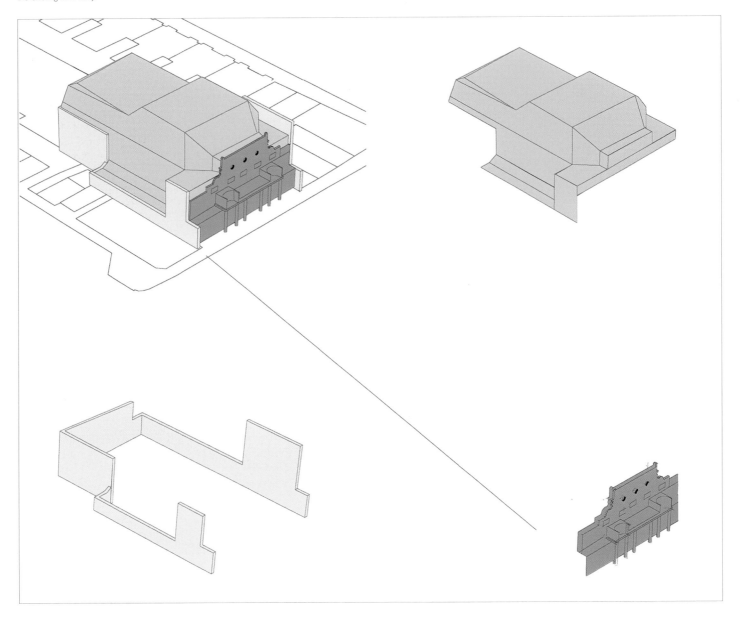

Below: Building pieces – the facade, the sculpted roof and the existing boundary.

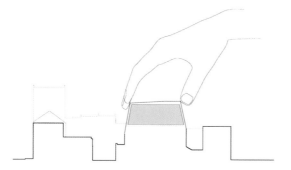

Left: The roof has been squeezed to comply with rights of light regulations and for neighbouring property.

and creating an exciting new venue that will hopefully inspire a variety of events. The intention is to provide, to some extent, the feeling of a third space – somewhere that isn't home and isn't work, but that is nevertheless familiar, communal and intimate, and will help reinstate, or translate the idea of the continuous performance as advertised on the building's billboards during the early part of the 20th century. There is a feeling that the cinema could once again become the physical heart of the local community.

Andrew describes the form of the smaller lozenge-shaped auditoria as being similar to a flight simulator and again it feels almost as if he is describing a film set, an intense experience. These boxes are to sit on springs within a concrete shell that constitutes the envelope of the building. The combination of these design and material decisions should provide the mass and void to absorb any superfluous energy and dissipate any residual transmitted vibration either from one auditorium to another or from the cinema to the neighbourhood outside.

The external form of the building has been developed from studies that examined the rights to light with respect to 17 neighbouring properties. Many of the adjoining properties on Haberdasher Street and Buttesland Street are privately owned, and during the planning application process there was widespread concern among this community that the building would have a negative impact on the local environment. The site is locked in and very tight indeed, and it is true that Waugh Thistleton were applying for what constituted a vertical extension to the existing form. The images which Waugh references, that have inspired the design process and informed the solution, include Lou Reed on the cover of *Transformer* wearing a pair of skin-tight trousers, a Stealth bomber and the Empire State Building in New York, which also acquired its form from a similar rights to light diagram. All these images illustrate just what a tight fit the solution needed to be and just how the envelope of the building has to be sculpted to respond to every facet of the adjoining properties.

Right: Street presence. Drawing of the two routes into the building.

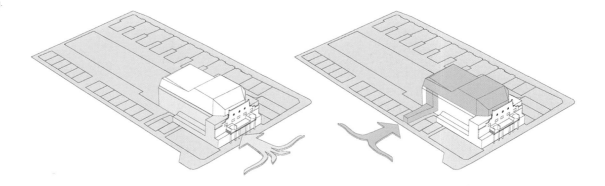

There is a photograph in circulation from around 1915 of two large coaches of men preparing to go on a trip. It is the Royal Oak outing, taken outside the Hoxton Cinema, and shows the facade as a frenzy of information: advertisements and comments, text and image. The facade is a backdrop to an image of local community, from the suited-and-booted men to the shoeless urchins to the right of the image or, to the left, the child looking away from the camera sporting a pair of enormous shoes that can't possibly be his. The hope is that the cinema will once again feel as if it is at the centre of local life. At the moment there is a blue neon sign above the entrance that lights up each night stating simply, 'The Cinema' – which, at the moment, it clearly isn't. It causes a faint pulse though, an expectation and intention, an introduction to the future.

Below: Front elevation facing onto Pitfield Street.

ARCHITECTURAL VOICES

Below: Section through the building showing the new auditoria.

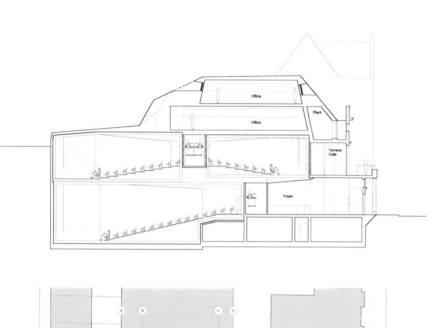

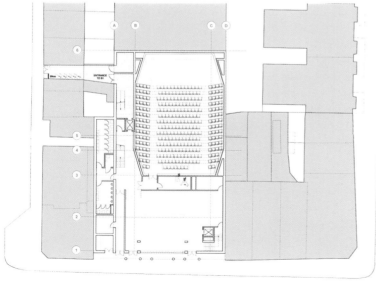

Above: A temporary washing area constructed directly above a drain in what was originally one of the cinema's open-air fire escapes. These escapes exist on both sides of the building and in recent years have been roofed over to provide additional storage space.

Left: Plan to ground floor.

The Power of the Real
interview with Peter Higgins

David Littlefield

Peter Higgins studied architecture at the Architectural Association, after which he worked as a set designer for the BBC. In 1985 he joined the design and communications consultancy Imagination and, in 1992, co-founded his own design practice, Land Design Studio. In 2000 Land designed the Play Zone element of London's Millennium Dome; since then, the practice has designed spaces and installations for the UK's Foreign and Commonwealth Office, the Natural History Museum and the National Maritime Museum at Falmouth, Cornwall.

Peter Higgins, architect and founder of interpretative design practice Land Design Studio, has carved out a curious and almost unique role for himself. Formerly of the BBC and design agency Imagination, Higgins is a story-teller who will draw upon almost every available technique to help further a narrative – whether in architecture, interior design, technology, curating, film or interactivity. Interpretative design, if that is how best to express it, is an emerging art form that has yet to gain a position of mainstream acceptance; it fits between architecture and curatorship; it is neither about the building nor the glass case; it is about distilling messages down to an essence in the hope that, once consumed, people can embark on their own journeys of discovery.

This 'in-between' sort of role has brought Higgins to an equally ambiguous or blurred relationship with buildings and spaces. He is highly sensitive to the power of architecture, and yet his installations might turn their backs on it; he is eloquent on the matter of architecture as the sensitive manipulation of light, space and materials, and is scornful of the designer's 'ego', but he simultaneously looks beyond the building for its real value. It is human history which exerts its gravitational pull on Higgins – history, memory, our interpretations of these things, and a reverence for the objects which we leave behind. To that extent, a building is merely a 'vessel' for a mental exploration. The building has no voice – it is, however, an echo chamber.

'We are interventionists,' says Higgins, who regards found buildings almost as source material. 'We inherit spaces that have often been built for entirely different imperatives than our own, and we imprint entirely different meanings on to them.' To Higgins, the meaning of a space is not necessarily uncovered by engaging directly with it – it might need to be mediated in some way, interpreted to give the visitor a head start, a set of clues and the inspiration to get stuck in.

Like artist Gerry Judah (see p 98), Higgins has visited Auschwitz. He was part of a small group of people and snow fell. That snow, in its way, mediated Higgins's experience of the site. 'It was cold, so bitterly cold, and it was the right way to experience the place.' The snow at Auschwitz operated on the same level as Daniel Libeskind's concrete garden at Berlin's Holocaust Museum, a space in which the landscape tilts and perpendicular lines are drawn away from the vertical; it is deliberately disorientating and enough to induce sickness in visitors. Similarly, Higgins's snow was symbolic of the *exposure* of the people who had lived here, both to the cold and to the whims of their captors. It was, however, an almost solitary experience and Higgins's job is to provide interpretative experiences for groups, many of whom pass through quickly.

Higgins is, for example, working with Edward Cullinan Architects on a new gateway and visitor centre for the Graeco-Roman city of Petra in Jordan. This desert site (28 square kilometres of landscape,

Below: A view of how the timbers of the Mary Rose, now almost 500 years old, will appear in their new enclosure in Portsmouth's naval dockyard.

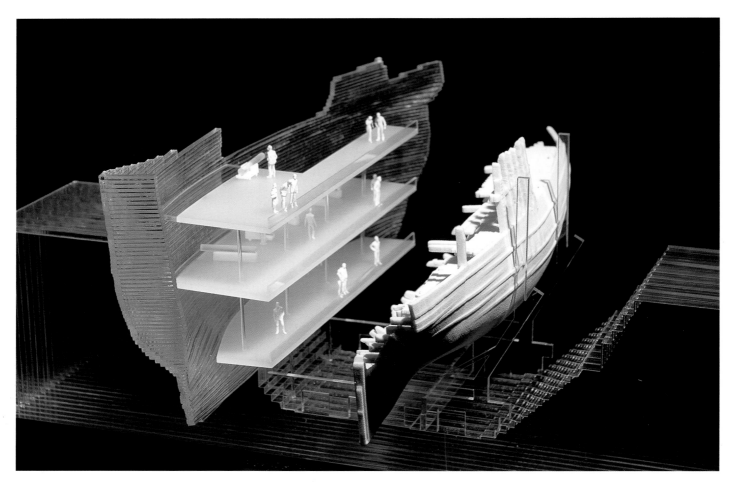

dwellings and temples carved out of the rock) defies 'interpretation'; it is too big and, with roots reaching back to 300 BC, too ancient to be represented by a single narrative or captured into something as simple as an exhibit. With only five display zones, Higgins estimates that he can capture the attention of visitors for just 45 minutes: 'We simplify it and take all the poetry out of it. But all the poetry is out there waiting for you. The experience of walking through that landscape, of standing in temples within shafts of sunlight, it is absolutely extraordinary. It takes your breath away. We cannot recreate that. All we can do is prepare you for it.' At this interpretation centre, therefore, Higgins begins his narrative in 1812, when the site was first discovered by Europeans. Petra is a place to be discovered by confronting it personally, and all people like Higgins can do is orientate visitors and give them a chance to comprehend what they are looking at.

At the heart of Higgins's practice is a belief in 'the power of the real' and the thrill of touch, especially when in contact with the objects of archaeological evidence. There is a judgement to be made here between what constitutes an object and how an object may differ from a building. Higgins resists the urge to objectify buildings and believes they should be accorded object status only when, as ruins, they cease to become inhabitable. To Higgins, buildings were conceived and constructed as containers for human activity, and those buildings created in a spirit of what he calls 'generosity' (that is, ambiguous, substantial and open to change) stand the best chance of being appropriated for new uses. It is even important that buildings refuse to become objectified because, if they do, curators will be ready to move in, prevent further change and set them within a glass case alongside other precious and jealously guarded artefacts.

Right: The timber-clad 'hull' of the proposed building for the Mary Rose will be incised with copies of personal marks made by the ship's Tudor sailors in lieu of their names. Produced in a pre-literate age, such marks represent a lost language.

Higgins is uneasy about the glass case although he accepts that, in an age of mass tourism and curiosity, items deemed to be of historical and cultural importance cannot be handled by the crowd. So he sets up technological solutions to help people scrutinise objects from a distance – by giving them the where-withal to zoom in on the real item or manipulate a virtual recreation. The idea is twofold. First, that technological mediators like holograms can assist in our under-standing of an object without the need for us to handle it. And second, that the wish to touch, the yearning triggered by the out-of-reachness of these things, might even deliver a more complete appreciation of those objects we can touch, especially 'non-collectables' such as burger cartons and matchbooks (things which are, says Higgins, the collectables of tomorrow and which, one day, will become untouchable and their weight, fragility and texture will be unknown to most).

So what does one do with the super-object, the Mary Rose and her contents which sank in front of Henry VIII in 1545? Higgins, along with interior designers from Pringle Brandon, is part of the team led by architects Wilkinson Eyre to present this Tudor fighting ship within a specialist enclosure in Ports-mouth. Due to the peculiarities of the way the ship sank into the mud of the Solent, just half of the hull remains and is now temporarily enclosed, the subject of a long-term conservation project. Quite apart from the remains of the ship itself, literally thousands of objects have been recovered from the underwater site – including, as well as bones, leather jerkins, dice, kindling and the world's largest collection of long bows. For Higgins, the value of the collection is that it represents a glorious snapshot of Tudor life, an uncurated, unplanned time-capsule of often worthless objects that are now regarded with fascination.

Right: Site of a planned enclosure and museum for the ship, which sank in 1545 and was brought to the surface in the 1980s. The outline of HMS Victory, Nelson's great battleship built more than two centuries after the Mary Rose, appears on the right.

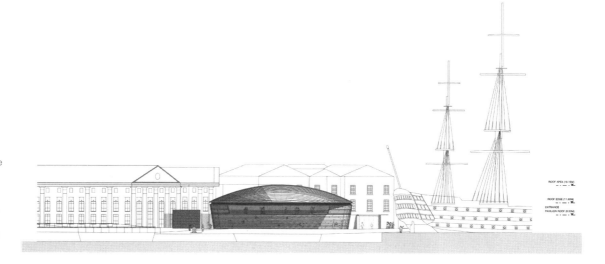

ARCHITECTURAL VOICES

Left: The proposed buildings have been conceived by Edward Culli-nan Architects, with interpretative design by Land Design Studio. 'The experience of walking through that landscape, of standing in temples within shafts of sunlight, it is abso-lutely extraordinary. It takes your breath away. We cannot recreate that. All we can do is prepare you for it.' Peter Higgins

Packaging and presenting these items within the context of what remains of the hull presents a problem; the design team proposes to create a glass echo of the preserved timber ship, on which these rescued objects will sit in roughly the positions they occupied five centuries ago. This glass facsimile of the Mary Rose replaces the missing half; it is a tactic reminiscent of Patricia MacKinnon-Day's pieces in Exeter (see p 82) which use glass to highlight absence and allow the solidity of the historic remains to stand alone.

Some of the more arresting relics of the Mary Rose are the marks made by the ship's crew in lieu of writing their own names. Produced in a pre-literate age, these marks represent a lost language (or at least a lost script) and their presence is a forceful reminder of the humanity that underlies any relic. This humanity, this person-to-person contact, is what appeals to Higgins at a profoundly fundamental level. It goes beyond curatorship and moves into the realm of wonder. Apart from any quality (such as generosity) which an architect or designer can feed into a building, Higgins looks for the ways in which places have been cared for, nurtured even. Like Petra or Derek Jarman's garden – for the latter's fragility and the care with which it was assembled – places which have been the subject of enduring human attention can be clearly recognised. Higgins speaks of 'resonance'.

Interpretative design is often misunderstood. It does not seek to replace what is there, but merely to enhance one's understanding of it. That is why Higgins's project at Petra is almost deliberately unpoetic and if Petra has a voice Higgins is prepared to let it speak for itself; his role is to prepare visitors to listen, not to tell them what they are likely to hear.

Below: Section drawing slicing through the centre of the building to reveal how the low-profile visitor centre minimises its visual impact on the ancient landscape of Jordan.

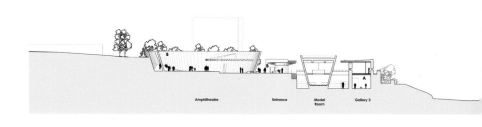

Amphitheatre   Entrance   Model Room   Gallery 3

Paved Entrance Court   Gallery 4 & 5   Gallery 3   Gallery 1 & 2   Administration

Above: Architect's drawing of the elevation of the proposed building looking north.

Right: Plan of the proposed visitor centre. The building appears as a hinge, or an opening door, embedded within the landscape.

Epilogue

Saskia Lewis

The gist of histories and statistics as far back as the records reach is in you this hour – and myths and tales the same;

If you were not breathing and walking here where would they all be?

The most renowned poems would be ashes … orations and plays would be vacuums.

All architecture is what you do to it when you look upon it;

Did you think it was in the white or gray stone? or the lines of the arches and cornices?

Walt Whitman, 'A Song for Occupations', [4], in *Leaves of Grass*.

It is true that without people to articulate them, exchange stories and interact with them buildings remain mute. However, buildings are the container. They hold in their skin the wear and tear that bears witness to the events that have taken place in and around them. Certainly, it is people who animate buildings, but the notion that buildings are inert and subservient may be misguided. They are designed, built and occupied by people, and once built they need to be tended to, looked after. It seems possible, even probable, that given this intimate symbiosis between people and buildings, these buildings might absorb some of the evidence of our existence, our narratives.

This book has been compiled as a series of reported conversations and case studies to explore how a dialogue has been created with buildings that adapt during a continuous history. There is much emotive suggestion and fond narrative contained within these pages. Buildings are discussed intimately,

informally, like people describing over a meal how they have interpreted the marks of history or atmosphere from environments that have seen others pass through. The fact is that we leave our mark on buildings and they, in return, leave their mark on us.

How you come to look at buildings with this type of intimacy is a story in itself. For my part, there is one step that I have known all my life between the kitchen and the sitting room in my family home. First it was the step that led up the stairs in the 17th-century farmhouse winding around the chimney on its southerly elevation. Later it was the step that took you to the outside oven and to the paddock to tend to the animals. In the mid-19th century, when an extension was built to the south, it became the step that negotiates the change in level between the two interiors. Everyone who has ever walked across it has contributed to the slow dip in its surface. When we are gone there will be others to continue the work. I have been aware of this carving ever since I can remember and am very fond of it. My parents introduced me to these quiet creations and to the idea of my contribution to a slow sculpture – I have my place in the history of this fabric and feel the presence of others who have done the same. In consequence, I have always imagined that buildings have tales to tell.

The impact of this type of observational attitude grew during my postgraduate studies and subsequent teaching posts. While studying architecture I began recording the impact of people on spaces instead of vice versa. I was practising what I considered to be observational architecture. Looking at worn space, evidence of occupation, of lives led. This was a rebellion against what I found to be the tyranny of the pristine. The immaculate, unmarked, untouched buildings in architectural drawings seemed neither to allow for, nor to anticipate *use*. This led me to propose an excavated building for my final thesis – a building that held the story of its advent in the decoration of its surface. The architecture and its narrative were one and the same.

Through teaching I have found that the narrative – the story behind a street, a building, a room, a detail that exists – is a way of describing and exploring the atmosphere of a space. Designs which students propose have increasingly lacked atmosphere, as has recent architectural conversation and construction, but in reality it is the atmosphere of a building that touches us. Without being able to read buildings, imagine the advent of their original design and use and subsequent adaptation or alteration, if any, we can't fully anticipate how our proposals may exist in the future. Buildings can become increasingly clever or complex and technology can offer dramatic new opportunities, but without atmosphere what can we hope to really be contributing to our environment?

The majority of buildings under construction and those recently completed, like the manufacture of products at the cutting edge, seem to have a sell-by date, an in-built redundancy, a premeditated obsolescence. They have a life expectancy of several decades but no more. There is no time for the patina of age to be acquired. On the other hand, there is something deeply admirable about buildings that have survived for centuries. They acquire a dignity with age, and if they have existed that long it is clear that someone in each generation has felt sufficiently inspired by what already exists to repair or adapt their basic form.

Design can be defined as a translation of experience, the *translation* of inspiration. In order to create extraordinary spaces with integrity and atmospheric presence we need to identify what we find valuable, what we are moved and inspired by. This is a book that has explored the echo of past lives in buildings with history, and the notion that the emotive patina that may be present in a building may contribute to the dialogue leading to its redevelopment for future habitation.

The true epilogue to this publication is yours. If you, the reader, have enjoyed these descriptions then it is for you to look around you now and discover your own stories, your own relationship to space, time and material.

January 2007

Below: A well worn step showing the passage of time.

Right: Suspended in time – narratives weave together and objects await their rediscovery.

Further Reading

Alexander, Christopher; Ishikawa, Sara; Silverstein, Murray; Jacobson, Max: Fiksdahl-King, Ingrid; and Angel, Shlomo. *A Pattern Language: Towns, Buildings, Construction*, Oxford University Press, New York, 1977.

An investigation and analysis into what makes successful architecture – written for and to inspire a broad audience that may be preparing to contribute more immediately to their environment.

Atkins, Marc and Sinclair, Iain. *Liquid City*, Reaktion Books, London, 1999.

This collection of mini-essays by writer Iain Sinclair, supported by almost ghostly photography from Marc Atkins, teases out the poetics of ordinary places in and around London, overlaying them with personal memories and associations that both enrich and transcend their physical presence.

Bachelard, Gaston. *The Poetics of Space*, Beacon Press, Boston, 1994.

The seminal work by the French philosopher on the ways that spaces embody poetry and psychological intensity.

de Botton, Alain. *The Architecture of Happiness*, Hamish Hamilton, London, 2006.

A well-researched book based on personal conviction about the ways that architectural style can influence the mood and imagination of buildings' inhabitants. The author argues that architectural 'language' is more than just the application of form and style – these things have emotional and psychological consequences.

Brooker, Graeme and Stone, Sally. *Rereadings: Interior Architecture and the Design Principles of Remodelling Existing Buildings*, RIBA Enterprises, London, 2004.

A collection of short case studies, based around the themes of analysis, strategy and tactics, detailing the techniques by which architects have grafted the new on to the old.

Calvino, Italo. *Invisible Cities*, Vintage, London, 1997.

This collection of micro-fictions, narrated by Marco Polo to Kublai Khan, contains descriptions of imaginary cities and the ways that architectural form and the behaviour and values of the inhabitants reflect one another.

Dodds, George and Tavernor, Robert (eds). *Body and Building: Essays on the Changing Relation of Body and Architecture*, MIT Press, Cambridge, MA and London, 2002.

A collection of essays demonstrating how the form and dimensions of the human body have informed architecture since the classical age. Rather academic, but accessible nonetheless, this book deals with subjects as diverse as posture, the geometry of Renaissance fortresses, the Greek brain and ideas of perfection.

Ede, Jim. *A Way of Life – Kettle's Yard*, Kettle's Yard, Cambridge, 1996.

An account of the conversion of a series of cottages in Cambridge lived in by Jim Ede and his wife – the things that inspired them, the collections they made and the inspirational atmosphere they created and preserved for the public at Kettle's Yard in Cambridge.

Giono, Jean. *The Man Who Planted Trees*, Peter Owen, London, 1985.

A very simple story of the alteration of a landscape by one man – an inspirational tale of the potential for positive interaction between man and his environment.

Harbison, Robert. *The Built, the Unbuilt and the Unbuildable: In Pursuit of Architectual Meaning*, Thames and Hudson, London, 1991.

Tackling gardens, monuments, fortifications, ruins and images of imaginary places, this work of intelligence and lateral thinking attempts to get to the root of how built spaces occupy the human imagination.

Jenkins, Simon. *England's Thousand Best Houses*, Penguin Books, London, 2004.

Brief introductions to buildings outlining their history, character, tales and giving a personal insight into their atmosphere.

Lee, Pamela M. *Object to Be Destroyed – The Work of Gordon Matta-Clarke*, MIT Press, Cambridge, MA, 1999.

Catalogues the inspirational and unique work of an artist who reinterpreted condemned buildings by slicing through them in order to alter their forms, views and volumes before demolition, as well as describing other fascinating and relevant things.

Pallasmaa, Juhani. *The Eyes of the Skin: Architecture and the Senses*, Wiley-Academy, London, 2005.

A modern classic, this slim volume of essays presents a thoroughly convincing case for assessing buildings for their non-visual merits – and considers the meanings implicit in shadows, taste, the role of the human body, peripheral vision and 'multi-sensory experience'.

Perec, Georges. *Species of Spaces and Other Pieces*, Penguin, London, 1999.

An eclectic series of essays and exercises that describe ways of looking and recording space and architecture. The book is littered with inspirational lists, projects, ideas and imaginings.

Rasmussen, Steen Eiler. *Experiencing Architecture*, MIT Press, Cambridge, MA, 2000.

Covering everything from scale and rhythm to sound and colour, this book subjects buildings to dispassionate analysis and teases out what makes them places worthy of human attention and delight.

Robb, Peter. *Midnight in Sicily*, Harvill Press, London, 1999.

A rich and evocative journey that touches on almost everything, as his sub-title suggests – On Art, Food, History, Travel and Cosa Nostra.

Robbe-Grillet, Alain. *Jealousy*, Grove Press, New York, 1987.

Meticulous observations of time, space, movement and worn surface are described in this drama between characters on a banana plantation. The text is narrated in the present tense by an unknown character with a disorienting cyclical dynamic.

Shonfield, Katherine. *Walls Have Feelings: Architecture, Film and the City*, Routledge, London, 2000.

Very possibly a unique book, this set of intriguing essays is based on a deep understanding of Modern architectural theory, a close reading of classic films (including *Mary Poppins, Rosemary's Baby* and *The Apartment*) and an analysis of the claims made by building product manufacturers in their brochures.

Tanizaki, Junichiro. *In Praise of Shadows*, Vintage, London, 2001.

Another slim volume, this book on aesthetics by the Japanese novelist examines the spatial, textural and material qualities of traditional Japanese buildings, contrasting them with the demands and values of Western (and Modern) design.

Tindall, Gillian. *The House by the Thames and the People Who Lived There*, Chatto & Windus, London, 2006.

One lone house remains from what was once a riverside terrace. Gillian Tindall uses this address to locate her research in a text that explores site, time, occupation and social history.

Woodward, Christopher. *In Ruins*, Vintage, London, 2002.

A highly personal and thoroughly engrossing account of the history of ruins and their cultural meaning.

Zumthor, Peter. *Atmospheres*, Birkhäuser, Basel, 2006.

An illustrated transcript of a lecture delivered by Peter Zumthor on 1 June 2003 in Germany – a touching and personal eclectic mix of inspiration and solution to architectural design.

Index

Aalto, Finn Alvar 201
Ackroyd, Peter 13, 15, 55, 146
Adam, Ken 43
Adam, Robert 15
Aitken, Kirstin 151
Albert-Birot, Pierre 84
Allen, Harry 14
Allford Hall Monaghan Morris Associates 167
Almeida, Fabio 180
Altman, Robert: *Nashville* 196
Amico, Claudia 148, *149*, 151
Arts and Civic Centre, Goole, Yorkshire 72, 80, *81*
Arts and Crafts Movement 78
Arundell 131
Asher, Jane 54
Atkins Walters Webster 51
Auden, W.H.: 'Musée des Beaux-Arts' 195
Auschwitz-Birkenau 12, 99, 222
Avebury 57

Bachelard, Gaston 84
Bage, Charles 184, 187, 190, 191-2, *193*
Baker, Phillip 83
Bank of England *99*, 102
Bankside Power Station, London *35*, 203
Bannister, Roger 164
Barry, Charles *35*, 36, *36*, 37
Battersea Power Station 120-3, *121-3*
BDP 17, 18, *82*, 83
BDP Lighting 85
Bedford, Eric 204, *205*
Being John Malkovich 43
Bell, Reverend Andrew 164
Benyon, Benjamin 190
Benyon, Thomas 187, 190
Betjeman, John 75
Bignell, William 39
Billingsgate market, London 39
Boathouse, The, Ladbroke Grove, London 180-3

Bolt, Robert 9
Bolt and Nut Supplies Ltd 19
Bomb Shelter, Brusselton, Western Australia 58-63, *58-63*
Botton, Alain de 10, 12
Boulton, Sid 14
Boulton & Watt 18, 19
Bow Wow Wow 44
Brecknell, Jonathan 49-50, 52
Brehler, Bettina 147
Breughel, Pieter: *Fall of Icarus* 195
Bryan, G. 167
Buck, Reverend W. Armstrong 89, *93*, 95
Buckland Court Estate, Shoreditch 72, 79-80, *80-1*
Burroughs, William S. 33
Buschow Henley *74*, *77*

Cadogan Estate 165, 167
Cage, John 195
Calle, Sophie 148
Calvino, Italo 9, 13, 46
Cambridge pub, Soho 39
Canadian National Vimy Memorial 54
Canterbury Cathedral *194*, 196
Canterbury Tale, A 196
Cappuccetto, Soho 44
Carter, Howard 22
Château de Paulin 124, 132-3, *132-3*
Chatterley Whitfield coalmine 14-15
Chelsea College of Art 139
Chermayeff, Serge 201
Chipperfield, David 203
Chirico, Georgio de 195
   Melanconia 196
Ciudad Guerrero, Mexico 174
Clayton, Malcolm 41
Clock House, Coleshill, Oxfordshire 104-19, *104-19*, *230-1*
Cochrane, Ray 104
Coleshill House, Oxfordshire *8*, 104-19, *104-19*

Collier, Eli *152-4*, 153-4, 157, 159
Collings, Matthew 30
Collingwood, John *68*, 69, 120
Collis, Richard 184, 189, 190
Colosseum, Rome 57
Cook, Ernest 107
Crosby, Clern 66
Cross Mill, Ditherington Flax Mill 187, 191, 192
CTP St James 17, 18

Damtsa, Virginia 24, 26
Däniken, Erich von 141
Dannatt, Adrian 30-3
Davidovici, Irina 75
Davidson, Lischutz 50
Davis, Paul 10, 21, 165, 166, 168-9, *170*
Davis, Paul, and Partners 164, 165, 167
De La Warr Pavillion 201
Ditherington Flax Mill 184-93, *184-93*
Dodd, Stewart 157, 162
Dresden 11
Duke of York's College 167
Duke of York's Headquarters 164, 167, *167*
Dunbar and Miles 33
Dunlop, Frank 66
Dunn, William 39

Earle Architects 39, 46, *47*
Ed's Diner, Soho 39
Edward Cullinan Architects 222, *226*
Edward Nash Architects 50, 51, 52, 53
Egan, Sir John 166
Einstein Tower, Potsdam 201
Eisenhower, President 174
Ellis Island 12
Emmett, Mathew 13, 204-7, *206-7*
Empire State Building, New York 219
Escape to River Cottage 152
Evans, Dan 109
Evans, Kit 107, 109

Evans, Marsha 109
Evans, Toby 109

Factory, The Shepherdess Walk, Nos.
    20-22, Shoreditch 72, 73-5, *73-4*
Falcon Reservoir 172, *173*
Farrell, Sir Terry 37, 204
Fawcett, Anthony 33
Fearnley-Whittingstall, Hugh 152, 158, *161*
Feilden Clegg Bradley Architects 172, 184,
    184-5, 189, 192
Firearms Act 1937 *28*
Foreign and Commonwealth Office 222
Form Design Architecture 39, 41
Foster, Norman 199
Francesca, Piero della: *View of an Ideal
    City* 195, *196-7*
Frankfurt Museum of Applied Arts 36

Gaete-Holmes, Richard *150*, 151
Galsworth, John: *Forsyte Saga, The* 38
Gandy, Joseph *99*, 102
Gibbs, James 124, 125, 127, 130
Gibo 180-3
Gidley, Ann 83
Ginsberg, Allen *27*
Goodridge, H.E. 51
grain elevators, Buffalo, USA 176-7, *176-7*

Hackney Phalanx 92
Hansom, Charles 51
Harbison, Robert 202
Harrap, Julian 198-203, *198*
Harrap Architects, Julian 172
Harvey, Alan *220*
Harvey, Harry *220*
Hawksmoor, Nicholas 198
Haworth Tompkins Architects 65-6, *68*
Herzog & de Meuron 37
Higgins, Peter 222-7, *222*
Historicism 37
Hitchcock, Alfred 43

Holland & Holland (gunsmiths) 26
Holocaust Museum, Berlin 222
Hopkins, Michael 35-7, *35*, *36*
Howard, Alec 165
Howell, Bill 65
Howick Place sorting office *142-7*, 143-7
Hoxton Cinema 206-21, *206-21*
Hume, Gary 216
Huntley, Ian 12

Imperial War Museum 99
Insall, Donald, Associates 167

Jackson, J.B. 78
Jarman, Derek 227
Johnson, Philip 49
Jones, Inigo 104
Jones, William 187
Judah, Gerry 98-103, 222
    Angels 98, *98*, *100-3*, 102
    Frontiers 101

King, Stephen: *Shining, The* 14
Kubrick, Stanley 14

Lacock Abbey *57*
Lan, David 66
Land Design Studio 222, *226*
Land Securities 83
Lasdun, Denys 197
Lawley, Rector Algernon 95, 183
Libeskind, Daniel 222
Lichtenstein, Rachel 86
Lloyd, Matthew 50, 86, 89, 91, *91*, 95, 96
Lloyd, Matthew, Architects *92-3*
Lloyd, William 39
London Bridge 9, 20
Lord's Cricket Ground 36
Louis XIV 38
Lovejoy's bookshop, Soho 39
Lucas, George 171
Lupton, Martin 85

MacKinnon-Day, Patricia 82, 85, *82*, 227
Malinowski, Antoni 65
Manchester City Art Gallery 35, 36, *36*
Market Hall, Accrington 148-51, *149-50*
Marshall, John 187, 190
Marsham Street, No. 2, Westminster,
    London 204-7, *204-7*
Mary Rose 223-5, *225-7*
Mary, Queen *8*
McLaren, Malcolm 44
McQueen, Alexander 180
Meier, Richard 36, 37
Melvin, Jeremy 132
Mendelsohn, Erich 201
Merchant Taylors' School 92
Middle Row Primary School 182
Middlesex House of Correction 143
Milky Voids 138-41
Millennium Dome 51, 222
mining engine building, Botallack, Cornwall
    136-41, *137-41*
Mitchell, Roger 26
Mode 182
Modernism 34-7
Monument, London 198
Moor Street Hotel, Soho 38-47, *38-47*
Moor Street Triangle 39, *39*, *41*, 44, *46*
Morgan, William 39
Morris, William 79, *79*
Moth, Ken 17, 19-20, 21, 22
Mozart, Wolfgang Amadeus 166
Munich 57
Murray, Matthew 17, 18-19, *21*
Murray, Peter 13, 54-7, 65
Museum of London 46

Nash, John 124, 125, 130
Nash Range 130
National Gallery Sainsbury Wing extension
    37
National Maritime Museum, Falmouth 222
National Maritime Museum, Greenwich 22

National Theatre 41, 197
National Trust 55, 107
Natural History Museum 222
New Covent Garden, London 39
New Wardour Castle 131
Nuremberg 12

O'Leary, Pat, *Environmental Graphics 79*
Old Guerrero (Guerrero Viejo), Mexico 172,
    173, 174-6 *173-5*
Old Wardour House 130-2, *130-2*
Olmsted, Frederick Law 176

Pace, George 35
Paine, James 131
Palace Green Library, Durham 35
Palladio 104
Park Farm, Devon 152-63, *152-63*
Parry, Eric 124-35, *124*, 132, 135
Pearce's Whim, Botallack *138*, 140, 141
Pedlar, Richard 51
Pembroke College, Cambridge *134-5*, 135
Petra, Jordan 222-3, 227
Pevsner, Nikolaus 35, 104, 167
Piper, Adrian 148
Plas Mawr, Conwy 22
Pleydell, Thomas 104
Pleydell-Bouverie, Bertrand 104
Pleydell-Bouverie, Bina 104
Pleydell-Bouverie, Doris 104
Pleydell-Bouverie, Molly 104
Poe, Edgar Allan: *Fall of the House of
    Usher, The* 17
Polanski, Roman 10
    Tenant, The 10, 11
Portchester Castle 198
Portcullis House 36
Post-Modernism 34, 37
Pratt, George 104
Pratt, Roger 104
Pringle Brandon 225

Pro-Cathedral, Clifton, Bristol *13*, 48-53,
    48-53
psycho-geography 146
Pugin, A.W.N. 72
Pugin, E.W. 72

Reed, Lou 219
Regan Miller Associates 18
Reilly, C.H. 92, *93*
Rich, Geoff 184, 186, 189
Richardson, Dane 62
Riflemaker 24-33, *24-33*
Riegl, Alois 72, 81
Riflemaker Becomes Indica 27, *30, 33*
Riflemaker Everyday Book & Diary 28, 30
River Cottage 152-63, *152-63*
Rodinsky, David 86, 89
Round Foundry, Leeds 17-23, *17-23*, 50
Round House, London 180
Royal Academy of Arts, Sackler extension,
    London 199
Royal Aircraft Establishment, Farnborough
    199, 200-3, *200-3*
Royal Court Theatre 66
Royal Hospital, Chelsea 167
Royal Mail Sorting Office, Victoria, London
    11, *142-7*, 143-7
Royal Military Asylum 164-71, *164-71*
Royal Military College, Sandhurst 167

Saarinen, Eero 176
Saarinen, Eliel 176
Saatchi, Charles 164, 167, 170
Saint, Andrew 92
Sanders, John *164*, 167
Sasdy, Peter 54
Satellite Architects 157
Scanes, William 83
Seal, Malcolm 154
Self, Will 146
Shakespeare 198
    Hamlet 197

Shawcross, Conrad *32*
Sherratt, Paul 14
Shervington, Helen 58-60, *59*, *61*, 62-3
Sheward, Darren 49-50, 52, 53
Simmons, Jean 114
Sinclair, Iain 86-9
Smith, Ray 160
Smithfield market, London 39
Smythson 131
Soane, Sir Arthur *99*, 102
Soane, Sir John *164*, 167, 198, 203
Soane Museum 30, 198
Soho, London 14, *15*
Souden, David 14
South Africa House 129
South Western District Office, Victoria,
    London *142-7*, 143-7
Spiller, James 92
Squire and Partners 143, 146-7
St Albans Cathedral Chapter House 35
St Anne's, church of, Limehouse, London
    198
St Barnabas, Hackney *10*, 86-96, *86-93*
St Catherine's Chapel, Exeter 83-5, *82-5*
St John-at-Hackney, London 86-96, *94-7*,
    183
St Martin-in-the-Fields 124-30, *124-9*
St Monica's Board School, Hoxton 72
St Paul's Church, Bow 50, 91, *92-3*
Steiner Waldorf School, Bristol 51
Stevens, Canon John 83
Stewart, Peter 34-7
Stirling, James 198
Stone Tape, The 54
Stonehenge 9
Sullivan Louis 176

Talbot, William Henry Fox 55, *57*
Talkback Television Offices, Newman
    Street, nos 20-22 72, London 75-9,
    76-8
Tanner, Sir Henry 143

Tate Modern, London *35*, *37*, 203
Tavernor, Robert 11, 12, 91
Taylor, Tot 24-5, 26, 29, 30
Tenant, The 10, 11
Thatcher, Mrs Margaret 37
Thomas, Percy, Partnership 48, 51
THX 1138 171
Tomkins, Steve 65, 69
Trafalgar Square 125, 127, *128*, 129

Ukeles, Mierle Laderman 14
Uncle Silas 116
Urban Creation 49, 51, 53

Venturi Scott Brown 37
Verhoeven, Julie 180, 182, *182-3*
Victoria, Queen 139
Villa Nueva, Mexico 173, 174, *178-9*, 179
Vimy Ridge 54-7, *55-7*
Vollmer, Joan 33
Vonnegut, Karl: *Slaughterhouse 5* 11

Walker-Hebborn, Tyrone 208-9, 210-11
Waugh Thistleton Architects 210
Waugh, Andrew 209, 214-15, 219
Way, Mark 146
Wells, H.G.: *Red Room, The* 13
Wesley Square shopping centre, Goole 80
West, Fred 12
Whitehead, Peter *27*
Whitfield, William 35
Whitman, Walt: 'Song for Occupations, A'
    228
Wholly Communion 27
Wickham, Cynthia 108
Wickham, Denny 109, *109*, *113*, 114
Wickham, Gemma 108, 109
Wickham, Michael 107, 108, 109-10, *111*,
    114
Wickham, Polly 108
Wilder, Ken 136, 139-41, *139-41*
Wilkes, John *28*, 30

Wilkes, John, & Son *24*, 25
Wilkes brothers 26, 30
Wilkins, Kate 46
Wilkinson Eyre 225
Willets, Funda Kemal 172-9
William Jones Maltsters 192
Wilson, Richard *20:50* 140
Woodward, Christopher 57
Wordsearch 54
World Trade Center, New York 12
Wren, Sir Christopher 167
Wright, Frank Wright 176

Yates, John 184, 187, 192, *193*
Yeo, Cherie 180-3 *181-3*
Young Vic Theatre 65-9, *64-71*

Zaira 9, 13
Zenobia 46

Acknowledgements

David Littlefield would like to thank everyone who gave their time freely in order to explore the ideas and buildings contained within this book. Each chapter is the result of many hours of conversation and being guided around empty (and often dangerous) buildings. In particular, I would like to thank English Heritage, John Collingwood, Paul Davis, Bob Tavernor, Ken Wilder, Feilden Clegg Bradley Architects, Squire and Partners, and developers Urban Creation. In particular, I thank Kerri for her support and patience.

Saskia Lewis warmly thanks the following for their participation collaboration and support in this project and for making the process and exploration so enjoyable: Miraj Ahmed, Jacqui Barhouch, Matthew Beilecki, Stewart Dodd, Shaun Earle, Family Evans, Family Fox, Jack Gordon, Alan Harvey, Martin Howarth, Jules at Vegas Design, Pat Larcombe, Theo Lorenz, Joel Newman, Eric Parry, Malcom Seal, Stephen Senior, Helen Shervington, Tot Taylor, Andrew Waugh, Denny Wickham, Matt White and especially Antonia Quirke for her kindness in casting a regular and supportive eye over the developing narrative.

I would like to thank in particular, my parents, Marya and Stuart Lewis, for sharing their observations, thoughts and time that we have spent together, most of all, thank you for the laughs.

Credits